Truthful Fictions

Truthful Fictions

Conversations with American Biographical Novelists

Edited by Michael Lackey

B L O O M S B U R Y

NEW YORK • LONDON • NEW DELHI • SYDNEY

Bloomsbury Academic
An imprint of Bloomsbury Publishing Inc

1385 Broadway	50 Bedford Square
New York	London
NY 10018	WC1B 3DP
USA	UK

www.bloomsbury.com

Bloomsbury is a registered trade mark of Bloomsbury Publishing Plc

First published 2014

© Michael Lackey, 2014

Library of Congress Cataloging-in-Publication Data
A catalog record for this book is available from the Library of Congress.

ISBN: HB: 978-1-6235-6741-5
PB: 978-1-6235-6825-2
ePDF: 978-1-6235-6182-6
ePub: 978-1-6235-6615-9

Typeset by Fakenham Prepress Solutions, Fakenham, Norfolk NR21 8NN
Printed and bound in the United States of America

For Julie

Contents

Acknowledgments

In the summer of 2011, my wife, knowing my admiration for Walter Benjamin, gave me a copy of Jay Parini's biographical novel *Benjamin's Crossing*, which focuses on the last year of Benjamin's life, when he was fleeing the Nazis. By this point in my life, I had read only a few biographical novels, such as Arna Bontemps' *Black Thunder*, Zora Neale Hurston's *Moses, Man of the Mountain*, William Styron's *The Confessions of Nat Turner*, Bruce Duffy's *The World as I Found It*, and Irvin Yalom's *When Nietzsche Wept*. But it was *Benjamin's Crossing* that made me reflect on the rich power of this aesthetic form, so I decided to contact Jay about giving a lecture on the topic of the biographical novel at my university. Over the course of the next few months, Jay and I had many conversations about the origin, evolution, and nature of the biographical novel. To get more insight into it, I organized a round-table forum with Jay, Bruce Duffy, and Lance Olsen at the University of Minnesota's Institute for Advanced Study. It was my conversations with Jay, Bruce, and Lance that inspired me to do this book. Therefore, my greatest thanks for making *Truthful Fictions* possible go to my wife, Julie Eckerle, Jay, Bruce, and Lance.

I am also immensely grateful to all the authors who allowed me to interview them. This was an incredibly demanding project, because I had to fly to many cities in order to interview sixteen writers. But instead of exhausting me, the interviews energized me, as all the writers were so eager and excited to discuss their work and the development of the biographical novel.

For financial support, it is simply impossible to imagine any institution being more generous than the University of Minnesota. The University gave me two Imagine awards and one grant-in-aid; the Institute for Advanced Study funded my round-table forum; and the University of Minnesota, Morris gave me two Faculty Research Enhancement Fund awards and one course release. All of this support has enabled me to complete this project.

Additionally, the university generously gave me funding for my research assistants, Rachel Balzar, Kelsey Butler, and Adrienne Haataja, who far exceeded my very high expectations, for which I am very grateful. A special word of thanks goes to Roger Wareham. In all my years doing research, never have I met a person in grants development who more passionately, tirelessly, and aggressively secures funding for faculty research. My university is lucky to have Roger.

I would also like to thank Sandy Kill, interlibrary loan manager at the University of Minnesota, Morris, who makes my job much easier because she does her job so well.

Finally, I want to thank my editor, Haaris Naqvi. From the beginning, he has believed in this project and in me.

Michael Lackey

Introduction: The Rise of the American Biographical Novel

Given all the biographical novels published over the last thirty years, we could probably assume that, if Robert Penn Warren wrote *All the King's Men* today, he would have named his protagonist Huey Long instead of Willie Stark. Indeed, Jay Parini, who was a friend of Warren's, claims that the novel would have been stronger had he done so: "In *All the King's Men*, written in the mid-forties, Robert Penn Warren felt tightly bound to the traditions of conventional historical fiction. I don't think he could see his way toward the contemporary forms of the biographical novel, or else he would have called his protagonist Huey Long, not Willie Stark."

Parini's remarks, of course, beg the question: What happened in the realm of ideas that made the biographical novel not just possible but also incredibly popular? To begin answering this question, let me explain what prohibited one of the twentieth-century's most likely writers from producing a biographical novel.

In her essay "The Art of Biography," Virginia Woolf maintains that the "novelist is free" to create, while "the biographer is tied"[1] to facts. Lytton Strachey and the new biographers of the early twentieth century revolutionized the biography by making liberal use of the creative imagination and fictional techniques in depicting a person's life, thus giving the artist/biographer the "freedom to invent" something new, "a book that was not only a biography but also a work of art."[2] But ultimately, Woolf concluded, this "combination proved unworkable," because "fact and fiction refused to mix."[3] It should seem odd that Woolf would reject the biographical novel, because she published *Orlando: A Biography*. But for Woolf, it is impossible to reconcile the act of creating a living character and representing a person accurately. Therefore, as a biographer, she sought to represent the life of Roger Fry as accurately as she possibly could in her biography of the artist. But as a novelist, she thought that tethering herself to an actual person's

---

[1] Woolf (1942), "The Art of Biography," in *The Death of the Moth and Other Essays*. London: The Hogarth Press: 120.
[2] Woolf (1942): 123.
[3] Ibid. For useful discussions of Woolf's complicated approach to biography, see Ray Monk's "This Fictitious Life: Virginia Woolf on Biography and Reality" and Mark Hussey's "Woolf: After Lives."

story would be death to her creative freedom. So while Woolf calls *Orlando* a biography, it is clear to her and the reader that it is fiction. After all, the subject is not a real person, but a fictional character that lives for more than 300 years, undergoes a non-surgical sex change from a man to a woman, and has a child. For Woolf, writers have to choose between the art of representing a person's life accurately, which would lead them to produce a biography, or creating a living and breathing character, which would lead them to produce a work of fiction. Blending the two in the form of the biographical novel is not an option.

For many biographical novelists, developments in postmodernism made it possible to fuse biography and the novel. For instance, Parini, Lance Olsen, Madison Smartt Bell, and Ron Hansen argue that it is no longer possible to treat historical and/or biographical representations as any more truthful than narratives of fiction because historians and biographers use the same rhetorical strategies, devices, and techniques as creative writers in constructing their narratives. Within this postmodern framework, fact is fiction, and consequently, history and biography, which were once considered to be separate and distinct from fiction, can no longer lay claim to being non-fictional. Michael Cunningham, Julia Alvarez, Joanna Scott, and Mark Allen Cunningham agree with this postmodern assessment, but they reverse the equation by underscoring the factualization of fiction. As Michael Cunningham explains, "there's no such thing as fiction, not in the absolute sense. Fiction writers work from our experience of the world and the people who inhabit it." If fact is not as factual as we once thought, neither is fiction as fictional as we once thought, which is why Cunningham concludes: "Some of us go to greater lengths than others to disguise that which we've seen and heard, but still, fiction can only arise out of what a writer has seen and heard. And so, it's really a question of degree." Contra Woolf, who claims that fact and fiction refuse to mix, these postmodernist writers argue that fact and fiction are inseparable, because fictional techniques play a crucial role in shaping fact, while facts provide the basis for fiction. This postmodern blending of fact and fiction is, in part, what made the biographical novel possible.

It was on November 6, 1968 that we first see prominent novelists in a contentious debate about the legitimacy of the biographical novel. The historian C. Vann Woodward moderated a forum with Warren, Ralph Ellison, and William Styron, and the topic was "The Uses of History in Fiction." When introducing the central ideas to be discussed, Woodward insists that there is a "distinction between the historian and the novelist."[4]

---

[4] Ellison, et al., "The Uses of History in Fiction." *Southern Literary Journal* (Spring 1969): 59.

Unlike the novelist, the historian cannot "invent characters, invent motives for his characters."[5] But Warren rejects this assumption because he holds that the past is always mediated through a specific consciousness, which means that historians, whether they realize it or not, use the creative imagination as much as novelists in order to construct their "historical characters."[6] Though Warren claims that historians and novelists are the same in that they use the imagination to access and construct their subjects, he does make a distinction between the two. The fiction writer "claims to know the inside of his characters, the undocumentable inside," while the historian "wants to find the facts *behind* the world."[7] Like Warren, Ellison rejects the idea that there is a distinction between "American historiography and American fiction," for "they're both artificial," which is why Ellison refers to historians as "responsible liars."[8]

Since Ellison considers history fiction, it would seem that he would favor the biographical novel. But such is not the case. At one point during the discussion, Ellison praises Warren for engaging history correctly in *All the King's Men*:

> I think that Red Warren, who has always been concerned with history, has offered us an example of how to confront the problem of history as the novelist should. I think that when he wrote about a great American politician who governed his state and refused to intrude into the area of the historian, he refused because he was canny enough to realize that he could never get *that* particular man into fiction. And yet, I believe that he did use that man to bring into focus within his own mind many, many important facts about power, politics and class, and loyalty.[9]

Warren's decision not to name his character Huey Long was aesthetically sound and pragmatically astute, because he was able to articulate some crucial historical "truths" about the dynamics of power, the psychology of politics, and the structures of class. Had Warren ventured into the realm of the historian by specifically naming his character Huey Long, he would have failed to represent the complexity and details of the man and he would have made himself vulnerable to attack from historians. Indeed, Ellison specifies what historians would do to novelists were they to encroach on the historian's intellectual terrain: "the moment you put any known figures into the book, then somebody is going to say, 'But he didn't have that mole on that

---

[5]   Ellison et al. (1969): 59.
[6]   Ellison et al. (1969): 61.
[7]   Ibid. Warren's emphasis.
[8]   Ellison et al. (1969): 62.
[9]   Ellison et al. (1969): 64–5. Ellison's emphasis.

side of his face; it was on *that* side. You said that he had a wife; he didn't have a wife."[10] Therefore, instead of naming the character after the original, as so many contemporary biographical novelists do, Ellison counsels writers to "lie and disguise a historical figure,"[11] as Warren did.

While Ellison's comments are about Warren's work, they are also a not-so-subtle critique of Styron's 1967 biographical novel *The Confessions of Nat Turner*, which differs from *All the King's Men* because he named his character after the original historical figure. This novel caused considerable controversy for exactly the reasons Ellison mentions: people claimed that Styron misrepresented Nat Turner and made factual errors about him. Styron was prepared for this objection, but ironically, he used the work of Georg Lukács to respond to Ellison and his critics. Citing a passage from Lukács' *The Historical Novel*, Styron argues that the novelist who has a commanding grasp of an historical period can alter certain facts in an effort to "reproduce the spirit of any age faithfully and authentically."[12] Later in the discussion, he insists that writers cannot totally dispense with facts and evidence. But he does use Lukács' work to say that novelists have the freedom to disregard "useless fact"[13] in order to get to a more substantive historical truth.

Styron did himself no favor by citing Lukács, for if Styron had read *The Historical Novel* in whole, he would have realized that Lukács would have dubbed *The Confessions of Nat Turner* an unambiguous failure. For Lukács, the ultimate goal of the historical novel is to portray a "great historical truth"[14] which it does through "the poetic awakening of the people who figured in"[15] momentous historical events. "What matters," according to Lukács, "is that we should re-experience the social and human motives which led men to think, feel and act just as they did in historical reality,"[16] and this is something that the historical novel is best suited to accomplish. Lukács favored the classical historical novel, because it effectively pictured the "derivation of the individuality of characters from the historical peculiarity of their age."[17] Within this framework, the author must clearly understand and accurately represent "history as a process,"[18] that is, the way historical concreteness functions according to rigorous and objective laws in shaping and determining the great socio-political collisions of a particular age.

[10] Ellison et al. (1969): 74. Ellison's emphasis.
[11] Ibid.
[12] Ellison et al. (1969): 66.
[13] Ellison et al. (1969): 75.
[14] Lukács (1962), *The Historical Novel*. Lincoln: University of Nebraska Press: 319.
[15] Lukács (1962): 42.
[16] Ibid.
[17] Lukács (1962): 19.
[18] Lukács (1962): 21.

Given this objective, the biographical novel is doomed to failure, because the focus on "the *biography of the hero*" leads authors to overlook or misrepresent significant historical events and truths, and thus "reveal the historical weakness of the biographical form of the novel."[19] Should a particular person be the focal point of an historical novel, this figure would be treated as more important than the historical transformation, which would necessarily lead to a distorted image of the society and the age.[20] Obviously, Lukács would fault Styron for centering his novel in the consciousness of Nat Turner.

The varying critiques of the biographical novel by Woolf, Ellison, and Lukács are important because they reflect the judgments of the literary establishment, especially those who determine the Pulitzer Prize in fiction. The first biographical novel to pose a serious challenge for the Pulitzer committee was Styron's *The Confessions of Nat Turner*. Significant is the fact that the committee did not yet have a suitable vocabulary or conceptual framework for making systematic sense of the biographical novel, which in part explains its difficulty in assessing it. The 1968 report notes "the Fiction Jury could not reach a unanimous opinion" about this novel, so it submitted a form with "a minority and a majority opinion and a possible compromise selection."[21] To come to terms with its own confusion, there is an extended discussion of Styron's novel. The report is six pages long and consists of twenty-two paragraphs. Styron's novel is discussed in twelve of those paragraphs, and it is the exclusive subject of ten. The only other novel to come close is Isaac Bashevis Singer's *The Manor*, which is mentioned in six paragraphs and the primary subject of only two.

As important as the length and focus of the report are the comments about Styron's novel, which shed considerable light on the committee's assumptions and expectations regarding fiction. Even though Lukács would have characterized and faulted *The Confessions of Nat Turner* as a biographical novel, both Styron and the committee saw it as an historical novel. This is clear from the decision of John K. Hutchens, one of the committee members, to cite Styron, who says that *The Confessions* is "less an 'historical novel'" than a meditation on history."[22] Lessening the degree to which *The Confessions* is an historical novel does not negate it as one. And it is worth noting that, when Styron defined his novel during the forum with Ellison and Warren, he used Lukács' *The Historical Novel* to do so. What Hutchens admires so much about the work is Styron's ability to do two things simultaneously: to

[19] Lukács (1962): 320. Lukács' emphasis.
[20] Lukács (1962): 321.
[21] Fischer and Fischer (2007), *Chronicle of the Pulitzer Prizes for Fiction: Discussions, Decisions, Dissents*. Munich: K. G. Saur Verlag: 294.
[22] Fischer and Fischer (2007): 294.

use rich, imaginative language in order to engage the reader and to represent the historical figure accurately. On the basis of these criteria, Hutchens concludes that Styron "has written what is, in my opinion, the finest American novel of 1967, and the one that promises to be most enduring as art and re-created history."[23]

Maxwell Geismar and Melvin Maddocks were the two other readers, and they disagreed with Hutchens on both accounts. Their comments are useful, because they indicate what the members consider the freedom a writer is allowed and not allowed to take with the historical record. Geismar and Maddocks claim that *The Confessions* is a flawed novel because there are "serious defects in the use of its historical material" as well as the "prose style." It might seem that these two problems are separate and distinct, but for these readers they are actually inextricably linked. Maddocks claims that the novel's writing is "too smooth, too literary."[24] This is a problem because such literary language lacks verisimilitude. According to Geismar, instead of replicating the "early nineteenth century language" of Nat Turner or Thomas Gray, the lawyer who took the rebel slave's confession, "Styron has added a large percent of romantic Southern rhetoric to the point of making the novel's prose so fragrant, redolent, and prolix as to be overblown and luscious."[25] The literary expectation is this: for a historical novel to be effective and legitimate, the language must accurately reflect the way people spoke from the represented period, and if the language fails to do this, then the author must have a faulty understanding of the historical period.

Most prominent biographical novelists reject the Geismar/Maddocks view. In their effort to represent a structure of consciousness or a historical reality biographical novelists frequently subordinate empirical facts to a symbolic truth. For instance, when discussing the construction of her fictional characters, Joyce Carol Oates claims that her "characters are more interesting, elastic and subtle than the real people." Indeed, she goes on to say that the actual historical figures are "not nearly as nuanced or subtle as my fictitious characters." This is the case because Oates uses her characters to access and represent a larger historical and cultural truth. In their assessment of a literary work's engagement with history, Geismar and Maddocks acknowledge that novelists can use fiction to illuminate the historical record, but they forbid tampering with the literal facts, which explains why they drew a damning conclusion about *The Confessions of Nat Turner*: "while William Styron may have the right to 'invent' historical incidents within

---

[23] Fischer and Fischer (2007): 295.
[24] Ibid.
[25] Fischer and Fischer (2007): 297.

the framework of recorded history, he has in this book taken some dubious liberties with history itself."[26] For Geismar and Maddocks, Styron has the right to invent scenes that illuminate the established facts about history, but he does not have a right to alter history itself. But for Oates, altering history is precisely what the biographical novelist does.

So contra Geismar and Maddocks, biographical novelists unapologetically take "liberties with history itself." But what enables them to justify this is not so much a cynical rejection of historical truth as a subordination of a particular narrative truth. Russell Banks best articulates the philosophy underwriting the biographical novelist's approach to history. In *Cloudsplitter*, Banks describes a road that the Brown family takes on its journey to the Plains of Abraham, where the family settles. After the publication of the novel, a local historian contacted Banks complaining that he made an error because the "road alongside those lakes in 1848 [...] wasn't built until the 1870s." Banks said that he had a map of the area from the time period, so he knew that there was no road there in the 1840s. But that fact did not matter, because he wanted to picture the Brown family going along the road, which was shaped like "the blade of a scimitar," as a way of prefiguring "the bloody swords that they would use much later." When I asked him to clarify and justify his motivation for taking this liberty with the historical record, he said that he at times subordinates a historical fact to "a dramatic truth." More specifically, the dramatic truth about the psychic life of the Brown family is more important than a literal truth about a road.

To put the matter succinctly, all three Pulitzer committee members did not yet have an epistemological or aesthetic framework that would enable them to understand or appreciate the biographical novel. Geismar and Maddocks failed to see how Styron's subordination of certain historical facts enabled him to access and represent more substantive historical structures and truths. As for Hutchens, while he praises *The Confessions*, it is clear that he considers it a historical rather than a biographical novel.

It might seem that 1980 marks the official arrival of the biographical novel, for it was in this year that Norman Mailer received the Pulitzer Prize in fiction for *The Executioner's Song*, which chronicles the last nine months of Gary Mark Gilmore's life. But there are two separate reasons why this is not the case. First, by virtue of Mailer's own definition, *The Executioner's Song* would not qualify as a biographical novel. If, as Woolf argues, the art of representing a person accurately is the primary task of the biographer while the art of inventing scenes to create a living character is the primary task of the novelist, then Mailer's novel would qualify as a biography but

---

[26] Fischer and Fischer (2007): 296.

not a novel. As Mailer claims in his Afterword, *The Executioner's Song* is a "factual account," a "*true life story.*"[27] The novel makes use of "interviews, documents, [and] records of court proceedings" to give readers "a factual account of the activities of Gary Gilmore,"[28] and when Mailer gets conflicting evidence about Gilmore, he chooses "the version that seemed most likely."[29] Given the absence of overt creative invention, it is difficult to justify calling *The Executioner's Song* fiction.

An example from Bruce Duffy's work will enable me to bring into sharp focus the distinction between *The Executioner's Song* and a biographical novel. While I have already discussed the postmodernist claim that fictionalizing reality is inescapable as the art of framing a character or story necessitates a creative shaping of material, biographical novelists do something more conscious and strategic. They invent stories that never occurred in order to answer perplexing questions, fill in cultural lacunae, or signify human interiors. For instance, Ludwig Wittgenstein had a conflicted sense of himself, for he was a Jew whose family became Catholic. In *The World as I Found It*, Duffy brilliantly pictures the famous biographical moment when Wittgenstein confesses to the philosopher G. E. Moore that he deceived him and others by concealing his Jewish heritage. Had Duffy only included scenes like Wittgenstein's confession, *The World As I Found It* would be an engaging biography and not a biographical novel. But to access and represent Wittgenstein's conflicted self, Duffy creates a scene much earlier in the novel with the Austrian philosopher in a Jewish theater, which features a play about the Jewish monster figure Yosele Golem, who is described as "a kind of beast or something." So captivated by the performance is Wittgenstein that "for five hard minutes he *was* the play, Yosele Golem."[30] During my interview, Duffy said that Wittgenstein is "so upset by a seemingly garish simple-minded scene—and so unconscious of his deeper emotions—that he passes out." This is the case because he was forced to confront in the theater "his true past," specifically his Jewish heritage. However, as Duffy told me, this scene never actually occurred. This is the kind of scene that does not appear in *The Executioner's Song*, which is why 1980 cannot be considered the official arrival year of the biographical novel.

This lack of strategic and overt invention explains the 1980 Pulitzer Committee's conflicted response to *The Executioner's Song*. The committee obviously recognized that there was a problem giving Mailer's work an award

---

[27]   Mailer (1998), *The Executioner's Song*. New York: Vintage Books: 1053.
[28]   Mailer (1998): 1051.
[29]   Ibid.
[30]   Duffy (2010), *The World As I Found It*. New York: New York Review Books: 145. Duffy's emphasis.

for fiction, for it tries to make the case for it as a novel in the first sentence of the report: "*The Executioner's Song* is subtitled 'A True Life Novel.'"[31] Something is not entirely right about this work, which is why the committee members feel the need to justify that it is actually a novel. Indeed, in its six-sentence report, the members strategically and repeatedly emphasize the way the novel expands "our conceptions of the limits of history and fiction" and "challenges our notions of fiction."[32] The members obviously want to underscore how the novel challenges our definitions of fiction so that they can justify their decision to give Mailer an award for fiction. This becomes most apparent when we look at the letter that the chairman of the committee, Frank McConnell, submitted to the advisory board. McConnell notes that one committee member, Anatole Broyard, "expressed some concern that Mailer's book may not really be a novel (whatever that means)."[33] McConnell obviously didn't agree with that assessment, which is clear from his parenthetical interjection. But Broyard was rightly "worried that giving the prize to" Mailer's novel "may raise unpleasant controversy and embarrass the Pulitzer Committee,"[34] because, if it is correct to say that *The Executioner's Song* contains no overtly fictional characters or scenes, then it would be difficult to justify awarding it the Pulitzer Prize for fiction.

The second reason why 1980 does not mark the official arrival of the biographical novel is the committee's subtle bias against the genre. The report says: "And although the story told is about real people, and based upon a great mass of documentary material, *The Executioner's Song* is an extraordinarily ambitious and powerful narrative."[35] Note the hint of surprise ("although") that a "novel" about a "real" person that uses "documentary material" could be a "powerful narrative." These are clearly people who have not yet read Duffy's *The World As I Found It*, Scott's *Arrogance*, Banks' *Cloudsplitter*, and Oates' *Blonde*. At this point, the literary establishment still needs to undergo a few more transformations before it could understand or appreciate the biographical novel.

The year 1999 represents a decisive move in favor of the biographical novel, for it was in this year that Cunningham's *The Hours* and Banks' *Cloudsplitter* were nominated for the Pulitzer, and that Cunningham's novel won the award.[36] Cunningham's novel is significant because it addresses the literary establishment directly. The novel features a prominent writer

[31] Fischer and Fischer (2007): 349.
[32] Ibid.
[33] Fischer and Fischer (2007): 348
[34] Ibid.
[35] Fischer and Fischer (2007): 349.
[36] Cunningham's *The Hours* also won the PEN/Faulkner Award.

(Richard) who receives an important literary award. For Cunningham's narrator, this prize "means that literature itself [...] seems to feel a need for Richard's particular contribution."[37] This is a wonderful way of articulating what happened with the Pulitzer committee. It felt a need at this time for the biographical novelist's contribution. After all, so many prominent writers published biographical novels by 1999 that it was impossible to ignore them.[38]

Most encouraging, however, is the content of the Pulitzer's jury report, which indicates a shift in the literary establishment's aesthetic expectations and theory of knowledge. For instance, when discussing *The Hours*, the committee notes that a "fourth character is Woolf herself," which contributes to the novel's "four-person complexity."[39] Instead of assuming that a real person as a character would be a liability, as the 1980 Pulitzer committee did, the 1999 members recognize that such a literary choice could be a huge asset. What, in part, made this possible was the committee's acceptance of postmodernism. Before 1999, postmodernism was never mentioned in any Pulitzer jury report for fiction. But in the year that *The Hours* received the Pulitzer, the committee praised Cunningham for presenting "the floating post-modern world and generation that a number of contemporary writers have tackled, but none so artfully and movingly."[40] Rather than strictly demarcating fact and fiction, biography and the novel, or a historical figure and a fictional character, postmodernists suggest that fact is fiction and that fiction is inseparable from fact. This postmodernist shift made the committee understand and appreciate a hybrid aesthetic form such as the biographical novel, which is why we could say that the biographical novel was partially legitimized in 1999. I say partially because in his interview, Cunningham acknowledges that *The Hours* is only a partial biographical novel, as Woolf is only one of four main characters.

---

[37] Cunningham (1998), *The Hours*. New York: Picador, 64.

[38] From the 1930s through the 1980s, Irving Stone published a number of biographical novels, but these works have a formulaic feel and have not impacted major contemporary writers. Not one of the writers I interviewed mentioned him. A few works that had a significant impact before 1999 include: Arna Bontemps' *Black Thunder* (1936); Zora Neale Hurston's *Moses, Man of the Mountain* (1939); William Styron's *The Confessions of Nat Turner* (1967); Gore Vidal's *Burr* (1973) and *Lincoln* (1984); Bruce Duffy's *The World As I Found It* (1987); Joanna Scott's *Arrogance* (1990); Jay Parini's *The Last Station* (1990) and *Benjamin's Crossing* (1997); Irvin Yalom's *When Nietzsche Wept* (1992); Julia Alvarez's *In the Time of the Butterflies* (1994); Madison Smartt Bell's *All Souls' Rising* (1995); David Mamet's *The Old Religion* (1997); and Anita Diamant's *The Red Tent* (1997).

[39] Fischer and Fischer (2007): 424.

[40] Ibid.

The convergence of history and fiction

At this point, I want to focus on concurrent developments in history and fiction that made the biographical novel possible and extremely popular. In the nineteenth century, history became an institutionalized discipline that conceived of itself as a science. As such, it distanced itself from literature by expanding and hardening the dichotomy between fact and fiction. Within this framework, historical fact became more dogmatically factual while imaginative fiction became more fantastically fictional. There were, to be sure, prominent nineteenth-century detractors, like Friedrich Nietzsche, who rejected the fact/fiction dichotomy by exposing the degree to which the scientific historian's established fact is really an anthropomorphic construction, thus suggesting that a (personal or communal) power interest played a much more crucial role in the formation of historical fact than the seemingly neutral and objective observers of history were willing to admit. But it wasn't until the 1960s, with the linguistic turn in multiple disciplines, the provincialization of western thought, the deconstruction of the correspondence theory of truth, and the valorization of postmodernism, that the fact/fiction binary was systematically and comprehensively dismantled.[41] Perhaps no writer, with the exceptions of Nietzsche and Wittgenstein, anticipated the postmodern fusion of history and fiction more than Walter Benjamin. In 1997, Parini published *Benjamin's Crossing*, a biographical novel about the final year of Benjamin's life. In this work, Parini brilliantly dramatizes one of Benjamin's most important contributions to intellectual history, and it is this contribution that would pave the way for the biographical novel: "Benjamin believed that the equivalent of a Copernican revolution in thinking must occur. Fiction would replace history, or become history."[42] By 1997, that revolution was well underway, which is why Parini could publish a biographical novel that simultaneously discusses and enacts that revolution.

---

[41] For discussions about the history of history, see Hayden White's *Tropics of Discourse, The Content of Form,* and *Metahistory: The Historical Imagination in Nineteenth-Century Europe* and Georg G. Iggers' *Historiography in the Twentieth Century.* For a discussion of the linguistic turn, see E. L. Doctorow's "False Documents," Richard Rorty's *Contingency, Irony, and Solidarity* and Judith Ryan's *The Novel after Theory.* For discussions of the provincialization of western thought, see Dipesh Chakrabarty's *Provincializing Europe* and Edward Said's *Orientalism* and *Culture and Imperialism.* For discussions of the deconstruction of the correspondence theory of truth, see Rorty's *Philosophy and the Mirror of Nature* and Michel Foucault's *The Archaeology of Knowledge* and *The Order of Things.* For discussions about the rise of postmodernism, see Jean-François Lyotard's *The Postmodern Condition,* Linda Hutcheon's *Poetics of Postmodernism,* and Ryan's *The Novel after Theory.*

[42] Parini (1997), *Benjamin's Crossing.* New York: Henry Holt: 62.

According to Mas'ud Zavarzadeh, the mounting post-World War Two incredulity toward metanarratives gave rise to a new form of fiction, one that effectively fuses fact and fiction. For instance, in 1965, Truman Capote published *In Cold Blood*, which has been misleadingly referred to as a "nonfiction novel," a phrase that Capote, in his self-promoting way, coined in interviews about his book.[43] For Zavarzadeh, the fictive novel provides an overarching interpretation of the world, an "epiphanic vision" that illuminates "the ultimate structure of reality."[44] But given the postmodern exposure of such metavisions as phantoms of an overheated imagination, the traditional approach to the novel no longer made sense, so the nonfiction novelists created a work with a "noninterpretive stance"[45] to the world.

With regard to literary history, and specifically the rise and legitimation of the American biographical novel, the Capote case has done more to muddle and confuse than anything else, which is clear from Beverley Southgate's recent study *History Meets Fiction* (2009). This is a superb work of scholarship that clarifies the intellectual developments that led to the blending of fact and fiction, history and literature. Less compelling, however, is Southgate's discussion of *In Cold Blood*, which he uncritically refers to as a nonfiction novel. If we think of a novel as fiction, then we could say it invents a world that is not required to literally represent historical events and persons. And if we think of history as nonfiction, then we could say it seeks to represent as literally as possible the events and persons that exist in the world outside the text. Given these two separate activities, Capote's work would be considered nonfiction, as he makes clear in his Acknowledgments: "All the material in this book not derived from my own observation is either taken from official records or is the result of interviews with persons directly concerned, more often than not numerous interviews conducted over a considerable period of time."[46] These prefatory remarks have led Southgate to say of Capote's book: "One could hardly better that as a statement of correct procedures for a contemporary historian."[47] But while Southgate considers the book typical history, he also calls it fiction. Startling, however, is Southgate's implicit definition of a novel, which is based not so much on an author's act of fictional creation as the reader's experience of a particular

[43] Hollowell (1977), *Fact & Fiction: The New Journalism and the Nonfiction Novel*. Chapel Hill: The University of North Carolina Press: x.
[44] Zavarzadeh (1976), *The Mythopoeic Reality: The Postwar American Nonfiction Novel*. Urbana: University of Illinois Press: 42.
[45] Zavarzadeh (1976): 42.
[46] Capote (1965), *In Cold Blood: A True Account of a Multiple Murder and Its Consequences*. New York: Random House: Acknowledgments.
[47] Southgate (2009), *History Meets Fiction*. Harlow: Longman/Pearson Education Limited: 34.

text: "*In Cold Blood* is a novel—*fiction*—inasmuch as it is an imaginative construction written to hold the attention of its readers, and make them want to keep on reading."[48] Given this description, novelists are different from historians and biographers because they know how to write in an engaging way. By this logic, if a historian or biographer were to write a captivating work, it would cease to be history or biography and would, therefore, become fiction. This obviously is a dubious definition of fiction. Given Capote's approach to the material and what *In Cold Blood* actually does, it would be more accurate to refer to it as a page-turning history or biography than a nonfiction novel.

At stake here is not what writers are doing as much as the scholarly definition of writing in the postmodern age, and no work has done more to bring clarity to the discussion than Linda Hutcheon's 1988 study *A Poetics of Postmodernism*, which is subtitled *History, Fiction, Theory*. It was this triad that enabled Hutcheon to formulate her most enduring contribution to literary history, which is the idea of historiographic metafiction. The postmodern theorist's recognition that history and fiction are human constructs enables writers to rethink and revise accepted versions of the past. Historiographic metafiction incorporates historical events into a literary work, but given its awareness of crucial developments in theory, it also reflects in a critical way on the questionable process of converting those events into an official version of history. In his interview, Lance Olsen incisively expresses how Hutcheon's historiographic metafiction can be used to illuminate his work and the biographical novel more generally. But Hutcheon's model can also be used to explain a major development from Capote's *In Cold Blood* to Mailer's *The Executioner's Song*. In *The Politics and Poetics of Journalistic Narrative*, Phyllis Frus claims that Capote's *In Cold Blood* and Mailer's *The Executioner's Song* are the first to take the label of the "nonfiction novel."[49] However, she argues that Mailer's novel goes beyond Capote's in that it contains critical self-reflections that call attention to the narrative construction of history and thereby tacitly undermines its own narratorial authority,[50] which is why Mailer's work is much closer to Hutcheon's historiographical metafiction than Capote's *In Cold Blood*. But because *The Executioner's Song* lacks the overt creative invention of a novel, it would actually be more accurate to refer to it as historiographic metabiography than historiographic metafiction.

---

[48] Southgate (2009): 35. Southgate's emphasis.
[49] Frus (1994), *The Politics and Poetics of Journalisic Narrative: The Timely and the Timeless*. Cambridge: Cambridge University Press: 181.
[50] Frus (1994): 181–4.

Literature and the subconscious

The questions at this point are these: what has made contemporary writers so willing to go beyond Capote and Mailer by inventing characters and scenes and altering historical and biographical facts in the biographical novel? And what has led ordinary readers and the literary establishment to accept such liberties? While there are many competing answers to these questions, one of the most important revolves around our growing understanding of the subconscious. Nietzsche articulates most clearly the idea that would have a decisive impact on both the content and form of post-nineteenth-century literature. In *The Case of Wagner*, Nietzsche formulates a two-tiered conception of the human, which significantly undermines the trustworthiness and authority of the knowing human subject: "all of us have, unconsciously, involuntarily in our bodies values, words, formulas, moralities of *opposite* descent—we are, physiologically considered, *false*."[51] There exist in our bodies words, values, formulas, and moralities that frequently conflict with our rational conception of ourselves. For instance, on a conscious level, we might say to others and ourselves: I am not a racist. But at the subconscious level, many of us have absorbed and internalized racist words and values, which make many of us "racist" despite our intentions to the contrary. Given the way words, values, moralities, and formulas of opposite descent invade our bodies without our consent ("unconsciously, involuntarily"), it is impossible for us to be physiologically true.

This model impacted post-nineteenth-century literature in two separate ways. First, many prominent writers shifted their focus from the realist's external world, which was now seen as superficial and untrustworthy, to the world of the subconscious, which was now regarded as more fundamental and primary. Second, many prominent writers used this two-tier model to illuminate contradictory political behavior. For example, Richard Wright's 1940 novel *Native Son* examines the contradictory psychology of a typical white American liberal. Mr. Dalton donates money to the NAACP, hires underprivileged blacks, and supports racial uplift. And yet, much of his fortune comes from the massive exploitation of blacks—he charges exorbitant rents for rat-infested apartments in all-black areas of Chicago. How is it possible to explain that a white liberal, who philanthropically hires Bigger Thomas, makes his fortune by systematically exploiting and violating blacks, such as the Thomas family which is forced to live in one of Dalton's

---

[51] Nietzsche (1967), *The Case of Wagner*, in *The Birth of Tragedy and The Case of Wagner*. Translated by Walter Kaufmann. New York: Vintage Books: 192. Nietzsche's emphasis.

slum tenements? In an essay titled "How 'Bigger' Was Born," Wright offers an explanation. What concerned him is less people's conscious and rational thought than "the implicit, almost unconscious, or pre-conscious, assumptions and ideals upon which whole nations and races act and live."[52] To put the matter starkly, post-nineteenth-century novelists were starting to realize that, if they want to understand the deepest and most important "truths" about humans, then they need to find a way to access and represent not what people consciously say and think about themselves, but the underground mental life, which frequently contradicts what people say and believe about themselves.[53] The deepest "truth" about Dalton is not to be found in his philanthropic statements and efforts, but his "unconscious, or pre-conscious" assumptions, which lead him to contradict what he says and does.

This focus on the subconscious is of crucial importance for Gore Vidal, who could be described as one of the most important figures in the development of the American biographical novel.[54] Vidal published *Burr* in 1973 and *Lincoln* in 1984, and he provides a way for understanding why contemporary biographical novelists feel free to invent scenes and characters in order to illuminate the life of an actual historical figure. According to Vidal, one gets "to the essence of a culture not by looking at what is said but by looking at what is not said, the underlying assumptions of the society, too obvious to be stated. Truth—or some crucial aspect of truth—resides in those silences."[55] The aesthetic task of the novelist, therefore, is to develop aesthetic techniques for accessing and representing a person's or a culture's subconscious.

Oates' spectacular novel *Blonde*, which portrays the transformation of Norma Jeane into Marilyn Monroe, brilliantly deploys and justifies one of the most important techniques for illuminating the subconscious. For example, when working on a scene for the film *Niagara*, Oates' Norma

---

[52] Wright (1998), "How 'Bigger' was Born," in *Native Son*. New York: Perennial Classics: 445.

[53] Wright's two-tiered portrayal unleashed a massive reaction against white liberals, which would reach its apex in the 1960s. For a wonderfully insightful discussion of this development, see Lawrence P. Jackson's *The Indignant Generation*.

[54] The line of connection between Vidal and contemporary biographical novelists goes through Jay Parini. Parini and Vidal were close friends, and in 1990, Parini published *The Last Station*, a biographical novel that has been published in more than twenty-five languages and made into a Hollywood film. Parini acknowledges that Vidal offered him useful suggestions for writing *The Last Station*. Parini is also heavily involved with Bread Loaf, the famous writer's conference at Middlebury College. Many of the most prominent biographical novelists today have had close contact with Parini and have been debating the aesthetics of the biographical novel with him for the last twenty-five years.

[55] Quoted in Jay Parini (1997), "Mentors," in *Some Necessary Angels: Essays on Writing and Politics*. New York: Columbia University Press: 15–16.

Jeane expresses concern to the director that her character Rose Loomis is formulaic and underdeveloped. This is typical 1950s Hollywood, which consistently portrays females as simplistic clichés. Oates' Norma Jeane wants to give her character depth, so she asks if she can rewrite some of the dialogue. The answer, of course, is no. So she decides to act the character in a way that would express Rose's complexity. To clarify her approach, Oates' Norma Jeane says to the director:

> It came to me last night. Rose had a baby, I think. And the baby died. I didn't realize it consciously but that's why I play Rose this way. She has to be more than the script says; she's a woman with a secret.[56]

Norma Jeane clearly does not consider this story literally true, for she says that she thinks rather than knows that Rose had a baby. More importantly, Rose's "secret" is not something that is consciously represented in the script or film, for it occurs on a subconscious level ("I didn't realize it consciously"). In preparing to act the character, Norma Jeane detects something in the behavior that requires an explanation, something that functions at the level of the subconscious to impact and determine Rose's mysterious behavior. The only way to make sense of the character is to invent a story that would clarify the visible action. The story may not be true in a literal sense, but it rings true insofar as it functions to illuminate the truth of the character's complexity. In this instance, projecting into being a subconscious secret creates a more plausible female character, one more truthful and authentic than Hollywood's cardboard women of the 1950s.

Just as Oates' Norma Jeane invented this scene in order to illuminate the "truth" of Rose's female complexity, so too has Oates invented this scene in order to illuminate the "truth" of Norma Jeane's female complexity. After Norma Jeane tells the director about her approach to Rose's character, he resorts to an *ad hominem* attack: "A *dizzy blonde* he'd want to call her. That was the quickest strategy of dismissal. Was he worried she'd undermine his authority as director, the way 'Rose Loomis' undermined the authority and manhood of her husband?"[57] Hollywood males have a subconscious agenda, which is to typecast Monroe into the role of the dumb blonde. But Oates' Norma Jeane knows the men's subconscious goal, which is to straitjacket women into the role of a weak, dependent, and harmless plaything, and she has strategically devised an approach to undermine the men's efforts. But the director, who assumes that Norma Jeane is as mindless as the female character in his film, cannot imagine that Norma Jeane has the intelligence

---

[56] Oates (2009), *Blonde: A Novel*. New York: Ecco: 330.
[57] Oates (2009): 330. Oates' emphasis.

to grasp and portray character complexity or to read and challenge his patriarchal agenda. To expose the director's flawed assumptions, Oates renders Norma Jeane's complexity, which gives the lie to the director's sexist assumptions. In essence, what sets Rose and Norma Jeane apart from the husband and director is their complexity and depth, the women's "secret" life of the subconscious that the men can neither see nor appreciate.

What Oates brilliantly does in *Blonde* is to create a fictional scene in order to express a subtextual biographical "truth." The scene she invents about Norma Jeane is not true literally because it did not occur, as Oates said in her interview with me. However, the "truths" about the patriarchal agenda of creating mindless female characters and Norma Jeane's effort to debunk male projections of women accurately reflect the kind of subtextual battle between the actual Hollywood and the real Norma Jeane. Therefore, the novelist's creative invention has enabled Oates to portray not a literal "truth" about Norma Jeane's day-to-day experiences on the set of a film but, as Vidal says, an underlying "truth" regarding the conflict between Hollywood's patriarchal assumptions and Norma Jeane's feminist agenda, "truths" that reside in the subconscious silences that inform and illuminate visible action.

The cultural shift from the deductive to the inductive imagination

The growing skepticism about and discontentment with the universal and the ahistorical certainly contributed to the rise of the biographical novel. From Nietzsche, through Wittgenstein, to the French poststructuralists, there was a mounting suspicion that ahistorical pronouncements, what Jean-François Lyotard refers to as metanarratives, are not only epistemologically untrustworthy but also politically dangerous. Zavarzadeh argues that it was this incredulity toward the ahistorical metanarrative that gave birth to the nonfiction novel, which immerses readers in a welter of historical facts and refuses to provide an overarching explanation to unify the particulars. Such approaches totally dispense with ahistorical claims. While many contemporary biographical novelists adopt the postmodernist view that all knowledge systems are human inventions, most do not dispense with the universal or the ahistorical. Different for them, however, is the nature of the overarching claim within a literary text. To bring into sharp focus the difference, let me return to "The Uses of History in Fiction" debate in 1968, because it reflects the major cultural shift that gave rise to the biographical novel.

Ellison makes the case "for the autonomy of fiction" which is why he says "that novelists should leave history alone."[58] For Ellison, the writer's task "is to create symbolic actions which are viable specifically, and which move across all of our differences and all of the diversities of the atmosphere."[59] This describes perfectly what Ellison does in *Invisible Man*. Like many twentieth-century American writers, Ellison addresses the contradiction at the core of the contemporary western polity, which could be stated thus: Contemporary western political systems seemingly support the rights of life, liberty, and the pursuit of happiness for all people. Yet, these same political systems have developed strategic methods for excluding large segments of the population from obtaining such rights. To illuminate the psychological epistemology that enables political leaders to justify their contradictory behavior, Ellison creates the Brotherhood. The political agenda of the Brotherhood is of ultimate importance for both the members and the leaders. Therefore, if individuals cannot advance one of the Brotherhood's objectives, they exist outside history. As such, they can be used and abused with impunity. The problem here is not that political leaders take sadistic pleasure in violating those outside history—this is Cross Damon's view of political leaders in Wright's *The Outsider*. Within the framework of Ellison's novel, the problem is that, given the construction of their inner eyes, the political leaders do not even see those who exist outside of their history-making agenda. As for the members of the Brotherhood, the political leaders frequently do not see them as individuals, because they only see them as instruments for advancing the goals of the organization. Within this context, as soon as a political agenda is established within a person's body, the psychological epistemology will determine what can and cannot be seen, what does and does not belong to history.

From the time it was first published, readers have suggested that the Brotherhood is really the Communist Party. But as Arnold Rampersad notes, Ellison pointed "out repeatedly that the Brotherhood is an invention. It is, indeed, no more the Communist Party than Invisible's college is Tuskegee Institute."[60] Ellison was adamant on this score because his approach to the novel was based on the power of the deductive imagination. Once Ellison details the way a psychological epistemology functions within the Brotherhood to render certain people and groups invisible, that model could be applied to many people and groups, such as the Republican Party, the Democratic Party, and the Communist Party. If the Brotherhood were the

---

[58] Ellison et al. (1969): 73.
[59] Ellison et al. (1969): 74.
[60] Rampersad (2008), *Ralph Ellison: A Biography*. New York: Vintage Books: 245.

same as the historically specific Communist Party, then his novel would no longer contain its most important "symbolic actions" that could apply to a wide variety of political parties.

During the 1968 forum, Ellison appeared defensive and aggressive in relation to Styron, but there was a good reason why. At stake was Ellison's approach to the novel as cultural criticism and social critique, and the rise of the biographical novel signaled the decline of the deductive imagination, which was central to Ellison's aesthetic. The deductive-imagination approach starts with an ahistorical precept, which can then, through an act of the imagination, be applied to specific political groups and people. Put more concretely, once readers understand how the Brotherhood's psychological epistemology functions, they can then use their imagination to apply Ellison's model to many specific parties, people, and organizations in the real world. But given the growing skepticism about universals and metanarratives, there was a shift away from aesthetic models that started with an ahistorical precept and a shift toward models that foregrounded the historically specific, which explains why the biographical novel became increasingly more popular with both average readers and prominent writers after the 1970s.

Central to the new aesthetic of the biographical novel is the inductive imagination. Unlike the so-called nonfiction novelists, who refuse to offer an overarching vision, biographical novelists immerse themselves in a historically specific figure in order to draw a more cross-cultural conclusion. To illustrate, let me briefly discuss Madison Smartt Bell's trilogy about Toussaint Louverture. These works intelligently and poignantly portray the bizarre forms of racist logic that enabled France to justify its brutal enslavement and violation of Haitians. Most ironic, of course, is that the democratic ideals of the French Revolution were not seen as applicable to blacks in Haiti. In a response to a historian's subtle critique and extensive praise of the trilogy, Bell indicates how his novels function to illuminate not just the political situation in Haiti but also the United States.

In his essay, Bell claims "Haitian society has gone much further toward solving the problem of racism, derived from the history of colonialism en masse, than has the society of the United States."[61] After citing examples to support his point about the persistence of racism in the United States, Bell says that the "root of the problem is a good two hundred years in the past, enlaced with the three revolutions that concluded the eighteenth century."[62] If

---

[61] Madison Smartt Bell (2001), "Engaging the Past," in *Novel History: Historians and Novelists Confront America's Past (and Each Other)*. Mark C. Carnes (ed.). New York and London: Simon & Schuster: 207.

[62] Ibid.

we want to make some progress in eradicating contemporary race problems, examining the situation in Haiti (as represented in Bell's trilogy) would supply some answers. This is the case because, while Haiti, France, and the United States had revolutions that supposedly extended human rights to all people, only Haiti actually extended such rights to blacks. For Bell, the "failure of the American and French Revolutions to extend their ideology to all people created fault lines in the societies that resulted from them, fault lines that still promise and produce earthquakes today."[63] Given this failure, the situation seems dire. However, literature can move us forward, for if we understand and internalize the lessons of the Haitian Revolution, this would enable us to bring to fruition the democratic ideals implicit in our own incomplete Revolution. As Bell claims in the concluding sentence of his essay, "we must embrace the Haitian Revolution before we can fulfill our own."[64]

Through extensive research and expert artistic representation, the skillful biographical novelist immerses readers in a historical situation. In the case of Bell's trilogy, this enables readers to see some of the root causes of the race problem in Haiti. Having understood the historically specific example, readers can then use the inductive imagination to do a cross-cultural analysis and application. The biographical novelist's approach is the perfect response to the old-school universalism informing Ellison's work, which Edmund White unambiguously denounces in his interview, and the noninterpretive stance of the so-called nonfiction novelists. Ellison claims that fiction "manipulates reality, as it tries to get at those abiding human predica-ments which are ageless and timeless."[65] The biographical novelists of the postmodern age are certainly less comfortable making "ageless and timeless" Truth claims. But neither do they abandon their role as social and political critics, so they clearly reject the nonfiction novelist's approach of refusing to take an interpretive stance. Literature that appeals to the inductive imagi-nation is the response to the two extremes. Instead of inventing a symbolic character or group that exposes and expresses a timeless truth (Mr. Dalton in *Native Son* or the Brotherhood in *Invisible Man*), biographical novelists derive a "truth" from the experiences of a concrete historical figure. But the "truth" that they derive is not a traditional universal, which would apply to all people in all places at all times. Rather, it is a cross-cultural and cross-temporal "truth" which we could refer to as a limited or provisional universal.[66]

---

[63] Bell (2001): 207–8.
[64] Bell (2001): 208.
[65] Ellison et al. (1969): 64.
[66] For an insightful and useful discussion of provisional and constructed universals, see the debates of Judith Butler, Ernesto Laclau, and Slavoj Žižek in *Contingency, Hegemony,*

For example, Bell does not make a universal claim that is supposed to illuminate all racist polities, including, let us say, Nazi Germany. His focus is on those countries that had democratic revolutions in the eighteenth century but struggled with extending human rights to blacks. A cross-temporal and cross-cultural application of Bell's insights about Haiti would enable Americans to illuminate the contradictory ideology on which our contemporary political system is based. We see this same strategy and approach in Banks' *Cloudsplitter*. Banks examines the racist views of nineteenth-century Americans, but he also explores the taboo topic of homosexual desire through his narrator, Owen Brown, who is a repressed homosexual. When I asked him if there was evidence to suggest that Brown was homosexual, he said no. However, he said that there were parallels between the race issues of the nineteenth century and the issues of homosexuality of the twentieth century. Through a cross-temporal act of the inductive imagination, it is possible to see how nineteenth-century racism can be used to illuminate twentieth- and twenty-first-century homophobia.

Developments in Oates' corpus best chart the transformation in the literary imagination. In *Blonde*, Oates insightfully pictures the contradictory psychology of prominent American politicians. As a liberal, it would seem that JFK would have a progressive view of women. But in his relationship with Monroe, he is "a patrician patriarch."[67] With regard to the inductive imagination, JFK is not merely a typical male of the 1960s. He also represents the contradictory psychology of a powerful male liberal of the 1990s. Notice how Oates draws a clear parallel between JFK and Bill Clinton. Marilyn enters the President's room, and he is on the phone talking to "a White House adviser or cabinet member."[68] Oates describes what happens in a way that unmistakably recalls the Monica Lewinsky scandal: "Gamely the Blond Actress began to stroke the President's penis, as one might stroke a charming but unruly pet while its owner looked on proudly. Yet, to her annoyance, the President didn't hang up the phone."[69] Published in 2000, this novel was written in the late 1990s, at the height of the Lewinsky affair. But what is crucial to note is the transformation in Oates' writing during this period.

Like Wright, Oates targets the contradictory psychology of white male liberals in her fiction. Also like Wright, she authors a work that requires readers to use the deductive imagination to critique the American polity. That novella is *Black Water*, which was published in 1992 and is like Warren's

---

Universality. For a rehabilitation of the universal within the context of literature and cognitive studies, see Patrick Colm Hogan's "Literary Universals."

[67] Oates (2009): 708.
[68] Oates (2009): 705.
[69] Ibid.

All the King's Men in that it does not name the protagonist after the original figure. This novella is clearly based on the 1969 Chappaquiddick incident, when Senator Ted Kennedy had a car accident that resulted in the death of Mary Jo Kopechne, who is named Kelly Kelleher in the novella. But instead of naming her character Kennedy, Oates simply refers to him as the Senator. Also, the novella is set in the 1990s, after the first war in Iraq had already started, and the incident occurs on July 4 rather than July 18, thus giving it much more political significance. These changes enable Oates to construct a symbolic character (a universal or metanarrative) that embodies the reckless patriarchal psychology of so many prominent political figures of the 1990s. And once this symbolic character is clearly defined, readers could then use the deductive imagination to illuminate the behavior of a wide range of powerful American males.

By 2000, with the publication of *Blonde*, Oates produced fiction that required readers to use the inductive rather than the deductive imagination. Oates names her character Marilyn Monroe, and while she never actually refers to the President as JFK, the historical correspondences make such a conclusion inescapable. That historical specificity functions as an argument confirming Oates' critique of the patriarchy. This is not the work of the fictive imagination, which can easily concoct a sexist character that could be used to critique powerful males in the real world. In the postmodern age, we are more skeptical of such fictional abstractions because they resemble ahistorical precepts or traditional metanarratives. What we see in *Blonde*, therefore, is an empirical portrait of a known philanderer, whose reprehensible behavior contributed to the death of an actual woman. But Oates' concern is not just the patriarchal politics of the 1960s. By subtly using details from the Lewinsky case to describe JFK's treatment of Monroe, Oates invites readers to use the inductive imagination to draw a clear link between the patriarchal politics of JFK and Clinton. What JFK did in the 1960s Clinton continued to do in the 1990s. Or, read the other way, we can use the records from the Lewinsky case in order to illuminate what occurred between Monroe and JFK. My point is this: There is something much more penetrating and persuasive about literature that requires an act of the inductive rather than the deductive imagination, which, in part, explains why the biographical novel has become increasingly popular.

To be more specific, *Blonde* is a much more compelling critique of white male liberals than either Wright's *Native Son* or Oates' *Black Water*, because she avoids the charge of using the fictive imagination to concoct a sexist character that functions like an ahistorical Truth. By naming names and fictionalizing factual figures, Oates produces a searing portrait that is much more difficult to dismiss as the product of a paranoid or a runaway imagination. And by inviting readers to use the inductive imagination to link the white male liberals of the 1960s and the 1990s, Oates makes her implicit argument and cultural critique both persuasive and relevant. The shift from the deductive to the inductive imagination not only makes logical sense, but it is also a necessary aesthetic move for contemporary writers who want to continue in their role as the culture's most insightful social critics.

The interviews

The interviews in this volume have more than just individual merit. They are valuable in relation to each other. For example, in 1997 Anita Diamant published *The Red Tent*, which was, as Terry R. Wright notes, "a publishing phenomenon."[70] This biographical novel imagines the life of Dinah, who is raped in Genesis. After the rape, there is almost no information about Dinah in the Bible. But in *The Red Tent*, Diamant imagines what happens to Dinah both before the rape (also absent from the Bible) and after, as she goes to Egypt, bears a son, becomes a midwife, and gets married. This international best-seller sold more than two million copies and has been translated into twenty languages. Given its extraordinary success, it only makes sense that subsequent writers would author biographical novels about female religious figures, so Sherry Jones published *The Jewel of the Medina* (2008) and *The Sword of the Medina* (2009), which picture the life of Muhammad's nine-year old child bride A'isha; and Rebecca Kanner published *Sinners and the Sea* (2013), which gives a name and a voice to the nameless and voiceless wife of Noah from Genesis. Both Jones and Kanner acknowledge their debt to Diamant, but they also take this subgenre of the biographical novel in a different direction. This is important, because if we want to chart and define the evolution and nature of this subgenre, it is useful to hear how these writers conceive their work in relation to each other.

But here I want to issue a word of caution and to clarify my decision to put the interviews in alphabetical order. There was a temptation to organize the interviews according to subgenres. For instance, Diamant, Jones, and Kanner have written biographical novels about female figures from a religious tradition, so I could have created a section that contained the interviews of these three writers. However, an equally legitimate subsection such as feminist biographical novels would have probably included Diamant,

---

[70] Wright (2007), *The Genesis of Fiction: Modern Novelists as Biblical Interpreters*. Aldershot and Burlington: Ashgate: 113.

Jones, Kanner, Oates, Scott, Alvarez, and Kate Moses. In other words, categories obviously shift dramatically on the basis of the overarching descriptor, and many of the novels and novelists categorized here could appear in multiple categories.

Even though I do not use a subgenre classification system to organize the interviews, I do ask writers to locate their work within specific traditions. One provocative and insightful subgenre could be the slavery insurrectionist biographical novel, which would include Bontemps' *Black Thunder*, Styron's *The Confessions of Nat Turner*, Bell's *All Souls' Rising*, and Banks' *Cloudsplitter*. Another subgenre could be the biographical *Künstlerroman*, which would include Scott's *Arrogance,* Oates' *Blonde,* M. Allen Cunningham's *Lost Son,* White's *Hotel de Dream,* Parini's *Passages of H.M.,* and Moses' *Wintering.* Many of the novels focus on anti-Semitism, which would mean that Scott's *Arrogance* would be in the same tradition as Duffy's *The World as I Found It,* Parini's *Benjamin's Crossing,* Olsen's *Nietzsche's Kisses,* and Hansen's *Hitler's Niece.* There is obvious value in asking writers to think about their work within specific traditions, but there is also a clear danger of pigeon-holing their work, which is another reason I have decided not to organize the interviews according to subgenres.

With regard to the interviews, it is important to note that these are not exact transcriptions. I recorded all interviews, which I immediately sent to my research assistants, who transcribed them. I then spent a few days editing them, eliminating redundancy and fluff and refining the language. Finally, I sent each edited version to the author, who had the opportunity to add, delete, or revise. The author then sent the final copy to me. This process varied from one writer to the next. Many authors only reviewed and edited one version of the interview. Others went through multiple drafts. I always left it up to the writers to determine when the interview was complete.

I see this work as merely a beginning. There are many more great American biographical novelists, but because of limited time and resources, I could not include them in this volume. For instance, I would have gladly interviewed David Mamet, Margaret Cezair-Thompson, Jerome Charyn, Therese Anne Fowler, Geraldine Brooks, Jim Shepard, Bruce Olds, Brian Hall, David Maine, and Barbara Mujica, just to name a notable few. I especially regret not having interviewed Vidal before his recent passing. But I believe this book honors him and his work by acknowledging and carrying on his legacy.

What really needs to be done is to clearly define what the biographical novel is uniquely capable of doing. In 1986, Milan Kundera breathed new life into the novel by encouraging us "to discover what only the novel can discover."[71] Shifts in our theories of knowledge have necessitated corresponding developments in the form of the novel, so what is needed are studies that clarify precisely what only the biographical novel can discover. Liam McIlvanney and Ray Ryan recently published an edited collection of essays titled *The Good of the Novel*, and they have rightly noted that "the novelness of novels is coming back"[72] in part because of the decline of theory. I have strategically avoided interjecting too much theory into the interviews not just because of its decline but also because most of the writers in this volume consider it mind-numbing and intellectually reductive. One writer went so far as to say to me off the record that the current crisis in the humanities is a consequence of theory's alienating, obscure, and anti-democratic jargon. In many ways, I have followed McIlvanney and Ryan's lead by posing questions that any serious thinking person who loves reading literature could ask: "What is it that the novel knows? What kinds of truth can the novel tell?"[73] My questions in these interviews are the same, but they narrow the focus by discussing specifically the biographical novel. My audience, however, is not just academics. These interviews should engage people in and out of the university, and they do what all novels should do, which is to expand our understanding of the world and each other, raise perplexing questions about life, and confirm that humans are insoluble mysteries.

---

[71] Kundera (1988), *The Art of the Novel*. New York: HarperPerennial: 5.
[72] McIlvanney and Ryan (2011), *The Good of the Novel*. New York: Continuum International: viii.
[73] McIlvanney and Ryan (2011): xii.

1

Fixed Facts and Creative Freedom in the Biographical Novel

Julia Alvarez

Lackey: Let me start by telling you about this project. I want to find out why the biographical novel came into being. Before the 1980s, there were only a handful of really good biographical novels by writers such as Arna Bontemps, Zora Neale Hurston, William Styron, and Gore Vidal. But starting in the 1980s this genre of fiction became very popular. Why did this start happening in the 1980s? And can we define the nature of this genre?

Alvarez: I wasn't aware of a trend developing. After all, we've always been writing about each other. Recently, I've been reading Horace's *Odes,* and he gives generic names to many of the people he addresses or writes about. But even though he's not using specific names, it is *very* obvious—as the footnotes often note—that the ode is about a particular, real-life figure. When Horace does use an actual name, it's in a complimentary ode. Perhaps in antiquity there were higher stakes: the temptation to disguise was due to the danger of banishment or death. Now we settle for litigation instead! But we human beings are curious critters, and writers are no exception: we are always trying to understand each other, and especially we want to understand figures who have had some renown, whether it's because they were so heroic or horrid. Perhaps this complicates your question, but I'm not sure that this is some new trend.

Lackey: But why not change the names? Why are we naming a character Virginia Woolf or Ludwig Wittgenstein in recent years? Why are contemporary writers more comfortable doing this? And why do authors feel like they can take this liberty more today than they could in the past?

Alvarez: *In the Time of the Butterflies* began with a blurb on the back of a postcard. A women's press was doing a series of postcards on women heroines around the world, and they asked me if I'd contribute a Dominican heroine. I chose three, the Mirabal sisters, who started the underground that toppled the dictatorship in the Dominican Republic. I realized I had more than a blurb to say about them! This led me to ask more questions and to collect information. At that time, not much had been written about them—a mention here and there in a history book. So, it was a process of discovery: finding and interviewing the people who had known them and who had survived the dictatorship, visiting the places that had been important in their lives. My initial objective was to write a biography about them. But as I went along, I realized that I had become interested in their characters—what made them become the figures they became, what made them stand up to the dictator at a time when so few men or—heavens!—women, dared to do so. Character, then, became my focus, and for me, that is the province of fiction: recreating what evolves in that character, the truth according to that character. At first, I kept all the names. But when the manuscript was finished, I got cold feet and I decided to make it a story about fictional characters in a fictional country. The person who actually talked me out of it was Minou, the daughter of Minerva, one of the murdered sisters. Minou said, "Julia, we've been behind you this whole time." She and Dedé, the surviving sister, had given me access to everything; Minou even sent me the original letters her parents had written to each other during their time in prison. "We want people to know their story," Minou insisted. "We want them to know about the Mirabal sisters; we want their story to get out." And I said, "*Bueno,* Minou, I'm a little nervous because I'm not holding anything back, and some of these people are still alive." Also, the last thing I wanted to do was upset Dedé, who had already been through so much. On the other hand, I wasn't writing to order, the airbrushed story. So the deal was that Minou would read the manuscript since she knows English, and anything problematical she would discuss with Dedé. If Dedé or the family were upset with my novel, I'd go back to the idea of a totally fictional world. Believe me, I sweated those couple of weeks not knowing what was going to be the verdict. Finally, Minou called me: "You have our blessing." Now that the novel has been translated into Spanish, Dedé has been able to read it for herself. When people ask her about the novel, she says: "Some things aren't exactly the way I remember, but Julia caught their spirit. She captured those times."

Lackey: So you started by writing a biography, but it eventually morphed into a novel?

Alvarez: You know, I didn't even know what it was going to be. I just knew I wanted to understand those sisters, to tell *their* story. But I didn't know how. Initially, I had this collage planned where I was going to use clippings from newspapers,. telegrams, things that were happening around the world to create this kind of kaleidoscope around their story. I even wrote a number of poems in the voices of each sister to go between the chapters of this projected mongrel novel! It was going to be genre-bending. But as I got further and further inside the characters, the artistry started to fall away—the idea of using news clippings, the idea of using poems. I was captivated by their characters.

Lackey: This is the same strategy that Jay Parini uses in *The Last Station* with multiple narrators. He refers to it as a kaleidoscopic perspective.

Alvarez: Yes! The truth is complex, multi-faceted, and one person's truth might actually negate another's truth. I realized this as I interviewed more and more people: Dedé knew the three women as a sister, their revolutionary friends knew them as fellow revolutionaries, guards who remembered them knew them as prisoners. And so we have what I think of as a Native American moment where the truth sits in the center, but depending on where you sit around the circle, you see this or that aspect of the truth. As a novelist you can find ways to put all or many of those aspects into the narrative. But that's what makes literature trustworthy, rich, opposed to propaganda or what you have in a dictatorship, whether political or canonical, in which there's "one official story," the hegemony of one approved point of view and required allegiance to it. Once you're creating "real" characters you can complicate and present many aspects of the life and experience, because you don't have the point of view of just that one character. You can include other characters who bring out other aspects of your protagonist. And you also don't have just that single layer of character. You can also use setting, imagery, plot, the rhythms of your sentences, any number of elements to present other aspects of your character and his or her reality. By doing so, you are actually respecting the complexity of being a human being, including darker and hidden aspects of your character. I love what Terrence, the Roman playwright, once said, "I am a human being, nothing human is alien to me." That could be the motto of a novelist.

Lackey: And so it is through the creation of multiple characters that you can get to this more complicated perspective, whereas in traditional biographies and histories, a singular perspective dominates.

Alvarez: Not just multiple characters that complicate and enrich the perspective, but other elements of narrative, as I just mentioned. Of course, a good biographer would continue to complicate the material; however, there is the danger of a certain take on the character. You have to present the facts and perhaps draw a conclusion. Whereas, in fiction—and this is what I love about it—you can actually create *competing* truths. You can show multi-faceted dimensions—no truth trumps the other. Joseph Conrad makes this point in the preface to *The Nigger of the "Narcissus"* when he says: "Art itself may be defined as the single-minded attempt to render the highest kind of justice to the visible universe by bringing to light the truth, manifold and one, underlying its every aspect." That's what fiction does. He doesn't say *one* truth. He says the truth, *manifold and one*, underlying its every surface. It's that rich complexity we experience reading a novel, the feel of the texture of reality, a world as fully dimensioned and mysterious as our own. This is something that the facts can't get at by themselves. This representation of the truth, manifold and one, was for Conrad, and is so for me, the *"highest kind of justice"* we can render this universe. But it might not always be factual justice.

Lackey: Is it psychological justice? Is it political justice?

Alvarez: That's why I think it's a wonderful phrase: "The truth manifold and one." It's not just the psychological or the factual, it's *"manifold and one."* All those layers of truths are woven into the narrative, which is why Conrad says that it is the way to render the highest kind of justice to our experience of being alive. Another quote I love is from Novalis, the German poet and novelist: "Novels arise out of the shortcomings of history." History can't explain the mystery of being a human being. It's not equipped to do that. But novels—that's what they do best. So when I want to understand the past, I go to them, I read them, I write them. Specifically, I write historical novels because I want to understand the past, or perhaps that is not totally accurate. I want to understand the *experience* of being alive in the past, which means being a human being alive in the past. With *In the Time of the Butterflies* I wanted to understand the dictatorship we had fled when I was a child, a dictatorship that had formed my parents, and thus the dictatorship which had indirectly formed me. I wanted to know why and how a whole generation and nation had tolerated this atrocious regime for thirty-plus years. Then, along come the Mirabal sisters. How and why did three women decide they could not bear it anymore? Where did they find this courage? How did they come to do this, given who they were, what no one around them had been able to accomplish? Many questions drove me to this material. People think that writers write because they know things. We write because we want to find things out.

But back then, there was hardly anything written about the Mirabal sisters. The fear and silence of those oppressive years were still with us. To find these things out I had to travel back to the Dominican Republic. I felt an urgency to contact the people who had known the girls, who could tell me the facts of what had happened to them. Originally, I intended to write a biography about the famous sisters, a factual document. But as I went along in my interviews, two things happened which moved me in the direction of a novel. First, I became more and more interested in character—the truth according to character, the province of novels, and second, the facts kept shifting depending who I talked to. I'll tell you about one instance: the legendary slap Minerva was supposed to have given the dictator at a dance when he got fresh with her. This story is told *everywhere*. There is even a popular merengue about the slap. I interviewed a handful of people who had been at the party. Some recalled the slap. Some remembered the pink imprint left on the dictator's right cheek. But Dedé, the surviving sister, told me there had been no slap. There had been words, an insulting remark on the dictator's part, a rebuff on Minerva's part that was "*como si le hubiera dado una galleta,*" as if she had slapped him on the face. The same happened time after time with one or another fact: someone's fact became another's fiction. I began to realize that "these facts" lay at the center, and the truth consisted of all these points around that circle. Everyone agreed there had been an insulting moment at the dance and a rebuff on Minerva's part. I chose to put in the slap because of the kind of truth that detail told. Facts are only a part of what really happened.

It's that kind of truth which is more than fact, but includes the facts, that I want to get to in a novel, the emotional, the *lived* reality of that moment and the drama, and the feeling of the character living it. And the fact is: the minute you start trying to capture an experience in writing, you begin making selections, leaving certain things out, highlighting others, even if you are writing biography. You want to create the *feeling* of that moment. But the feeling of that moment is not just the facts. If that were the case, just give people the transcript and have the deadpan camera record the information.

Even in our own experience of history, or what will be history to the future, and now it's just "our own times," we experience it as a story we tell ourselves of what is happening to us: we are a certain character, with our unique point of view, a certain background, living in a certain context, a particular setting, with a certain set of friends: all these elements are also the elements of storytelling, and they complicate and enrich the "facts" that are happening all around us. So when you are creating a character, and recreating moments in history through that character, you've got to create all that context on paper. For me, a novel is the best vehicle for conveying the feel of that moment, the drama of the moment, the emotion of the moment, the fact of the moment, the setting of the moment, the smells of the moment—for that particular character you are trying to make real. And sometimes, that reality can begin to seem more real than our own reality!

I've noticed that with the Mirabal family itself. I am now a part of the family; they have all read the novel. Sometimes, they start talking, and I think they're *remembering the novel*. There are things I recall in doing the research that Dedé said, "Oh, I don't know about that," or "I wasn't there," or, "I never knew that," but now she *remembers* the full-blown scene, which I made up from the details I got elsewhere. Or which I made up out of whole cloth because no one alive could tell me what exactly happened that resulted in said fact. So even our own memories are storytellers. We remember things that never really happened or that never really happened to us.

Lackey: Let me shift to another question. I've heard many professors criticize contemporary biographical novels. They say that creative writers are merely summarizing and paraphrasing histories and biographies and then calling their works novels. How would you respond to this critique?

Alvarez: It's not easier to write biographical novels; it's not a slacking off of the imagination, second-rate creativity, just a different set of difficulties and challenges. When you're writing within a certain set form you have to make it *breathe*. You have to make the sonnet sound like a real human voice speaking within that form. You've got to make it fluid, and you've got to move within its restraints. The same principle applies to biographical fiction. You have these set points that you can't change. There are certain things that are givens, and certain information which you intuit. You want to present your character accurately, authentically; you want to honor the truths, manifold and one. But you also have to create them on paper, render them real. I could have just reported on Dedé's Mirabal sisters, and that would have been just one perspective. But I found my challenge was to go around that circle and take in as many points of view as I could. I certainly had fixed facts: *this* happened and then *this* happened. But how did the character evolve from here to there? How did she who was here and reacted in this way become capable of doing this contradictory thing later? So that's where the truth according to character comes in. Maybe in a totally invented fiction, and I doubt there is such a thing, you yourself are fixing those points. But once those fixed points are there, you, too, have to work within the constraints you've set up. I suppose you can always go back and move this point over here, and then you'll have to recreate the whole web, because you tweak one thread and the whole weave changes. So you're just working with different kinds of difficulties and challenges. You still have to create that world and that life and that interior character on paper—that's still the same: bringing to life your characters (historical or not). And that's never easy. No shortcuts. Good writing is hard work.

Lackey: This reminds me of Virginia Woolf, who argues that the novelist's primary responsibility is to character. The author must use the imagination to create a figure that is brimming with life and authenticity. It is this obligation that explains why, according to Woolf, it is impossible to mix fact and fiction, to mix biography and the novel. In an effort to create a character's rich interior life the novelist cannot be restricted by the mundane facts of an individual's biography, which requires a person to focus primarily on representing a historical figure accurately. How do you respond to Woolf's critique? Can you offer some reason why she couldn't see her way toward the biographical novel? Or conversely, can you explain what has happened that has enabled so many writers like yourself to do what Woolf thought impossible?

Alvarez: One could argue that all of Woolf's novels are loose biographies of the world and the people who surrounded her. True, Woolf doesn't write about a particular known historical person, but she's writing about places and people and situations not all that different from her own. As a novelist, you write about a character because he or she intrigues you. You want to understand that character's interior life, what forms and informs that character. What was it like to be that character? If you have a historical figure, you already know some of the circumstances that shaped that character. If you have a totally fictional character, you invent those circumstances—it's just a different set of forces shaping your character, but character is what you are interested in. And in creating your character, real or fictional, you're always writing out of the material of your own life, your own biography. If you're writing about Napoleon, say, and you have him eat an orange, you never saw him do that, right? But maybe you had a father who was dictatorial and aggressive, and you remember how he used to devour oranges. So when you write about Napoleon eating that orange, you access that memory of your father to inform your description of Napoleon. The same goes for a totally fictional character, who is pushy, bossy. When you describe that character, you access what you remember from your own experience. And I also bet that your interest in Napoleon or a bossy protagonist has everything to do with your experience with that kind of character in your own life. That's what makes a particular character, whether historical or not, entrancing to you—your own biography. So I think.

Lackey: But here's the dilemma as Woolf represents it. In "Mr. Bennett and Mrs. Brown," she discusses the task of the novelist, which is to picture a Mrs. Brown. Arnold Bennett fails because he focuses on superficial externals rather than rich interiors. But for Woolf, if a novelist wants to make a character live, he or she must access the character's interiority; that's where the spirit lies. But to make a rich and living character, the novelist must abandon the impulse to represent Mrs. Brown accurately. The actual Mrs.

Brown becomes insignificant, irrelevant. You make an important point by saying that novelists work within constraints. There is a form, like a sonnet, but within these constraints and restrictions, the artist can breathe life into the work. Woolf seems to be saying that the restriction of representing the character accurately would deaden the life of a character. But I think you would say that it is possible to have restrictions, and yet to breathe life into the character just the same.

Alvarez: Absolutely! But I think that it might be a misunderstanding of character here. It assumes that a character who is famous, a public persona, is a fixed entity who doesn't have all the variety, contradictions, and tremulous life and possibilities that the rest of us have. I think we're all telling ourselves a story in our head about who we are, a story that keeps changing as we get this bit of information. We also are telling ourselves a story about every person we encounter, from what we know about that person, what we've been told, and so on. And since we can't have every bit of information about that person, we are always connecting the dots, always creating them in our heads in order to understand them. This is what Woolf is so wonderful at doing with her characters. And that can be done with a historical character as well. There are the certain constraints with the historical figure, facts that shape the narrative, or his/her character, but once you've set up a fictional world, there are constraints on your protagonist as well; you have to work within that world you've created. The key thing for the novelist is to breathe life into that character.

Lackey: But doesn't that act of breathing life into a character take the novelist away from the actual reality of the historical figure?

Alvarez: Oh, I don't think so. That historical figure was not a statue, but as various, complex as we are. I don't think of it as moving away from my historical character, but moving deeper and deeper into that character, peeling the onion as it were. After a certain point, you feel you've touched bottom. That's why, after I had all factual information I needed to be able to connect the dots, I didn't want to keep talking to Dedé about her sisters. I didn't want to go checking back and forth because the characters had assumed their own momentum and their own voices, and their own interior life. They had begun to be real on paper.

Lackey: And yet, you were still committed to representing the actual figures as accurately as you could?

Alvarez: Yes, but this act of representing accurately should not be seen as a box. To clarify, let me tell you about Mate. I wanted each character to have a very particular voice. Mate was the youngest, and therefore, the most girlish of the sisters. But how do I convey that? What *form* would best embody her voice, her youth? And I thought, oh, a diary form because there is something very young and fresh and evolving about that form. I also needed a voice in this novel that would provide readers with the little details, the news of the day, what she had for breakfast, what so-and-so was wearing, the kind of information that a Minerva would probably ignore because she is so caught up in ideology. So I gave Mate this voice, and later, when Dedé read the novel, she said to Minou: "How did Julia know that María Teresa liked to keep diaries?" That gave me chills! Here, we're entering very different territory from the traditional, academic, analytical framework in explaining a writer's process! For me, it was an experience similar to *santería* in our Caribbean culture. In this animist religion, the *santera*, or priestess, is mounted by the spirit of a dead person, who uses the body of the *santera* to communicate to the living. The *santera*'s voice, walk, appearance are transformed by this possession. I was so involved in each Mirabal sister as I wrote her chapters that I could feel viscerally when I was straying away from that character or trying to take her in a certain direction she wouldn't go. I was taken over by the life of that character. It's this kind of obsession or possession which I can't explain, but I felt as I was writing the novel. This might be what Dedé meant when she said that I *captured* the spirit of her sisters. That was the best compliment I received. Dedé didn't say I had recorded every fact as she remembered it, but that I had *captured* her sisters' personalities.

Lackey: At this point, let me shift to another question. Many biographical novels include a preface, an afterword, or a postscript with a disclaimer saying that the work is fiction, which is not to be confused with biography or history. In your postscript, you say that, on one hand, you lack the talent of a biographer, which is why you cannot give us the Mirabal sisters of *fact*. But, on the other hand, you claim that the Mirabal sisters of your creation are true to the spirit of the real Mirabals. The distinction, as I understand, is between fact and spirit. Can you define what you mean by spirit? And can you discuss some of your research techniques for accessing and writing strategies for representing that spirit?

Alvarez: I did traditional research about the history of the era: I read histories of other dictatorships in Latin America. I conducted oral interviews. I visited all of the locations in the book, including the prison, the torture center, the church where they had gotten married, the houses they lived in. I felt I needed visceral contact with everything in order to get into the voices and inner lives of the characters. But I read things that were not immediately, directly relevant: diaries of young girls in war-torn places;

memoirs by resistance fighters in Latin America and in France during the Second World War. It was also odd what made each sister come alive for me. When I first started writing in Patria's voice, I thought she was going to be the hardest for me because she's so religious. Conversely, I thought Minerva, because I love her revolutionary spirit, would be the easiest. But she was the most difficult to access. To get into Patria's character, I listened to a lot of organ music when I was writing her chapters. I wanted that sense of that spiritual soaring in her voice. I tuned into it by hearing that music and reading certain books, like Ron Hansen's *Mariette in Ecstasy*, which was very helpful. So, the research is not always direct information-gathering. But everything helped, researching *santería*, researching women who had been part of any number of resistance movements, including the resistance movement of French women during World War Two. Luckily, a whole book of their interviews and memoirs had just been published as I was working on my novel. It was very helpful to hear from these women, because they gave me insights about my own characters. These French women's admissions reminded me that even heroic women are complex, driven by fears, hopes, petty at times, brave sometimes by accident. I didn't want to create ideological pawns or stock historical figures, the prose equivalent of marble statues.

Lackey: Can I ask you a question about the Minerva character? Why was she so difficult to access?

Alvarez: Because she was driven, so idealistic. I knew there was more. But I couldn't seem to find my way inside her. That is, until I read Benazir Bhutto's memoir, *Daughter of the East*. Bhutto was Prime Minister of Pakistan, a heroic figure, a charismatic leader, a seemingly strong woman publicly, but in her memoir she confesses to panic attacks when she went out in public; at certain points in her life she's paralyzed by her fears, her fatigue, her flagging beliefs. Reading that memoir sprung open the character of Minerva for me. It explained some of the comments I would hear about Minerva, towards the end, as the pressures on her mounted. She wasn't just this flat, one-dimensional character, a total believer.

Lackey: Was she a broken character by the end? Or, could she recover?

Alvarez: I don't know. I think we die many deaths within our lives, and resurrection isn't always guaranteed. We do have the living dead, examples all around us. No done deals, at least not while we are alive. I think keeping parts of a character mysterious is part of the respect you render any character that you create. The complexity of a possibility; they're not a finished self, a set quantity...

Lackey: No formula.

Alvarez: Yes, right. That's such disrespect to your characters, when the plot is driving the story, and we just feel like the poor characters are yoked, carrying that plot forward. And I suppose that's what Virginia Woolf meant, that she didn't want to harness her characters to pulling the plot of what had really happened forward. She feared that she wouldn't have the license to create the full-dimensionality and complexity of the characters if that sort of burden of history were upon them. But I don't think that's even the way historical characters experience the history they're living as they're living it.

Lackey: In your postscript, you suggest that the imagination has the power to redeem the lives of the Mirabal sisters and the epoch in the life of the Dominican Republican. Can you clarify what that means?

Alvarez: You make meaning. It won't solve anything. The story won't save us, but the *telling* of the story is redemptive; we understand; we can bear the suffering. When everything has fallen apart, in that broken world, we learn how to be human again through the telling of the story. We are saying, this, too, is human; this, too, we can bear and understand. "These fragments I have shored against my ruins." I know the word *redemptive* has religious overtones, and I'm not trying to be hokey or self-aggrandizing, but telling the story can help us bear the unbearable.

I can think of two stories that explain this idea of redemption in the way stories can explain things, and explanations can't. One comes from Anna Akhmatova, that little piece she wrote, *Instead of a Preface*, about standing outside the prison where her son is incarcerated during the terrible years of terror. This weary woman who is also waiting in line recognizes Akhmatova and sidles up to her, and asks if she, Akhmatova, can describe this. And Akhmatova replies that, yes, she can. The last sentence, describing the weary woman's reaction, is something like, a smile passed over what once had been her face. For that moment, humanity is restored in that face and between the two women.

The other story is one that John Bartlow Martin, who was the US ambassador to the Dominican Republic after the dictatorship, tells about in his book, *Overtaken by Events*. He travels the country, asking people what kind of help they need to build a democracy. Martin meets with these teenagers in this one little outlying city, and when he asks them, they reply, "Build us a library so we can have some books." And he says, "Well, what books?" After a long pause, a thin, quiet one in a white shirt with large, brown eyes says, "Books about Trujillo." Martin is surprised. "Why?" And the young man replies, "So we can understand what happened to us." And that's what

I think stories can help us do: make meaning so we can understand what happens to us.

My sister was a therapist for many years in Boston working with political refugees who had fled their countries, people who had suffered devastating losses, who had seen their families killed, whole villages destroyed. She said that many of them were suffering from post-traumatic stress disorder. They didn't even have the language to articulate their experiences. She told me that she knew they were coming back to the human fold when they could tell her the story of what had happened to them. The horror, the horror. I survived it. I'm here to tell you the tale. There's something about the telling of the story that makes it—even if it's inhuman—possible for us to hold its heart-breaking reality inside us and among us. We share in our common suffering humanity—that to me seems redemptive.

Lackey: Shifting focus, I would like to briefly discuss Dedé. There is a wonderful scene picturing Dedé undergoing a transformation. She has just read that Virgilio Morales is a communist, an enemy of the state. But then she reflects on the disparity of the representation of Lío and her experience of him, and this leads her to become more critically aware and, not coincidentally, immediately after this experience she begins to realize she has overlooked so much in all that she has read in the past. Do you think the biographical novel demands a more complicated form of literacy than the traditional novel, as it forces readers to engage and negotiate fiction *and* history? And can you discuss how the biographical novelist educates readers into more complex forms of literacy?

Alvarez: I have never thought of this before, a more complex form of literacy … I think that any good novel demands a new kind of literacy from us. A weak novel, historical or not, just confirms all our habits of thinking, speaking, seeing the world through the lens of clichés. But a great novelist creates a whole new kind of literacy, in part from the use of language. Think of William Faulkner, James Joyce, Gertrude Stein, Virginia Woolf. More recently novels like *The Buddha in the Attic* by Julie Otsuka or *Room* by Emma Donoghue. They teach us new ways of reading, of seeing the world. They push the parameters of being a human being by mapping areas of the human psyche that had been there before, but only as potential, as possibility. That Emily Dickinson line suddenly lit up in my head, "I dwell in possibility"! So I think the best writers widen our possibilities as human beings.

Lackey: Let me give you an example. I am teaching *In the Time of the Butterflies* right now, and in your novel, you address foreign policy, how the United States initially supported the resistance in the Dominican Republic.

But then the United States withdrew its support. Part of the problem was Communism. If it is a choice between a dictator and Communism, the United States will let the dictator rule. For a teacher this is wonderful, because it gets my students into a conversation not just about what is going on in the novel, but also in the world around them. And in your work, especially in your postscript, you discuss the link between literacy and freedom, between the capacity to read and the ability to be free. It is through biographical novels that I have most success getting students to understand that link. Put simply, your novel demands not just that we read the text, but that we learn how to read our lives, how to read the political.

Alvarez: But don't you think that all good books force us to see and do that? Maybe the application to the political is a little fuzzier, but we learn to be critical thinkers, and that's why I think reading is so key. We develop the muscles of the imagination, which are also the muscles at work when we are compassionate, sensitive, and attentive. I think the best literature exercises our souls, perhaps even helps create them.

Lackey: I agree, but I think biographical novels resonate with students more powerfully than many other novels. Faulkner's *Light in August*, Woolf's *Mrs. Dalloway*, and Ralph Ellison's *Invisible Man* certainly teach us to read and think more critically and intelligently. But because your novel is so historically specific, my students can connect with the material in a way that many times they cannot in other excellent but less historically specific novels. I have been thinking about this because I have been teaching so many of these biographical novels and I have been stunned by the power they have over students.

Alvarez: What is it making them do what you say?

Lackey: It's getting them to think in more specific and complicated ways about domestic politics and foreign policy. This is something undergraduate students have a very difficult time doing. You have made characters and issues come alive for them, and in the process, the students want to understand these characters, these people, the Dominican Republic, and so much more. They want to understand how American foreign policy affects their lives and the lives of others, which is leading them to ask really smart and interesting questions.

Alvarez: This reminds me of the Middlebury mission to encourage students to go abroad for a year. One of the places they can come to, after graduation, is *Alta Gracia*, a sustainable coffee farm and literacy center in the mountains of the Dominican Republic that my husband, Bill Eichner, and I established in 1997. When students spend a year living there as volunteers, they begin to understand "underdevelopment," which up to then has been a textbook term. Poverty is no longer an abstraction. It wears the "human face divine," that wonderful Blake phrase. They are profoundly changed.

And I think that's the thing that happens when you read. When you enter a character, you see how issues affect a specific human being, one life, or one group of lives. I remember when I was writing *In the Time of the Butterflies*, being intrigued by the question: how do people come to courage? Reading those memoirs by women in the resistance in France, I was struck by how many came to their activism because of a specific person. A knock on their door, their neighbor from whom they had once borrowed butter, who had helped them when their baby had had colic, saying, "Can you help me? Can you hide my little daughter?" And although they hadn't wanted to get involved, it was no longer an issue, it was a human being whose life they understood and shared. Historical novels return us to the people the history happened to. We experience what it's like to be that person living at that moment. And that's the way we experience our own time—as I mentioned earlier—from our specific character. And that same complexity with which we are experiencing our moment in time, we have to accord to those characters in the past as well.

Your remarks made me think of something else. Years ago, I was working with the Poetry-in-the-Schools program. I called myself a migrant poet, because I would go wherever I was sent as a visiting writer, usually an elementary or high school. These were short six-week residencies. At one of these gigs, I met a British playwright who was having the students write up scenes about moments in history they were studying. Then the students acted them out. He had all these facts and figures that proved that, if students depicted a specific historical event, such as Lincoln deciding to go to war or Benedict Arnold siding with the Brits, they would retain the information much more readily. So when the final exam came, these students would all be able to write vividly about these events. But if these facts remained abstract and dry in a textbook, they just weren't interested. Somehow those moments that they had recreated were the ones they were apt to remember, think about, and want to learn more about.

Lackey: To conclude, do you have any final thoughts about the biographical novel?

Alvarez: I recently read a review of a new biography of Karl Marx, and the reviewer said that the author had provided a template of how we might approach great figures: "demystifying the words and deeds of those too often lazily deemed sacred." I think biographical fiction has been doing that demystification all along. It's part of a cultural shift, a new demand for transparency about our public figures. We see this shift when we compare figures like President Roosevelt and current politicians. In Roosevelt's time, the subject of his polio was *verboten*. Nowadays, if you are a public figure, your health records, your tax returns, your private life—it's our public right to know about. But no matter the talk shows and reality shows, the investigative reporting, there isn't anything that so powerfully recreates the interior life of a character, the complex stream of thoughts and feelings in response to whatever is happening as a good biographical novel. There is a natural kinship between biographies and novels, both are interested in character. Maybe, and I'm not sure about this, the biographer wants to get at the truth of a character, and the novelist at the truth according to character—it's a slight distinction but critical. But the minute we try to set up definite markers about where one genre ends and another begins, we're in trouble. It's a shifting landscape, just like it is inside the minds of every human being, as we live our lives, creating our internal world as we go along, part fact, part fiction, and all kinds of hybrids. It reminds me of that question people always ask me: do you dream in English or Spanish? They think they're going to catch me drawing a fixed line. But if I'm having a dream and the chair of my department comes to my door, she speaks to me in English. If my Papi comes in the same dream, he speaks to me in Spanish. There aren't these fixed markers. I understand the urge: we want to quantify, keep literature contained in neat little genre boxes, a kind of bad high-school English teacher's reductive need to nail down the winged life. We live in possibility, a messy landscape. We are trying to do the impossible, actually, to recreate life itself in language, and we need to range freely and creatively within the fixed contours of a particular character in order to make her or him come alive again in the imagination of our readers.

2

The Truth Contract in the Biographical Novel

Russell Banks

Lackey: Let me start by telling you about this project. There have been many biographical novels written over the last thirty years, and my goal as a scholar is to figure out why this has happened, but it is also to define the nature of the contemporary American biographical novel. For this novel to be possible some major developments in literature had to occur. To indicate that this is the case let me briefly discuss Virginia Woolf's essay "The Art of Biography." For Woolf the novelist is free to create, while the biographer is tied to facts. Lytton Strachey and the new biographers of the early twentieth century revolutionized the biography by making liberal use of the creative imagination and fictional techniques in depicting a person's life, thus giving the artist/biographer the freedom to invent something new: a book that was not only a biography, but also a work of art. But ultimately, Woolf concluded, this combination proved unworkable because fact and fiction refused to mix. Can you explain why it is now possible to blend fact and fiction in the biographical novel as you do in *Cloudsplitter*?

Banks: It's difficult for me to explain because in a way the question, as you phrase it, presupposes that I was aware of there being an opening available for that kind of fiction. Or even that I was writing a kind of fiction when I was writing the novel. In fact, I have to say I wasn't aware that I was until you wrote me and sent me your questions. And I could then see, yeah, I guess you're right. Whether and how an occasion for the writing of biographical fiction, or a legitimization of it, preceded the writing I can't say. Not calling it by any name, I was aware of and had spoken about the biographical novel in public with other people, like Joyce Carol Oates with regard to her book *Blonde*, which is about Marilyn Monroe, and E. L. Doctorow and his work. It seemed to me a given that I could write from inside a historical figure. I could write a "life" of that figure, using that figure's life, but I would be writing a dramatic narrative, a work with a dramatic shape and intent, rather than a biography of that character.

Lackey: You get inside the character. Do you think this is one of the defining features of the biographical novel? That writers are now trying to get to the interiority of a character more?

Banks: Yes, but I don't think that is unique to our time. I think it's unique to fiction. What fiction does from Cervantes forward, really through the novel more than any other form of fiction, is validate and dignify the subjective experience of an individual human being. And the best way, of course, to do that is to get inside that person's head and see the world through that person's eyes. Until I started working with film about ten or fifteen years ago I thought that in the film world the director was the closest person to the novelist. But after I was working closely enough with everyone involved, I could see the differences between the director and the cinematographer, the screenwriter, the actor, and so forth, and I began to realize that the actor more than the director was like the novelist. Because the actor inhabits the characters, feels his or her way inside the character, and then looks out through the character's eyes. And that is essentially what a novelist has to do.

Lackey: Were you ever tempted to change the character names in order to give yourself some more freedom?

Banks: Not in the case of *Cloudsplitter*. I have done it in other works. I had a novel published recently that is clearly set in Miami, but I changed the name of the city so that it wouldn't be a novel about Miami. This is an interesting contrast perhaps. I realized, if I call it Miami, it is going to be strictly a story about the peculiarities of Miami. It won't be universal. It won't be a story about every city in the world, at least the Western world. And so I invented a new name for the city, even though I was at times describing Miami, Florida, and it gave me much more freedom to invent my story and also to universalize the story. The opposite is the case with the historical figure.

Lackey: But in doing that you are now tied to a lot of facts, right?

Banks: Yes I am, but there's so much also that isn't known and that's one reason why I've told it from the point of view of Owen Brown. The facts are so well-known I'd just be retelling them if I told it from the point of view of John Brown. But he is an emblematic and iconic figure, and it is much more difficult to penetrate and identify with a character like that than to tell a story from the point of view of his little-known son Owen. There are other reasons as well. But I'm not really answering your question. Can you rephrase it for me?

Lackey: I'm questioning here the kind of liberties you can take as a novelist when you decide to name a character after the original figure. There is a question of ethics here. On the one hand, you want to give your readers a story, a living character. But on the other hand, do you have the freedom just to alter history in any way you want?

Banks: My feeling is that I'm using history in order to tell a story. I could as easily use a journalistic account from yesterday's newspaper or another work of art. My real purpose is to generate and tell a story. It is not to correct history or write an addendum to the historical or biographical record. It is simply to appropriate the material that history has dropped at my door, somewhat the way Shakespeare certainly felt entitled to do or the way Homer felt entitled to do. This is something storytellers have done since the beginning of narrative. If history drops it on your doorstep, it's there to be used. I don't feel that I have any higher ambition in terms of using history than that provided by the requirements of story. My respect and use of historical facts are really based on my need for plausibility. I can't violate what is commonly known or I will lose the reader's suspension of disbelief, which depends on plausibility. It's the same with geography. If I set a story in New York City and I have Broadway running from the Upper East Side down diagonally across to the Lower West Side, I'm going to lose the suspension of disbelief that my reader has acquired from the plausibility of my description of New York. The same thing applies to historical figures. If I have John Brown not being executed in 1859, but living on to see Lincoln become president, I would lose my readers. My novel would lack the kind of suspension of disbelief that my kind of realism depends upon. That is the only concern I really have. I don't have any particular concern for the historical record as such. There are many things in that novel that are not part of the historical record but that a scholar or biographer of Brown would know didn't occur. He or she would know, for instance, that John Brown never heard Ralph Waldo Emerson deliver his talk on heroism at the Charles Street meeting house in Boston.

Lackey: Why did you include that scene?

Banks: I included the scene for dramatic reasons and for reasons of character in the story. I wanted to divide Owen Brown from his father John Brown over a figure like Emerson, who was an abolitionist, but a pacifistic man and nowhere near as radical as John Brown. And I knew, although I didn't have any text to confirm this, that Brown would probably take a

critical view of Emerson. Even though Emerson's essay on heroism is calling
for a man like Brown to rise up out of the population and deal with the issue
of slavery. And Owen Brown would find him much more sympathetic. So
it was in order to split the two characters in the story over the same figure,
Emerson.

Lackey: There was a famous forum in 1968, run by the historian C. Van
Woodward, with Robert Penn Warren, Ralph Ellison and William Styron.
They talked about the ethics and wisdom of the biographical novel. Ellison
was the most passionate. He said that the biographical novel is a mistake,
and he had two separate reasons for this view. First, he said that there is no
way you can get to the complexity of the original person. So if you make
the decision to name the figure after the original, you're going to necessarily
misrepresent the complexity of that person. Second, the moment you name
the figure after the original, you are stepping into the historians' realm, and
they are going to attack you. They are going to say that the mole wasn't on
that side of the face or they're going to come back with some little detail and
say you made this mistake. How would you respond to Ellison's critique?

Banks: I think he is flatly wrong about the complexity of character. That is a
critique that doesn't make any sense to me. I don't even know what it means
to say that a historical character has greater complexity than a fictional
version of that historical character. Even a historical or biographical version
is still, at best, an imagined portrait of the character. So who is to say that's
more complex than a fictional character? He might as well say that fiction
can't capture the complexity of a human being. It doesn't make any sense,
that critique. His second critique, that you're making yourself vulnerable
to criticism from so-called experts, also seems wrong. There is a case in
Cloudsplitter where I ran up against a local historian—they're the worst.
They really know their little square of the universe. I have an episode in
Cloudsplitter where the Brown family for the first time in 1848 goes up to
reside in North Elba, New York in the Adirondack Mountains and they are
on an old road going alongside a long, narrow chain of lakes. They come to
an opening between the mountains and there it is—the Plains of Abraham—
and that is where they are going to live. After the novel was published,
an elderly woman named Mary Mackenzie, the town historian for North
Elba, wrote letters to newspapers, to *Adirondack Life* magazine, and to me
personally, and then telephoned me, outraged that I had placed the Brown
family on a road alongside those lakes in 1848 because that road wasn't built
until the 1870s. I happened to know that fact because I had an old map and
indeed there wasn't any road there then. There is now, it's been there since
the 1870s. But I wanted the image in the novel relatively early of this family

seen from above going along the edge of these narrow lakes that are like fiords, with mountains coming down directly into the water, so that I could describe them as going along the blade of a scimitar and deploy the image as a prefiguration of the bloody swords that they would use much later—200 or 300 pages later—in Kansas in the Pottawatomie Massacre, which was an incredibly graphic part of the novel. I wanted to anticipate that with the image of the lake. So I violated history.

Lackey: So could we say that you subordinate historical truth at certain moments in favor of a certain kind of symbolic truth?

Banks: Yes, exactly. And in favor finally of a dramatic truth. And a story. That is really my primary concern, and I'm not concerned with history except insofar as I need it for plausibility. And, therefore, the small parts that only a local historian in upstate New York would know—it doesn't bother me that that fact was inaccurate. I did it deliberately because I wanted the image. The image was more important to me than the roadmap of North Elba in 1848.

Lackey: This leads to one of the more difficult questions I want to pose to you about history. In most of these biographical novels, there is a preface, an author's note, an afterword, or an epilogue, and they all have a disclaimer declaring that their work is fiction and it is not to be confused with biography or history. Of all these recent biographical novels you make the strongest claim by saying "*Cloudsplitter* should be read solely as a work of fiction, not as a version or interpretation of history." But this prefatory claim is difficult to square with your Owen's definition that he is giving us the secret history of John Brown. For those of us who have read your novel closely and carefully, we tend to agree more with your Owen Brown than with you. How do you respond to this?

Banks: What do you mean you agree more with Owen Brown? You think you are getting the secret history of John Brown? You are getting Owen Brown's, a fictional character's, version of the secret history of John Brown. There is still another, I'm sure, and there are still probably a hundred more secret histories of John Brown yet to be told. The historical Owen Brown had no awareness of Owen Brown the fictional character. Don't forget, too, that Owen Brown in the novel is telling this story from around 1903, when in fact he died in 1889. So right there, by authorial fiat, I violated history. Anyone who knows the story of John Brown well enough knows his son Owen, born in 1825, died in 1889. I let him live on into the twentieth century so that his story, John Brown's story, would lose some of the antique quality it might have had otherwise and would point toward the twentieth century, to our own time. Even to the twenty-first century, where it's now being read as a portrait of the terrorist that can be applied to our understanding of our present time. Owen Brown's claim to be telling the secret history of John Brown—his own and his father's secret history—is a fictional character's claim. It's not Russell Banks's claim.

Lackey: This gets to one of the central questions at the heart of this project. What is it that the novel can give us that traditional histories cannot? Someone like E. M. Forster says that the novelist can chart the subconscious short-circuiting into human action. This is something that the novelist is uniquely qualified to do. Milan Kundera has argued that the novelist can represent a phenomenological interior. Biographical novelists today have been charting a new way of understanding history. So when I read your disclaimer, it is a bit disheartening because these novels are hugely important in that they can unlock history in different ways than traditional history. But we have to be really systematic and precise by saying: this is what the novelist does, this is why it's different, this is what it is uniquely capable of achieving.

Banks: It might not be that easy to apply to history in the way that you are suggesting. I oftentimes argue with people who've said that in *Cloudsplitter* they've found some historical error, as it were. I don't regard it as error, just as a different use for history than a historian or a biographer might have. I'm not able, for instance, to understand the War of the Roses through Shakespeare or the Trojan War through Homer, or the Civil War through *Gone with the Wind*. I think you make a big mistake if you use literature in order to understand history. I would apply it instead to our understanding of humanity and what it means to be human. The novelist can humanize a historical figure by inhabiting the character in a way that a biographer and a historian can't. But that's in the interest of humanity, extending our understanding of human beings, not history.

Lackey: That might not give us a literal historical truth, but it does give us a certain kind of phenomenological truth, doesn't it?

Banks: Yes, so long as we the readers of the novel can test its claims for phenomenological truth against our own secret phenomenological truth and not find it inauthentic or wanting. In fiction, it's always the reader who validates the truth of the text, or lack thereof.

Lackey: Postmodernism has radically impacted the novel in recent years. We used to think that there was a clear distinction between fact and fiction. But postmodernists have argued that the moment we step into the realm of language, we are in the world of fiction. Traditional histories and biographies were once considered non-fiction, but postmodernism has exposed both as fiction. Thus, the dichotomy between biography and the biographical novel has collapsed in recent years.

Banks: And I think that's fine. I follow that collapse with a certain degree of enthusiasm actually. Maybe now we can claim that historians and biographers have no special claim to that material, that they have no reason to say this is their material and not mine too. History and biography are interpretive, and they're subjective. So there is no absolute historical or biographical truth that resides in the historical or the biographical record, the data. That material is up for grabs.

Lackey: And now that it is up for grabs, this gives fictional writers a new kind of license. Is this one of the reasons why the biographical novel has become so popular with prominent writers?

Banks: It could be. There is an increasing speed to the use of that material, and I think that it is simply because it gets justified and validated by all the writers that you're working with here. There's enough of them out there now so that some twenty-five year old kid coming along and writing his novel wouldn't feel in the slightest hesitant about going ahead and doing it. I could point to a dozen biographical novels today, but I couldn't when I was writing in the sixties and seventies. I couldn't point to a whole lot of books other than Styron's and one or two others.

Lackey: So one of your arguments is that because there are so many people doing this, it becomes more possible. But actually I would argue that there is a key turning point, which involves your novel. In 1999, your *Cloudsplitter* and Michael Cunningham's *The Hours* were both up for the Pulitzer. It seems that the literary establishment said in this year: these biographical novels are doing something unbelievably original, so original, in fact, that they are worthy of this country's most prestigious award.

Banks: That's what I was saying. There are enough models that have been validated by the critical and academic establishment that younger writers don't feel any hesitancy about extending and continuing that tradition, deepening it, which is great.

Lackey: Let me shift to a question about Jay Parini. Parini recommends that contemporary biographical novelists stop making the prefatory disclaimer that their characters are fictional. Rather, he recommends that authors say the following, "Everything in the following pages is authentic, which is to say that it is as true as I could make it—take it or leave it." Can you define your approach to the biographical novel in relation or opposition to Parini's approach?

Banks: I know Jay, he is a good friend, and I think he is being a little facetious there. But I also understand his desire to get rid of these little prefaces. I wish I hadn't put mine in. But given the time when the book was published, it felt necessary.

Lackey: Would you change it today if you had?

Banks: Yes, I think I would. I don't think I would leave it in. That is an interesting question and my answer is: unless my publisher insisted, I'd leave it out.

Lackey: But why would you leave it out today?

Banks: For the very reasons that you're pointing toward. Because there are so many other books using historical and biographical figures as characters, literary characters. If you call it a novel on the cover of the title page, that should be enough. What that implies is a contract with the reader. If it's called a memoir, it has a different contract. But my contract with the reader is that *Cloudsplitter* is a novel because it says so on the cover and title page: some of it is drawn from history, some of it is drawn from biography, and a lot of it is made up. Some of it is drawn from my own personal life. But for my purposes, the way it should be read is as a novel, and the books against which it should be measured are novels. The same way you read *Moby Dick* you read this—if I can be that grand. We don't apply the terms and standards of history or biography to it. If it were memoir, the author would have to say on the title page, "A Memoir of Owen Brown," or "The Autobiography of Owen Brown." That would bind him to a different contract with the reader. And if it was indeed the memoir or the autobiography of Owen Brown, and he invented large bits and pieces of it, like many recent and somewhat notorious memoirists, he'd be guilty of violating that contract.

Lackey: Let's turn to Owen for a moment. Assuming that your Owen is to be fictionally believed, that he is giving us the secret history of John Brown, can you explain the kind of history he can give us that traditional historians cannot? In other words, can you specify the kind of truth that the biographical novelist can access and/or represent?

Banks: What a novelist is doing in inventing a character out of historical and autobiographical material is creating an individual who is different from the character invented by the biographer or historian. What's the difference between the character I invent, John Brown, and the character Robert Penn Warren invented in his biography of Brown, for instance? Warren basically attacks Brown for being a horse thief and puts him down in every possible way. Now you could compare Warren's biography to W. E. B. Du Bois' biography, in which Brown is a hero of the highest order. In my version of John Brown, he is an incredibly complex human being: both good and bad. He is not cynical, but he is manipulative, controlling. He is slightly mad and is probably bipolar, but he is a character that is invented for the purposes of telling a story—entirely a larger and different purpose than a biographer would have. And you could also say Warren and Du Bois each had an agenda that was political with regard to the issue of race. I did not. The novelist does not have an agenda. The novelist does not have a message, doesn't have a historical truth to bring to bear on the book or on the character. The novelist is trying to present, in a sense I suppose, a higher truth, a truth of what it is to be a human being, period. A more universal truth, let's say. He uses the data of this character's life and embellishes it sufficiently and reorganizes it and restructures it in such a way that it can both be data and a portrait of human beings who are very different from John Brown. It could be a portrait of the reader. I'll give you an instance of how this works. I don't think a biographer of John Brown would receive a letter like one I got after *Cloudsplitter* was published. It was written by a woman who had served twenty-four years of a life sentence in Bedford Hills prison for women for crimes she committed as a member of the Weather Underground in the sixties and seventies. She was involved in a robbery in which two guards were killed back in the early seventies. She read the novel and wrote me the best fan letter I've ever gotten—a three-page, typed, single-spaced response to the novel—because she believed that Owen Brown's life and story were her life and her story. She is a late twentieth century person, Jewish, from New York, her father is a powerful and liberal lawyer. She was a radical person, but this was her story. I don't think she would have felt that if she had read a biography of John Brown instead.

Lackey: So you are saying that it is not necessarily that the biographical novelist accesses and represents a different truth, but that it engages the reader in a different way.

Banks: Absolutely. Yes, so that the reader believes the story is about the reader. I mean, we do that with every novel we read—call me Ishmael—we all are Ishmael when we pick that up and start reading it. We're not Ahab. We are the character who is telling us the story and whose story it truly is. And Owen Brown in many ways is like Ishmael. I was quite conscious of that in fact in the structure of the story and in the telling of the story. It is a different contract—I guess I wanted to go back to that term too—between the writer and the reader. My contract with the reader is that in some important way I want the novel to be about you, the reader, when you read it. Just as, when I'm writing it, it's about me; I'm living in that fictional world. I'm inhabiting these characters, looking out their eyes. There is an interesting interview I read some years ago between Michael Ondaatje and the actor Willem Dafoe, and it goes back to what I was saying before. After the filming of *The English Patient*, Dafoe was interviewing Michael for a magazine and Dafoe said: "What does it feel like to see your characters looking differently than the way you imagined them. Looking for instance like me, the actor." Michael said: "Actually, in the end, I don't know what my characters look like because I'm inside them looking out. I don't know what they look like any more than I know what I really look like. I know how tall I am and so forth, but I don't really know what it's like to be in a room with me, to look at me from outside." And it's the same thing with my characters. Michael is absolutely right: you're inside, you're inhabiting the characters the way an actor inhabits his. That's why actors are so insecure about their looks. They don't know what they look like, and unlike novelists, for them everything depends on their looks.

Lackey: At this point, I want to shift to a slightly different topic. One of the fascinating things for me throughout the novel was Owen Brown's homosexual desire, especially for Lyman Epps. There was this scene building up to this moment when Owen is going to tell Lyman, and it turns out horribly. Was there any documentary evidence to suggest that Owen was homosexual?

Banks: No. I had an interesting conversation about that with Ed White after the book was published. He was a big fan of the book and he said he thought it was a great portrait of a mid-nineteenth century homosexual, working-class man for whom there was no vocabulary to describe his own longings and desires. There wasn't even a vocabulary to describe him socially. I was quite aware of the fact that there was nothing in the record to suggest that he was homosexual, except for the fact that he was single his entire life, which wasn't that uncommon then or now. That is the secret history of Owen in a sense, but it's a secret even from himself. Because he has no language for it, he himself doesn't know. It's not available to him. He doesn't live on the streets, and he'd have to find it there. There's that big scene that takes place in Boston Common where he clearly is drawn to the heat and light of what is illicit sex or deviant sexual behavior of one sort or another, and he is drawn toward it and he doesn't know how to relate to it in any way. He is an extremely naïve and almost innocent man in that regard. But I was quite aware that I was using it, that I was tunneling my way into that aspect of the nineteenth century, in particular where religion and politics have no space for homosexuality.

Lackey: This is another common denominator among these biographical novels. An honest and open engagement with and discussion of homosexual desire has given us a whole new understanding of historical events, as in Bruce Duffy's *The World As I Found It* and *Disaster was my God*, Parini's *Last Station* and *The Passages of H.M.*, Cunningham's *The Hours*, and White's *Hotel de Dream*. Can you briefly discuss the role homosexual desire plays in *Cloudsplitter*, not just in terms of Owen's repressed and latent homosexuality, but in terms of the larger religious context and social structure?

Banks: It has freed up the novelist in a way. A biographer or historian wouldn't be able to describe from inside the experience of being homosexual in a repressed and sexually controlling society. There was no record of it, no letters—there couldn't be with someone like Owen, a working-class man in a deeply religious family. All the novelists you mention have felt that freedom and exercised it. And why not? These novelists are telling stories that a historian and biographer can't tell, because the historians and biographers don't have the records that would give them permission to do so. You know the biographers of Henry James stumble all over the place trying to avoid or confirm whether he was homosexual. But a novelist can go there and not be restricted the way biographers and historians are by the record, by the letters, notes, and recorded conversations. We have this freedom, so why not exploit and utilize it, why not exercise this freedom?

Lackey: But it also tells us something from a slightly different angle about this whole time period. And I think this is Ed White's point, isn't it?

Banks: The present time period?

Lackey: Well, no. What I'm thinking about is how your Owen struggles with no vocabulary for this experience inside of him? You're examining this character in battle with himself. There is no vocabulary for his experience and there are also stark prohibitions against his desire. He can't even really entertain this desire as a legitimate possibility. This gives us a new entrance into a nineteenth-century psyche.

Banks: I like that, but also a contemporary psyche. I know one of the thoughts I had initially, before I really ended up exploring his sexuality, was simply the question of plausibility. I knew that I would have maybe fifty male characters, and that I would deal with several of them up close. As a modern American in the late twentieth century, I cannot say I know fifty people and none of them are homosexuals. There is a certain percentage of the population that is homosexual. So it would be implausible for me to have fifty characters, and not one of them be homosexual. I can't tell a story about America and expect it to be believable if I don't have anyone in it except upper middle-class white people. The absence of black people and of poor people and so forth would be too telling. I'd have to acknowledge their absence in some way. I could have them absent, but I have to acknowledge that they're absent. I think that is what Toni Morrison is getting at in *Playing in the Dark*, the absence of blacks in nineteenth century American literature. It is the absence which is so telling. In *Cloudsplitter* I went there because I had something I wanted to say about homosexuality in the nineteenth-century. I went there because I knew it would be unrealistic for there not to be a homosexual among my major characters. And since Owen was the one I knew best and was most sympathetic to, and in a way the profile of his life as I had laid it out and was working with, the givens, it made it very possible—it didn't make it necessary—that he would be homosexual. The others married, the others had children, but he never did. The intensity of his attachment to his father was really something to consider too. And so I let it continue to develop as I went along in the writing of the novel, and it became increasingly important and interesting to me and ended up maybe telling something about the present. And here it goes back to your earlier thesis. Maybe my interest in it was contemporary. But as a result there is a dimension of nineteenth-century sexuality that comes into the novel that is not in the histories and not in the biographies of Brown. It's hard to imagine homosexuality in the mid-nineteenth century among working-class people without having a novelist guiding you.

Lackey: You also made this point that maybe John Brown was bipolar. That's a new category for explanation, and so a novelist has a little more freedom to go back and use that category to try and open up that character in a new and original way.

Banks: That is true, and it took me quite a while to begin to realize that. I would say to myself, "Oh I think I see what's going on here." And it wasn't because of what the biographies told me. It was because of what my character was doing and how he was unfolding in front of me in the novel. I began to see some of this behavior feels a lot like bipolarity. The depressions he would go through, the withdrawals, the mania, the grandiosity, the incredible physical energy and then lethargy, back and forth. So in a way it helped me to structure the story more plausibly in late twentieth-century terms—psychological, neurological, and medical terms. And we can begin to understand it through our present lens.

Lackey: Near the end of the novel your Owen makes a startling claim. He says that he believes that his and his father's actions would be a "history capable of establishing forever the true meaning of the nineteenth century in the United States of America." Styron makes a similar claim about his Sophie in *Sophie's Choice*, that her experience best represents the meaning and nature of the twentieth century. Can you talk first in the abstract about the way fiction functions to represent the nature and meaning of a century, and then can you specify how this functions specifically in *Cloudsplitter*?

Banks: That is a hard one to answer.

Lackey: Which is why I saved it for the end of the interview!

Banks: Well, you see it's really Owen Brown's claim, not necessarily mine. Who in *Sophie's Choice* made that claim?

Lackey: It is actually a claim Styron made in an interview like this.

Banks: I don't know that I would make that claim. Owen does. But I myself couldn't claim that. John Brown is an iconic figure that has been in the American imagination since 1856, really since the late 1840s in the Kansas Border War. He was a very famous figure when he was still alive all the way down to the present. Sometimes he is portrayed as a thieving madman, as by Robert Penn Warren, at other times he is a noble, sentimentalized, racial hero as in Du Bois's case. I was drawn to Brown initially because he is buried down the road from where I live in the Adirondacks, but also because of the fact that he was viewed by many African Americans as a heroic figure, even above Lincoln, by people like James Baldwin and Malcolm X and going all the way back to Du Bois. He was viewed by whites, however, even liberal whites, primarily as a madman, however well-intended. But neither side disagreed about the facts. The facts have been known from the day of his death. There has never been any real argument about the facts. And that was really interesting to me because that meant that he was basically a figure in our imaginations, and we could project our own historical version or vision on to him. So I went there with that in mind, and not because I wanted to tell the story of or create the lasting image of nineteenth-century America, except insofar I do believe that the story of race is the one story in American history and in our imagination that we cannot seem to get rid of.

Lackey: So you are claiming that this novel is not just about the past, but it's also about the present. And when we think about the 1850s, this is when—in the Christian imagination—we're going to flip on slavery. Christians before the 1850s almost exclusively support slavery because you have to believe in slavery since the Bible, in its literal sense, supports it. But in the 1850s Christians came up with new arguments and they flipped on the issue of slavery. We're going through that same flip right now, but it is about homosexuality. And so your introduction of homosexuality into the novel has resonance for the nineteenth century because it helps open up the nineteenth century, but it's very contemporary because we are seeing the flip happen right at this moment.

Banks: You are exactly right. I approached the theme of homosexuality in the novel not out of an attempt to be accurate about the nineteenth century, but out of what I see around me. This is not a secret. Every family has two or three members who are homosexual. This is the most normal thing. I mean, I just love this switch that Senator Portman from Ohio just made—he "discovered" his son was gay. That kid has to be in his twenties, and the father just figured it out. I just love that flip. And it's just fascinating to watch it happen, I mean, fascinating and sad too because we had to wait so long for this moment. But you're right, I was looking at Owen's sexuality through the lens of contemporary reality because it surrounds me and it had to exist then too. It can't be that different, but how it was expressed and how it was experienced had to be very different. And so I had to make that translation, and that took a leap of imagination really. That's why I was so gratified by Ed White's response to it. He said, this is a totally believable portrait.

Lackey: He created that in *Hotel de Dream* though.

Banks: Yeah, that's right. It's obviously something that concerns him enormously.

Lackey: Did you have that conversation with him before he wrote that novel?

Banks: Yes, I believe so.

Lackey: That's interesting and useful, because I'm going to be interviewing him in two days. And with that, let me thank you for sharing your thoughts with me, as I will pick up with Ed where I left off with you.

3

Big Revolutionary Bangs in the Biographical Novel

Madison Smartt Bell

Lackey: Let me start by telling you about this project. I'm trying to figure out why, starting in the 1980s, so many prominent writers began to author biographical novels. I am also trying to define the nature of this genre of fiction. Your work is unique, as it is not entirely clear that it would qualify as a biographical novel. Your trilogy focuses primarily on Haiti rather than a single figure. However, it is possible to say that your novels chart the development and rise of Toussaint, which would make them biographical novels. Assuming for the moment that your trilogy could qualify as biographical novels, can you explain why you decided to write about Toussaint?

Bell: Sure, but I'm curious what you think the criteria are for biographical novels?

Lackey: Previously, writers like Robert Penn Warren would change the protagonist's name. So while the main character of *All the King's Men* is Willie Stark, we all know it is based on Huey Long. You kept the name Toussaint, but in classical historical novels, the author would usually change the name. The decision to keep the name is one of the key factors. The second thing is the invention of characters and scenes in order to illuminate the historical person. So there are two things: retaining an original figure's name and using fictional elements in order to illuminate the biographical figure.

Bell: A lot of biographers perforce use fictional technique and actually fictionalize some things in what purports to be biographies. If you have dialogue, for example, it is not likely to have been recorded verbatim anywhere, and some biographers use that. Also, I don't think this genre of fiction is totally new. Gore Vidal did a number of books like this.

Lackey: That's right, he published *Lincoln* and *Burr*.

Bell: But to return to my own experience. I wasn't particularly thinking about embarking on a new genre with certain criteria. I've never thought of writing that way, unless I'm functioning as a critic, which I sometimes do. But I don't write imaginative literature with those motives.

I became very interested in the trajectory of Toussaint Louverture's career when I first discovered it, and that was in probably 1983, well before the enormous wave of interest in the Haitian Revolution on the part of scholars in the United States and some other countries had manifested itself, although it was probably beginning to happen in small cells at universities here and there. So that was an interesting coincidence by itself. When my book came out it in 1995 it caught the wave as it was beginning to swell and put some energy into it, and rode it for the next ten years with the publication of my next two books.

Lackey: Did you ever entertain the possibility of changing Toussaint's name?

Bell: No.

Lackey: Why not?

Bell: I don't know why not. Most of my imaginative writing processes are entirely unconscious. I grope for a feel for how I'm going to write a book. In the case of *All Souls' Rising* it took a long time; I had the idea in 1983 and I didn't really start writing it until 1991 or 1992. In 1983 I read a little biography of Toussaint called *Citizen Toussaint* by Ralph Korngold, which had come out in the forties. And I thought it was an incredible story. Toussaint is an amazing person, a very mysterious personality. I thought in 1983 that this would be my next novel, but there was considerable difficulty doing the research. I had never really done anything quite like that before.

I discovered that, because I was a great admirer of Toussaint, I didn't want to falsify anything about him, which meant that I couldn't really invent anything about him or very little. This was an unconscious rule. He is an opaque figure in all three books, which is not so bad, since he was that way in life as well. I would not let myself have the character Toussaint in my book do or say anything that I didn't either know, or could reasonably conjecture, he had done or said. The exception for *reasonable conjecture* allowed me to conjure up a few episodes that fit with my sense of his personality and who he was. In most of those instances, I would reason that, given Toussaint's response to a particular situation, he must have been thinking thus and so. But I didn't let myself go overboard in that direction. So in order to have more freedom creating a fictional narrative, I surrounded Toussaint with fictional characters who are drawn from all the different strata of the incredibly complicated colonial world.

Lackey: At what point did you start to include these fictional characters? Was this when you first started to write the novel? Or, did you start writing about Toussaint and then realize that you need to create these other fictional characters in order to fill lacuna within his character and culture?

Bell: No, my first way into the book was to invent two fictional characters. One is a Maroon, Riau, and the other is a European doctor who just arrived, and that's an ancient device: a situation that's going to be unfamiliar to the reader is developed by a character who is not familiar with it himself, so he has to learn everything as he goes along—and teach the reader. That's the role of Doctor Hébert in *All Souls' Rising*. The character completely submerged in the African culture of Saint Domingue is Riau, and in the original draft of the book, Riau has the first word and narrates the first chapter, talking this very strange language out of a very unfamiliar kind of self; he has a different kind of psyche than the Europeans do.

I began to use these two characters as counterweights on either side of the personality of Toussaint, who had absorbed a great deal of African and European culture by the time he was grown up. Legend has it that he was the descendant of an African prince and I am confident he was a Vodou practitioner himself—quietly, but I feel pretty certain that he was, although later he prohibited it. (Prohibiting Vodou while practicing it at the same time is a tradition for Haitian heads of state.) On the other side, Toussaint was educated by the Jesuits who had a big hospital near the plantation where he was a slave and where he worked from time to time. He worked there as a nurse basically, and learned a lot of European medicine from that situation. And Toussaint was unusually close to his master Bayon de Libertat. They seemed to have been about the same age (the late Gérard Barthélemy has a theory they were cradle companions) and in a lot of ways operated like partners. Bayon was a Mason, and Toussaint was a Mason, which was quite unusual for a slave.

On either side of Toussaint, I just started building off of the European character, the doctor, and the Afro-Haitian character, Riau. Each has his own social circle so to speak and it grows, and pretty soon I had a cast of thirty people surrounding Toussaint, as real people would have had at the time, trying to figure out what his motives were and what he was going to do next.

Lackey: So do you see those characters as helping us to better understand Toussaint? Or, do you think of them more as giving us a representation of Haiti at that time?

Bell: Well, both.

There are three books, and you can read them in any order you want. Taken one at a time, they revolve on the basis of plots that have to do with fictional characters, but if you read them all the way through, the protagonist emerges as Toussaint Louverture, the sort of "master protagonist" of the whole group. So I had this design that should render the whole larger than the sum of its parts.

Lackey: What can you give readers of Toussaint that they couldn't get in a traditional biography?

Bell: I can bring characters and events to life—that's what I have been told by some scholars. The Haitian Revolution is now an overcrowded field, and these days the graduate students I run into are likely to be better informed than I am at this point. So I now have this pool of expert readers. One of them said to me, "When I read your books I had already read all the sources behind them, so I knew where you were getting this stuff, but there's something about seeing it dramatized that is just really great."

Lackey: So literature makes the material alive, but it does not necessarily give readers more in terms of knowledge?

Bell: Well, I'm not sure. Toussaint was a very secret person and he also was a contradictory personality. He had a benevolent aspect to him. He was socially progressive, and in that sense he was really years ahead of his time. But he could also be extremely ruthless in a Machiavellian way, though his ruthlessness was usually carried out through proxies.

After I spent considerable time in Haiti, I realized that "reality" functions in a different way there. The whole idea of an integrated personality that has to preserve all of its characteristics all the time is far less important there. A Haitian psyche can run to one extreme one day and another the next, without the kind of internal dissonance that we would experience doing that.

Each one of the fictional characters touches Toussaint a little bit and makes some aspect of him visible to the reader. In the end it's like seeing something form out of a cloud. I don't want to say that this was a conscious intention because it really wasn't, but somewhere half way through the entire project I saw, "Okay, this is what's happening, I'll know about this factor from now on."

Lackey: Is this capacity to represent a split self by vacillating between a public discourse and an interior monologue what makes the biographical novel so different from a traditional biography?

Bell: Yes, and it should be noted that I wrote a biography of Toussaint Louverture, which came after the novels. In doing that biography, I had a whole new set of inhibitions, because I couldn't invent anything. So, in spite of my claim that I felt very loyal to him in writing the novels, I have to admit that I invented some stuff. In a biography, any speculation has to be labeled as such, whereas in the novels I could just do it according to my belief that it was plausible.

Lackey: Why should I trust that you, as a novelist, are giving me something that's different and even more insightful than a traditional biographer?

Bell: I think, honestly, you probably shouldn't. What's curious is that a lot of scholars prefer the image of Toussaint from the novel—the whole situation from the novel—than the biography, where I committed myself to certain interpretations of facts that the academic experts don't agree with. It's almost inherently contradictory, but I think anytime you fictionalize a historical figure from a different period the fictional version is going to have more charisma for the reader than whatever has been reliably established by orthodox historical record.

Lackey: So the difference is ultimately how the reader is impacted?

Bell: No. What I want to say here is that there is inevitably some falsification, because what you're getting is *my impression* of Toussaint. You're not actually dealing with the person. You can't be, because he has been gone for 200 years.

Lackey: But it's not necessarily a falsification for the sake of falsification. With many biographical novelists, it is a falsification in order to get to some deeper or more complex truth. Would this be an accurate way of saying what you do?

Bell: Yes. I just don't want to invest a lot in the claim that there is really truth there. I made an honest effort to be faithful to the historical person, in part because I admired him. But I don't think you can be completely faithful to the historical personage because inevitably you do start adding stuff; you start completing the character in different ways that require you to make up stuff that, frankly, you don't know. That was brought to my consciousness forcefully when I wrote a biography about the same person and realized "I can't do all that prestidigitation if I'm writing a 'real' biography. I can make arguments in favor of these readings of events, but I can't *create* them as behavior or thought."

Lackey: Were there any constraints in writing the biography? Constraints, for instance, coming from the publisher?

Bell: No, the publisher didn't bother me at all. It's not set up like an academic book, either. The published version is not footnoted, although I annotated my manuscript as I wrote. When I get questions about sources I tend to just offer the annotated ms. I was writing a trade book for a general audience and the publisher left all verification up to me.

Lackey: Was there an internal censor at work in your mind as you were writing the biography, which subtly established different kinds of restrictions and constraints than writing a biographical novel?

Bell: Let me illustrate with an example. There is this very important episode late in Toussaint's career when his adopted nephew Moyse raises a rebellion against him. The rebellion is put down and Moyse is captured, and Toussaint actually let him go. This is the only time in his entire career that he ever released an enemy. He must have thought that Moyse would leave the country. In the novel, I believe it's all represented like that: his sentiments for Moyse, which are comparably affectionate, lead Toussaint to this act of mercy. But Moyse keeps running around the Northwest causing trouble, so eventually Toussaint had proxies round him up and shoot him.

In the novel I can present that organically, with some bits of frank description of Toussaint's internal process about this matter. But in the biography I just have to build a case for the probability that these were Toussaint's motives.

Lackey: A number of professors criticize contemporary biographical novels, saying that creative writers are merely summarizing and paraphrasing histories and biographies and then calling their works novels. How would you respond to this critique?

Bell: I think you have to go one book at a time there. I don't think you can generalize so much. Some of the lazier ones are probably like that.

Lackey: But you would say that yours are more than just summary and paraphrase?

Bell: There are so many invented characters in them. In a curious way you see less of the historical figures, because they get less time on stage in those novels. Also, I was less comfortable with manipulating historical figures. With my many fictional characters I could operate more freely. But there comes a point where the character controls itself to a degree, even if you invented it. They have a nature and you can't make them go against that nature. It wouldn't be believable. But we fiction writers are very used to that constraint, and it's not that taxing.

I think if you go back to genre, the historical romances for example, those probably meet the condition of being paraphrased from the historical record with minimal re-creation or reimagining of the character. There's always a kind of continuum from the mass-market fiction of that kind toward the "serious and literary" end of the spectrum, and there's even still, I think, a prospering genre of historical romances that people read. The curve that leads into a separate set that's accepted as literature, like Russell Banks' *Cloudsplitter*, which is a development of ideas about society that are everywhere in Banks's whole opus. In this book, he uses John Brown and his circle as an avatar, a means for expressing his social concerns.

I think a book like Banks's, and I would say mine too, are written out of a kind of necessity for the writer. In my case I can certainly claim necessity because it was an incredibly difficult job. It took twenty years, and once I was embarked on it, it began to carry me along with its own momentum. I kept choosing to do something easier; I made that choice probably eight times before I really went into it. It was hard but it was worth it.

Lackey: Let me briefly address the ethics of the biographical novel. Even though your work is acknowledged to be a novel, is it possible that it infringes upon the rights of the subject under consideration? Can you talk about the ethical responsibility you have to the actual Toussaint, that is, the obligation to represent his life accurately? Also, can you define the kind of liberties you feel justified in taking with the facts about a historical figure's life? And can you specify the kind of liberties that you could not take?

Bell: I didn't want to falsify anything about Toussaint or the several other historical figures, the real Europeans and African leaders. For the most part, those characters don't get the same kind of intimate internalized treatment as the others, because I didn't feel comfortable inventing stuff about real people. So I think I did experience that as an ethical consideration. I did want to represent the life accurately…

Lackey: But it's not the actual factual life because you created characters, so what kind of life are you talking about? Is it the psychological life? Is it the historical life?

Bell: The psychological life you really can't do because you can't know that. I had to do it a little bit in order to animate the character of Toussaint, so I did just what was necessary. But there's not a lot. You get a lot more inner experience from fictional characters surrounding Toussaint and the other historical personages than you do from the historical figures themselves, because I just didn't have the confidence and I didn't want to lie.

Another thing that evolved out of that problem was the chronology at the back of each book, and I created that chronology for my own use, keeping track of things. Later on I decided to append it so the reader could use it to follow the incredible complexity of events. But the chronologies also enable the reader who cares to distinguish what absolutely happened and what has been fictionalized. So that to me seemed to be pretty valuable, and in the later volumes I also was allowed to append letters and documents, many of which are used in the dramatized scenes in the text, so that the reader could see what the source material actually was.

Lackey: There was a huge controversy on the publication of Styron's *The Confessions of Nat Turner*. Your novel addresses very similar issues. Why did Styron's book inspire so much rage while yours did not? And how is your novel similar to but also different from Styron's?

Bell: We are both white southerners writing in the voices of black people experiencing slavery. That's the extent of the similarity as far as I'm concerned. I read *Nat Turner* when it came out, but the novel repelled me.

Lackey: Why?

Bell: Well, it seemed to me I was comparing it to the work of Robert Penn Warren, and I didn't believe the voice. Styron's representation of Nat Turner's voice seemed to me to be totally false. When I saw that question in your list I went and looked up the ostensibly authentic confession of Nat Turner, as you can now easily find on the Internet.

Lackey: But that is not actually Turner's voice. It is a lawyer's voice, who took Turner's confession.

Bell: I have read as much as I could find about that lawyer, Thomas Gray, and there's not very much, which makes this such a complicated situation. Gray was a lawyer who was down on his luck and broke. He was essentially a public defender, trying to turn a buck. His *The Confession of Nat Turner* was a commercial property, which he sold. He published it and sold it to make money. And he expresses a lot of horror and indignation about what happened—the violence committed by Turner and his group. At the same time he insists that Turner did speak that way, and his own interjections which he records are very few; there are only three or four questions posed by Gray in this whole thing. He claims that he set down Nat Turner's words exactly as they were spoken, without reprocessing them to a higher level of rhetoric, although a reader's first presumption would be that he must have done the latter. And he professes a lot of respect for Nat Turner's capacities. He says over and over, this is an extraordinarily intelligent, capable person with a lot of inner strength and he insists on all that, at the same time he is disgusted, repelled, and horrified by the slaughter. So I don't know. As a reporter, Gray is quite conflicted. But to me there's a little glimmer of authenticity down in there somewhere. Nat Turner was literate, we know that. He read stuff, he was solitary, and he was religious.

And I think it's conceivable he may have actually had a style of spoken rhetoric like what Gray set down—acquired from books. I don't think it's impossible.

Lackey: In my interview with Joyce Carol Oates, she addressed this question of a believable voice. Oates said that the Marilyn Monroe in her novel *Blonde* is more nuanced, subtle, and complex than the actual Marilyn Monroe. She is even more poetic. More importantly, Oates is unapologetic about this because she is using the Monroe character in order to access different types of truths about this person's internal, cultural and political reality. So she thinks that she can take liberties with the actual historical record so long as she tries to represent some other kind of truth, whether it is an interior truth, a political truth, or a cultural truth. Is it possible that someone like Styron knew full well that his rhetoric was overblown, that he was doing this so that he could access a different kind of historical truth? And what makes him so different from you? After all, you invent characters, and in the process, alter the historical record.

Bell: Joyce is bolder than I would be in just frankly claiming the historical figure and remaking it to suit her own artistic purposes. I say "artistic," not historical. I think she's inventing, not reporting in this case, and I don't think she'd disagree. Of course Marilyn lends herself peculiarly to this kind of treatment. "Marilyn Monroe," as opposed to Norma Jeane Whoever, was a huge target for everybody's projection.

Back to Styron—to me credibility in the voice is very important, and to me the voice of Styron's Nat Turner is incredible. It rings false in my ear—like wrong notes in music.

Lackey: Is it just because it's overblown rhetoric, or is it because it's inconsistent with who you knew this man had to be at a particular time?

Bell: I think Styron wrote that book as if it was him in that situation, and this is one of the reasons people hated it so much, particularly the black intellectual establishment at the time. It doesn't really work to just zip somebody of Styron's mid-twentieth-century sensibility into Nat Turner's skin. The way that the whole narrative is sexualized strikes me as being fundamentally false, as well. There are a lot bigger tensions than that in the historical situation than Styron is, ostensibly, representing. For the same reason, white people didn't like the book so much either.

Lackey: Somebody must have liked it, as it won the Pulitzer.

Bell: I'm guessing the book was best reviewed by the East Coast "intellectual establishment" of that day, where people's understanding of race relations in the South was remote. On the East Coast, reading a book about the relations between the races in the antebellum South would be like reading a book about medieval Afghanistan. Those readers have no direct experience of anything like that. So there is a kind of exoticism operating. A certain readership could buy into it as a fantasy, basically—and without realizing it. But to me that's what it is, a fantasy. It expresses what was going on in Styron's psyche at the time, which happened to take into itself a lot of anxiety in the general white culture about the end of the American apartheid and the implications of that end. Faulkner wrote about this too, more than once, notably in *Absalom, Absalom!* The idea that if you let this black population completely out of its cage, inevitably there would be "cross-breeding"—that really worried some people back then. Now that it's happened, we realize that it's not really a problem, but it has taken a long time for the anxiety to dissipate. There was still a very significant fear surrounding this subject, as late as Styron was working. And I think it is an anxiety that permeates the work, and at this point rather unfortunately dates it.

Lackey: There seems to be a dilemma here because on the one hand you have, as an artist, this responsibility to create a living character. But the biographical novel introduces a new feature into that aesthetic matrix, which is this: your objective is also to represent a historical person accurately. So let's assume, just for the moment, Styron would have changed the character's name from Nat Turner to John Thompson. He would have had more freedom, and he probably wouldn't have been attacked as much because he wouldn't have been held responsible to the voice of an actual figure. The problem with these biographical novels is that you have two conflicting objectives: to use the creative imagination to invent a living and breathing character and to represent a biographical figure accurately. And if you do not accurately represent the person, people are going to come back and attack you. Had Styron changed Turner's name, do you think the novel would have been more positively received?

Bell: People probably would have paid less attention. Using the actual name is a kind of truth claim, but at the same time by including the actual transcript of Nat Turner's confession, he shows how vast the difference is between what he did and what Turner said or did. That's a clear way of saying, "I've vastly transformed this character." And I think he did transform the character, to the point that for me Styron's Nat Turner is a nervous white guy in an Afro-American bodysuit.

But to go back to what you said about Joyce. I haven't read *Blonde*, but I've read a lot of her other work, and she'll appropriate a historical figure without any of the fretfulness I've described in my own case. She'll tell you frankly that these are no longer the people that they were. She takes them into herself and expresses them as completely transformed.

Lackey: That would be true before 2000. But with the publication of *Blonde* something changed because if you look at her 1992 novella *Black Water*, Oates changes the name of her protagonist from Ted Kennedy, who the novella is clearly based on, to the Senator. She changes a lot of things so that she can take many liberties with the story.

Bell: That happened late in the game, it sounds like. Perhaps there were some libel issues to worry about.

Lackey: I'm not so sure. It seems that 1999 is the watershed year, because two biographical novels were up for the Pulitzer in that year, and one won it. And this is when you see a major transformation in Oates' fiction. By 2000, she is no longer thinly disguising her characters. She names them Marilyn Monroe, Henry James, Mark Twain, and Ernest Hemingway. She has a new short story coming out, and one of the main characters is Robert Frost. Something has happened that has led many of our country's prominent writers to name their characters after the original figure, and I'm trying to figure out why that happened.

Bell: One of the same things that's happening at the time is reality TV, where you have people doing whatever they do on reality TV. There is a lot of talk in the general culture about the erosion of the distinction between the fictional character and the real person. Whether Joyce Carol Oates watches reality television or not I don't know—but things that are that large in popular culture have a way of seeping into everything, whether it's by direct contact or not. I think reality TV depends on our prurient interest in being able to look at real people in a fish bowl.

Remember the Loud family in the seventies? That was the first one of those things, a documentary called *An American Family*. They were a "typical" nuclear unit, supposedly: well-adjusted, happy. Here's the suburban dad, wife, two or three kids, there were teens. And they allowed these cameras in and I think everybody thought they were going to have a real-life Ozzie and Harriet, but really what happened was the whole thing imploded as they were filming it, and perhaps because they were filming it. And people were fascinated by this, but horrified too. Nobody did it again for twenty years. The next instance was *Survivor,* and the whole first group was set up on a game-show model—but now you have plenty of people turning their whole lives over to this voyeurism. Whole clotheslines of dirty laundry reeled backward out of the screen!

It's the normal thing that happens now. Honestly that aspect of the thing doesn't interest me that much. I find subjects that express things that I need to express for internal reasons mostly, or sometimes personal psychological reasons. Often, certainly with the book on Toussaint, there's a mixture of my own needs for expression, which are largely unconscious in my case, and certain social goals. If I'm writing about revolutions against slavery, that also applies to the race situation in America today. But the story plays out very differently in Haiti afterwards because of the success of their revolution there.

Lackey: This relates directly to my next question. A lot of people say that these biographical novels, which usually deal with figures from the past, are really not about the past. They are primarily interested in the present, and people have said that about your novel. But there is another way of thinking about the dual temporality of the biographical novel, and I want to mention a non-biographical novel to clarify my point. Junot Diaz's *The Brief Wondrous Life of Oscar Wao* looks at the forming of a nation, the formation of what is going to become the Americas. He suggests that the Americas arise out of a certain spiritual or mental sickness, and that sickness lingers into the present. So his novel is not just an attempt to illuminate the past, but also to illustrate how we are still suffering from the same kind of spiritual and mental illnesses that gave birth to the Americas. Would you say that something similar is going on in your novels?

Bell: Yes, probably. I didn't really set out to do that, or not very deliberately. I was trying to faithfully recreate this eighteenth century world. That was my goal. And I remember I became pretty friendly with my French translator. I once said to him, "Basically what I'm trying to do here is to write a nineteenth-century novel," which consciously I was. That's the golden age of the novel and I wanted this to be a book that was like that. And he looked a bit startled and said that my novel is totally modern. He saw it as a very contemporary work, and I'm sure he's right.

There's something about taking a step or two away from your own time that's liberating. In terms of models I think my three books resemble *War and Peace* more than anything I can think of. I didn't think of that until very late. We forget, because Tolstoy is a figure in our somewhat distant past, that *War and Peace* was a historical novel for him. He has real historical figures in the novel too. They aren't principal characters, but still in one dimension it is a book about the different qualities of Napoleon and his Russian adversaries.

Lackey: There have been many biographical novels about slave insurrections. Arna Bontemps published *Black Thunder* in 1936, which is about

Gabriel Prosser; Styron published *The Confessions of Nat Turner* in 1967; you published *All Souls' Rising* in 1995; and Banks published *Cloudsplitter* in 1998, which is about John Brown told from the perspective of his son Owen. Why is the insurrectionist such a suitable figure for a biographical novel?

Bell: The one novel on that list that I hadn't read before our conversation was *Black Thunder*, and I felt guilty about that so I got a copy and I haven't finished it yet. The circumstances in which that was written were very acute for Bontemps. He just lost a job for reading books basically. It was the 1930s, but you can be shocked all over again by that stuff and in fact it never was "okay." So Bontemps is in Watts, which fifty years later would be the site of a sizeable black insurrection, if you want to call it that, and really riding out conditions of extraordinary oppression—not slavery, but replicating a lot of the conditions of slavery, including the punishment of slaves for literacy. Bontemps had just lost a teaching job because he refused to destroy his library, incredible as that may seem. So there's an authenticity to his position which neither I nor Banks nor Styron could understand or appreciate.

For Banks and for me, we approach the situation from a different angle than Bontemps certainly, and I think Russell found an authentic way to do it. *Cloudsplitter* gives a credible representation of the historical John Brown, a person somewhat like Banks in a way: somebody who saw a toxic social problem in his time and wanted to solve it, rectify it, by any means necessary. Russell is actually more forward-leaning politically than the average literary novelist. There's always been a social edge to his work, a rogue belief that writing a book about something can actually change the world for the better. So I think *Cloudsplitter* is eminently that. I think that, in Haitian terms, Russell wanted to call back the spirit of John Brown to operate in our time.

Lackey: Yes, but he also claims that he updates the issue. By bringing together the issues of homosexuality and race, he was able to draw a link between the past and the present. In addition to struggling with prohibitions between blacks and whites, he also examines the sexual prohibitions between two males, which we see in Owen's relationship with Lyman Epps.

Bell: I actually don't remember that part as well as I should. Did he make that up?

Lackey: Yes, he made it up. His argument goes like this: if you think about the population, about ten percent of the people are gay. This was not addressed in nineteenth-century fiction, but he said that such homosexual impulses had to be there. So if you have thirty characters in a novel, a few of them are going to be gay. He wanted to bring this issue into this nineteenth-century novel because it is something that would not have been there had it been written in the nineteenth century. But because of the freedoms we now have, we can address it. We can access history in a new way, based on new categories of experience and understanding.

Bell: That seems dangerous. Nietzsche told us that we can't see around our own corner. You can't take off the lens that you're looking at history through, and in fact history itself is an unreliable thing. Because in anything that represents itself, only certain things are told. A small percentage of whatever happened is reported, and that is true of every case. The most unbiased historian even, never mind the novelist, is going to report according to biases that are simply unconscious or not perceived as biases because they are, at that moment, the "norms" of the society that the person is operating in. To take a ludicrous example from the eighteenth century, there was a lot of effort expended on pseudo-scientific studies setting out to show that Africans were a missing link between monkeys and men. That black people were half-animals, and therefore using them as beasts of burden was a perfectly legitimate thing to do and actually good for them. This was considered scientific fact by some at the time.

But if Russell wants to take risks I wouldn't, I think that's a good thing. He is so well established now as a social realist that people have forgotten he began as an avant-garde experimentalist. In terms of what he's done in the past, exporting some of our present attitudes to an earlier time is a fairly modest undertaking.

Lackey: Getting back to the original question, why is there this interest in insurrectionists among biographical novelists?

Bell: I think Bontemps suggests very strongly that he is in the same situation as the black insurrectionists. And he could actually say that convincingly. For me, Russell and Styron—we are on the opposite side of the racial barrier. That barrier becomes much more permeable and I think eventually will completely dissolve. But it's still there, and it keeps reappearing whenever you think you've overcome it. In Styron's case it was probably peculiarly painful, because he was a Southern white male of the pre-Civil Rights period, striving mightily to reconstruct himself as a good liberal. I honestly think he thought *The Confessions of Nat Turner* was a kind of testament to that, but it's not. Instead what it really shows is all the unresolved anxiety and all the things that are *not* worked out in his effort to adopt that position. And that's why the book has been rejected by so many people.

Lackey: There are two separate arguments about this. One argument suggests that he had all these unresolved issues within himself and his novel, which led to the major backlash. The other argument is that he published the novel in 1967 during the rise of black power and black separatist movements, and it was the timing that led to the backlash. Had he published it in 1979, it would not have been so badly received. What do you think?

Bell: The situation in which you write something defines what it is. If he had written that book ten years later it wouldn't have been the same book because it wouldn't have been under the same pressure during its composition.

Lackey: So when you say he wouldn't have written the same book do you mean the book would have had exactly the same words but it would have been received differently, or that he would have changed the words and scenes?

Bell: I don't think he would have written it in quite the same way because I think the electricity in that book is the electricity of the particular moment when he wrote it. You can see that there was an explosion about to happen. It's really difficult for anyone who was an American at that time to have much clarity and detachment because we are all implicated. We can go through these motions to purge and purify and shake off the reptilian hide of our part in the American apartheid, but it doesn't entirely work. It's all part of who we are. So for somebody like me or Russell, we have the advantage of writing in a less volatile time and with some detachment. But the motive, I think, is to work out a sense of responsibility for how the way we live now was created.

Lackey: To conclude, let me briefly discuss one theory about the split self. One of the arguments about the biographical novel is that it depicts two different dimensions of the human. On a conscious level, most people will say that they are not racist. But on a subconscious level, people carry traces of racism inside of them whether they are aware of it or not.

Bell: Yes, it's hard to get rid of.

Lackey: Within this framework, it no longer makes sense to say, "I'm not a racist." Rather we should be saying, "I'm trying to get rid of these traces of racism within me." That would be a more realistic response. Now some people have made the argument that what the novelist, especially the biographical novelist, is trying to access and represent is the split self, specifically that subconscious part of the self that continues to harbor unpleasant realities like racist attitudes and beliefs. Would you agree with that?

Bell: Yes, I think that's certainly true. I would say that's true in my case. I know that I write very unconsciously. To me it's like where the good energy comes from.

Lackey: But writing unconsciously is different from trying to access or represent in your work this deeper level of the subconscious as it's impacting the conscious and rational way of understanding the world. Your characters have these two levels. They might say on one level, "Look, I'm not a racist. I'm a decent person," but at a deeper level they still carry traces of racism. And what the biographical novel can do that no other work can really do is to examine this kind of split self.

Bell: I'll give you an example. During my first trip to Haiti I started communicating almost entirely in French and some incipient Creole. My whole identity got dislocated. It helped that there weren't many people around for me to see. All the faces I saw were black faces. I was actually covering a band, Boukman Eksperyans, and I was in their dressing room with them doing a sort of group prayer in a circle. In the middle of this I noticed a little makeup mirror propped up somewhere, and I looked in it and there's just the face of this white guy in there, which was my own face. But my reaction was to say: "What's that white guy doing here?"—before I realized, with a terrible shock, that it was me. At that point I thought that I'd probably been cured of racism, but I think that might have been too optimistic.

Russell and I both are very familiar with Haiti. He spent a lot of time there in the seventies and eighties, and his masterpiece novel, *Continental Drift*, is about Haiti during that time. But to try to give a better answer to the question you asked earlier—I think writers are attracted to these insurrectionary figures we have mentioned on the basis that different outcomes might have been possible. For example, there's Terry Bisson's novel *Fire on the Mountain,* which explores what the United States might have turned into if John Brown's insurrection succeeded.

Not only were different outcomes possible in Haiti; they actually happened. Haiti's got all of the million problems we always hear about, but they don't have automatic racial animosity toward white people at all really. They don't have a sense of victimhood in the way African Americans in the United States still do. As a fundamentally peace-loving person I don't like to declare what I'm about. One of my Haitian friends expressed a kind of frustration about her black American friends, regarding that same sense of victimhood. She said she couldn't understand how they were because Haitians aren't like that. So I said jokingly, "It's easy for you because y'all killed all the white people." And we both go, "Hahahahahaha," and suddenly she stopped and said, very seriously, "Yes, you're right." And her husband told me in a different conversation, "There are certain offenses that can only be wiped out in blood."

I think, unfortunately, that's true. In Haiti the score was completely settled, and they got a clean slate, and then they were unable to take complete advantage of it because of the behavior of the surrounding powers, which continued to run slave economies for another fifty years; that's really the problem. So it didn't go in a totally good direction for them, but they really actually did solve the race problem, which we have not done. It is happening, but it is taking us centuries longer because there wasn't a real cataclysm like the Haitian Revolution. And so I think for novelists writing about those slave insurrections of our past in the United States it's like going back to the Big Bang. It's like there *could* have been a Big Bang but there wasn't—and a kind of fascination with what kind of society we might be living in if John Brown's or Nat Turner's efforts had succeeded.

My feeling, eccentric perhaps, is that until September 11, 2001, the worst social problem in the United States related to the legacy of slavery: that is, the ongoing oppression of a black underclass, which populates our ghettos and our prisons—so many of our other inequities flow from that. After that date our big problem is perceived to be outside our borders: these hordes of alien people who (for bad reasons or good) would like to shoot us down. To me, though, these are variations of the same theme. Both depend on the dehumanization of the other. The extreme *jihadis* do it to us, and we certainly do it right back to them.

The best that fiction, historical or otherwise, can do is to foster understanding by permitting us to experience the lives of others in the imagination. But to do that honestly, in authentic good faith, is a great challenge.

4

Building the Imaginative Record with the Biographical Novel

M. Allen Cunningham

Lackey: There have been many biographies and studies of Rilke, as I'm sure you know. Why did you write a novel about Rilke? And what can you as a novelist communicate about him that a biographer and/or a scholar could not?

Cunningham: With Rilke, ultimately, one can only write "around" him. He is peculiarly suited for biographical fiction because he consciously "fiction-alized" *himself*. It was his life-project to live and breathe his art, to *be* his art. He acknowledged this project all the time in his letters, which themselves are literary masterworks, stunning in how they simultaneously achieve confession, intimacy, and a kind of artistic secrecy, always drawing a veil over the life, casting the life purely in terms of artistic development or impediment, putting the life's *work*, the image of the life *as* work in the foreground. In a 1922 letter to a young admirer, Rilke refers to a "figure" he's been "building" for many years (he was 47 then, and settled at Muzot, his rustic tower in Switzerland). The message in this letter is that "the figure" is more conse-quential than Rilke the real, prosaic man. He tells his correspondent, in so many words, "If the figure means something to you, if the figure is the reason you've written to me, then good, let us both believe in it." He says, "Who knows who I am? I change and change. But *the figure* is worthy and lasting." This sort of "figure-building" is the main substance of most of the 11,000 Rilke letters we have—Rilke was, in a way, his own biographical novelist. Rilke the Man, whoever he may have been, disappears completely into Rilke the Work. We do know a great deal about the circumstances of Rilke's youth and development, his peregrinations over the years, his friendships and the driving concerns of his work in any given phase—but all of this we know in purely *Rilkean* terms, either through his own first-person accounts or through contemporaries who just reinforce those Rilkean terms. The "created" Rilke, it seems, is the only Rilke there ever was. And so his life, one realizes, became a literary masterpiece in itself. This is one very central element of *Lost Son*. The novel plays with the existence of "the figure," and dramatizes, in certain sections, what it meant to build that figure. In approaching the life, the life's spirit, novelistically, one can lay bare, from the start, the *imaginative* nature of the narrative. The novel can work rather transparently as variations on the themes that Rilke embodied: the place of the imagination in the modern world, the life lived as *story*, the dialogues and tensions between generations, and the swirling together of the artistic and historical past and the present. So for me, it was never so much a matter of what I could communicate about Rilke *per se*, but more a matter of exploring Rilke's life and aesthetic as those things exemplify larger, more timeless questions and concerns. In reading many Rilke biographies early on, I recognized a very clear arc to this remarkable life, and yet I found that the arc was never drawn quite the way I saw it—not in any one single book. It seemed to me that, by placing the life in the more open, liberating, freely imaginative space of a novel, the life-arc could be rendered in a richer, emotionally vivid way. Once released from the rigid chronology of fact that makes up a biography, the life could be "heard" in the more musical way that I was hearing it. The eerie symmetries within the life, the chronic conflicts within the life—these could be expressed using a novelistic scale, in this case mainly language, image, and rhythm, three things that were of primary importance to Rilke himself. So, for example, the narrative arc of *Lost Son* begins in the early trauma of Rilke being raised as a delicate little girl, a surrogate daughter coddled in dresses, only to be packed off to military school at age ten, an experience of unmitigated misery that would haunt him all his life. And the arc ends with Rilke, after a lifetime of striving to live as a poet, finding himself drafted into the Austrian infantry, stuck in a military uniform all over again, having gone so far in his art—having written four of the great *Duino Elegies*—and yet having nothing to "show for it" in a worldly sense, still lacking all control over the circumstances of his life, still being forced into this other identity that is so alien to his nature. These kinds of symmetries occur everywhere in Rilke's life story, and I think they're lent a special drama and intimacy through a fictional, poetic, non-chronological treatment. The treatment itself can serve as a kind of homage, too, which hopefully has its own poignancy. Simultaneously, something larger can be said—something about *art as work*, about life lived in service to art-making or the imagination, about generations, about the passage of time, and the life of works of art over time.

Lackey: Does it violate or in some way distort the actual person's life to take these kinds of liberties in order to make the story more emotionally vivid and aesthetically pleasing?

Cunningham: Well, if I were a biographer it might be a violation. Generally, a biographer's job is to isolate an actual person from a public persona, parsing verifiable facts from autobiographical constructs. As I've said, though, this is all but impossible when it comes to Rilke, because here you have somebody who was not just some pretender. He wasn't *pretending* to be a poet down to his very tissue—he simply *was* that kind of poet. Of course, Rilke has his share of suspicious biographers, people trying to locate and penetrate some little crack in the mask. I find that very interesting. To me it says a great deal about our attitudes toward the imagination, suggesting a kind of hostility toward a devoted life, a reflexive mistrust of a lifestyle that would hold art above all. But as it turns out with Rilke, the "mask" is all we've got. The testimonies of the people who knew him corroborate the existence of this person wholly consumed and characterized by his art. "He was poet and personality even when simply washing his hands," as Rudolf Kassner said. The "mask," therefore, becomes the face itself, and the suspicious biographer's work is probably a lost cause. And for me as a novelist, it's not my work to verify facts or try to tear away masks. My work is more personal. It's simply about communicating what the life means to me, sharing something of how I *read* the life and all its complexities. So, playing with the structure, manipulating the chronology, is more about finding a way to explore certain ideas and to use this life as a template, not necessarily to say something new or factually revelatory about Rilke. I think of it as a method of launching into more universal concerns.

Lackey: What kind of universal concerns?

Cunningham: I just mean that an authoritative portrait of the poet was never the intention in *Lost Son*. I was creating something more essentially personal, a letter sent to a ghost is how I've often thought about this novel and about my process in writing it. *Lost Son* is more about the shadow Rilke casts than any definitive persona he left us for biographical rummaging. *Lost Son*, you might say, is about Rilke's congenital bewitchment, which engendered his art, and which we can recognize everywhere in the art. Simultaneously it's about the sense of bewitchment that his art engenders in others. Like hundreds of thousands of fellow readers, I was under the Rilkean spell as soon as I read *Letters to a Young Poet*. *Lost Son* is about the experience, really, of being haunted—what it means, in the largest sense, to be haunted by art, and to be changed, electrified, absolutely sensitized through witnessing the way art haunted another. This is the reason the novel features a bewitched narrator recreating large pieces of Rilke's story through a second-person lens. So when I say "universal concerns" I'm saying that my intent, as a biographical novelist, is to overlay the well-known story of this life, all the basic components of the story that you'll find in any Rilke biography, with my personal imagination in a way that will create some intimacy for the reader, and hopefully some new understanding about how every significant life or life's work preceding ours is the very stuff upon which we build our own life in the present. Whether we're conscious of it or not, this is what we do. It's not only us artists who do it, though I believe we do it, necessarily, a little more consciously, deliberately looking to the past and past achievements all the time. No, we all make use of these inherited lives. We build our meaning on these foundations. The Rilke in my novel is a reflection within a reflection. He's a personification of the experience of being haunted. Hopefully the novel transmits something of the beauty of this truth: that we own the past. It is *ours*.

Lackey: There are various types of biographical novels. For instance, Anita Diamant, Rebecca Kanner, and Sherry Jones have written about the lives of religious figures. Madison Smartt Bell and Russell Banks have written about the interior lives of people who led rebellions against slavery, such as Toussaint Louverture and Owen Brown. Can you define the kind of biographical novel you have written?

Cunningham: The first term that comes to mind is *Künstlerroman,* a novel about the development of the artist. There are many biographical novels that would fit this description, like Colm Tóibín's *The Master*, about Henry James, or Brian Hall's *Fall of Frost*, about Robert Frost. Also, *Lost Son* operates in dialogue with Rilke's own novel, *The Notebook of Malte Laurids Brigge*, which is itself a *Künstlerroman*, a story about the formation and inner spiritual terrain of a young poet. Malte, of course, is a fictional character where Rilke is not. It should be noted, though, that Malte is largely autobiographical.

Lackey: Some prominent figures have either rejected or condemned the biographical novel. In a 1939 essay Virginia Woolf argued that "the novelist is free to create, while the biographer is tied to facts." Combining the two is impossible because "fact and fiction refused to mix." For Woolf, writers have to choose between the art of representing a person's life accurately, which would lead them to produce a biography, or creating a living and breathing character, which would lead them to produce a work of fiction. Blending the two in the form of the biographical novel is not an option. Given this claim Woolf would say that *Lost Son* is a failure. How would you respond to Woolf?

Cunningham: Well, I would say to Woolf, "Surely you don't believe, as an artist yourself, that we ought to proscribe the boundaries of our art—or any art—at the outset, pre-emptively? Surely you recognize that it is only through our brazenness—and even our failures—that we ever get anywhere." Having read Woolf's essay, and knowing her as a writer, I believe this is actually more in line with her thinking. Her essay, as I read it, is about the endemic restrictions of *biography*, not necessarily of fiction. She does say that the biographer should not liberally employ the techniques of the novelist because doing so can never produce something meriting the appellation of "art." She does not expressly assert, however, that novelists *cannot make art of biography*. Toward her conclusion, she implicitly defends the prerogatives of the artistic imagination. She says that while the biographer has to work with "perishable" facts, the artist's imaginative work consists of "firing out what is perishable in fact" and "building with what is durable." That's a message I believe in. The "facts" are there for the artist's use, provided the artist penetrates, by way of imagination, to an imperishable truth at each fact's core. Should a self-styled biographer manipulate facts and strive through "freedom of invention" to create a work of art? No. I'd agree with Woolf there. But a novelist is free, free, free to play and push and experiment.

Lackey: But do you have an ethical responsibility to the subject you are exploring? Take, for instance, Tóibín's *The Master*. He pursues an interpretation of James as a closeted homosexual. We have little information to verify this approach. Of course, we can all have our suspicions. But at what point do we violate the subject by taking too much freedom? And if there is a point at which you can't take a freedom, what is that? Can you define it?

Cunningham: There is a line that shouldn't be crossed, sure. I think it has something to do with an iconoclastic agenda, or an overly psychologized approach, which ultimately reduces a personality or character to a set of psychological explanations. That's a dangerous retraction of the imagination, and it leads to not very good fiction because it robs a story of complexity. As I see it, the biographical novel is an ideal form for ramping up the human complexity of a given biographical story, to reveling in complexity. That is my way, anyway, of paying honor to the truth as a biographical novelist. The historical and factual template I'm working with is hugely important. But while recognizing that importance, I also want to avoid any attitude or stance that will rob the story of its humanizing complexity. This is an especially interesting thing when it comes to Rilke, because he's an extremely polarizing figure. For some, Rilke is a "saint" of modern poetry. For others, he's this loathsome shirker of his human duties, somebody who abandoned his family in order to focus on his art. In many commentaries and biographies, you'll find that the writer's stance is one way or the other. But that just doesn't work for me as a novelist, as someone who is interested in the deeper human story. The truth must be much more complex than that, and so a novel is ideal for laying out these contradictions—even delighting in them. Art, I believe, abhors the authoritative. Or, as Jules Renard put it, "The scholar generalizes, the artist particularizes."

Lackey: So the biographical novelist's work is all about representing complexity and thereby immersing the reader in the ambiguities and conflicts of a life story. But biographers and historians, by contrast, take a stance, thus placing themselves above the subject matter. Is that what you are saying?

Cunningham: The job that biographical novelists have cut out for them is to try to work totally free of judgment or agenda, whether agenda means iconoclasm at one extreme, or hagiography at the other. Both extremes are problematic, and if either one inheres too much, the work is not going to resonate as a novel. Instead it's going to have the superficiality of a defended thesis—of an anachronistic position, or, just as bad, a shallow topicality. The biographies of Rilke tend to be quite positional in their approaches. They do, generally, take a stance of some kind—defending the artist/saint or excoriating the fallible husband and father. The really good ones, though, manage to avoid this kind of thing. Here I'm thinking of Prater's *A Ringing Glass* or Wolfgang Leppmann's *Rilke: A Life*.

Lackey: So what's the difference between these especially good biographies and your novel?

Cunningham: I think in part it's this dual dimension in *Lost Son,* in which Rilke's story is constantly overlaid by a more personal story of this figure in the literary future dialoguing with this ghost. Certainly, there are informational things to be found in *Lost Son* that can be obtained from the factual record too. Readers will come away from my novel knowing a lot about the factual circumstances of Rilke's life. But Rilke's story as *fiction,* as this relentlessly complex human narrative that is sensual in detail, poetic in perspective, intimately imagined, and aesthetically configured as a series of rhyming biographical events—that amounts to a contribution to the *imaginative* record concerning Rilke. I think that's something worth making special note of in any discussion about biographical fiction. With any life-story that's been around for some time, that's been passed along in various forms down a few generations, we develop a historical record and, alongside that, we develop a complementary imaginative record, a body of understanding that is somewhat folkloric—disarming, alluring, complicating—in its effects. Which is not to say that this imaginative record is always necessarily unfactual. In the case of good biographical novels, it often cleaves very closely to facts while taking logical imaginative liberties. I can think of any number of serious biographical novels that contribute greatly to the imaginative record—DeLillo's *Libra*, about Lee Harvey Oswald, comes immediately to mind, and so does Brian Hall's *I Should Be Extremely Happy in Your Company,* about Lewis and Clark and Sacagawea. This imaginative record is something to value in itself, because it exemplifies mind meeting mind *aesthetically* across time—that is, in the most complex and characteristically human way. We should value the imaginative approach as well, however, for the reason that such an approach can actually *contribute* to the factual record. These things intersect and interrelate and enrich each other.

Lackey: How would you say the imaginative record enriches the factual or historical record?

Cunningham: Well, let's look at methods of research. My research for *Lost Son* involved reading everything I could—biographies, commentaries, all Rilke's written work, his correspondence, the accounts of his contemporaries and intimates. In those ways my methods were no different than a scholarly biographical researcher. But I also conducted a more impressionistic kind of research, a more sensory-oriented style of excavation, which, after a certain point, became my central mode of inquiry into this life. This meant, for instance, going to Paris and sitting for a few days in the *Bibliothèque Nationale*—simply sitting where Rilke sat during his first days there in 1902, and which he wrote about so unforgettably in *Malte*. In fact, the whole ordeal of trying to get into the library in the first place was itself a form of immersive research. Admission to the reading room involved two interviews, proof of publication, proof of research goals—a real vetting—and this ordeal put me literally inside the shoes of Malte Laurids Brigge, Rilke's brainchild and shadow self. About the library, Malte says, "In here I am safe. One must have a special card to get into this room." He says it proudly, and somewhat disbelievingly. Malte, this anxiety-ridden, impoverished foreigner hiding out among the books, is trying to convince himself that he's one of the elect, that he's not just another down-and-out street urchin like the ones he sees every time he sets foot on the sidewalks. Being myself a fairly cash-strapped young writer, and having to convince the gate-keepers of my "worthiness" and "win entrance"—this put me in a state of special receptivity. It sensitized me to little glimmers of Rilke's imaginative experience in these places. Other days, I simply wandered around the 5th Arrondissement just the way Rilke had done. All this led to a number of discoveries that were very important to *Lost Son*. But I would go farther and assert that this kind of process, being so different from the biographer's, yields different kinds of serendipitous insights which can be, in themselves, valid contributions to the *scholarly* record. For instance, Eugène Atget is a well-known Parisian photographer who lived and worked in the city at the same time as Rilke.

Atget, however, has never been discussed in relation to Rilke's poetic corpus or his novel *Malte*. As a novelist, I turned to Atget's photos for inspiration in recreating the Paris Rilke first knew, because Atget's work documents the generally unseen or ignored parts of Paris that Rilke was writing about so powerfully in *Malte*. In Atget you find organ-grinders and half-demolished houses, some of the very same imagery described in Malte's notebooks—and photographed in the very same period that Rilke was working on his novel! There's an incredible overlap of sensibility between these two artists, amazing parallels. But it turns out that these men were not only working in parallel, but they actually *resided* in parallel for a while. They both lived in the very same building at the same time, number 17 Rue Campagne-Première— neighbors in sensibility *and* in fact! This seems to me to be a major crossing of artistic paths. Did they ever meet? Did they know of one another's work? I don't believe anyone knows. But this significant connection between them is something no biographer has noted. In one sense, it was my loose impressionistic wandering that led me to stumble on these facts. In another sense, my novelistic process inevitably led me there.

Lackey: So you are saying that your different approach to research as a biographical novelist leads to new ideas that are distinct from those of the biographer. Also, this approach gives your writing a different feel because it reflects or captures the mood of the space that Rilke inhabited. You can recreate something that the biographer and historian can't.

Cunningham: Yes, and this gives the lie to the argument that biographical fiction simply tampers with the facts. The novelist who has undergone this very intensive, impressionistic process has experienced something that can't be argued with. You can't argue with the imagination in that sense. If a novelist is not writing in a strictly factual way about some aspect of a life, the novelist may still be writing in an *imaginatively accurate* way. And oftentimes that imaginative accuracy gets at something that's ultimately more significant.

Lackey: Why?

Cunningham: One thing I changed in *Lost Son* is that I kept Rilke's father in residence at number nineteen Heinrichsgasse in Prague. In fact, Josef Rilke didn't die in the same apartment where he'd lived with his family. But in keeping him there in *Lost Son*, you reinforce a larger truth about how every time Rilke interacted with his father, it was a return to all these disturbances of his shadowed youth. It becomes much more vivid if he returns to the actual apartment. And does it matter that Josef Rilke lived elsewhere in those years? The altered fact remains defensible because it in no way distorts the known character of Rilke. It remains true to the Rilke that somebody else, even a Rilke scholar, would know and recognize.

Lackey: This brings to mind your author's note, in which you say that you take some liberties with the facts of Rilke's life. And yet, you insist your portrait of him is true to the poet's inner character. Can you specify the kind of truth you seek to picture in your novel?

Cunningham: I'd say it's a musical truth. What the biographical novelist does is more like the composer than the scholar. The composer takes the existent notes in a musical lexicon and arranges them, inflects them, sustains them, contracts them in a new, dynamic composition, an artwork that is tonally unique. The biographical novelist's notes are "the facts" of the particular life about which he or she is writing, and the time in which that life was lived. Now, we don't begrudge the composer for moving notes around. It's what we expect. We understand that this is how music is made. But when it comes to the question of biographical fiction, our cultural or institutional attitudes can tend toward a kind of tonal fundamentalism, a severe literal interpretation of the facts relating to a life. To arrange those facts, to manipulate a few of them, seems deeply suspect—but only because we're forgetting that the aim is music, a novelistic composition. There can be a kind of desperate, proprietary need to cling to "the facts" for the sake of scholarly rigor, etc. This has its place in the realm of scholarship, absolutely. But in the realm of art, the novelist knows that "the facts" are always mutable; the facts are never *not* a product of interpretation, and he or she revels in that, makes the most of that. Where the scholar might despair, the novelist makes music.

Lackey: Beyond the question of manipulating facts, what would you say to the contention that biographical novels are extraneous or redundant? That perhaps they occupy a lesser position in the literary hierarchy because they are not purely invented?

Cunningham: I'd say that, just as the novelist understands the mutability of facts, he or she also understands that no story is fully "known," that every story can be told and retold a million different ways, from a million different angles, with a million different shades of meaning. The novelist knows, moreover, that no story is wholly "invented." All stories have their basis somewhere. I'd suggest that to doubt the imaginative powers required to produce a serious biographical novel is only to betray one's own lack of imagination. It's like believing that we stand at the end of history and of human discourse, that we understand all there is to be understood, that knowledge is a finite, attainable quantity. It's like believing that we can shut whole realms of human experience away in a file drawer, or that something as quintessential as the human imagination should be subservient to the dogma of a literary marketplace.

Lackey: Consistent among many biographical novelists is the tendency to use the life of a figure to illuminate an historical period. In *Lost Son* your focus seems to be almost exclusively on Rilke's personal relationships, interior life, and creative work. Would it be right to say that *Lost Son* is not concerned with history?

Cunningham: I think it is concerned with history but only in a very personal and even spiritual way. Is it concerned with the Zeitgeist of the *fin de siècle*? No, not by any means. There are biographical novels that capture a particular historical moment beautifully, such as Bruce Olds' *Raising Holy Hell*, which is a collage of historical documents inserted into a fictional narrative. This gives the reader a wholly dimensional view of a particular character, in this case John Brown, as well as a sweeping understanding of American history.

Lackey: But you're not doing that.

Cunningham: *Lost Son* was always conceived as being very personal rather than historical.

Lackey: Do you think Rilke was unconcerned with history?

Cunningham: For the most part, yes, he was unconcerned with history. There were a few moments when he got swept up in the energy of his own time and would try to comment on it in some way. Around the outbreak of the first World War, for example, he wrote a few pieces of verse in response to all that was happening, and for a while thought of himself as the poet of this warrior god that had been let loose. It seemed quite out of character, though, and it didn't last. *The Notebooks of Malte Laurids Brigge* deals with a number of themes and questions about history generally, but in that book these concerns are always looked at through this narrow lens of Malte and his ancestors.

Lackey: Earlier you mentioned the use of the second-person in *Lost Son*. Throughout the novel your narrator addresses Rilke in the second person, which has at times a disorienting effect because it seems like you are addressing the reader. But this technique builds nicely for the epilogue as you cite the famous line from the "The Archaic Torso of Apollo": "You must change your life." If I understand your novel and your Rilke, cultivating the art of reading is as important as creating a work of art. Therefore, using the second-person narrative form to merge subject and reader is an excellent strategy for urging readers to enter the artwork in the same way the artist does, thus encouraging readers to become creators of their own lives. Can you explain why the second-person approach is suitable for the biographical form of the novel? Is there something unique about Rilke that makes the second-person appropriate here?

Cunningham: I really like what you say about urging readers to enter the artwork in the same way the artist does, because that was certainly my intention in using the second-person—or anyway, in deciding to keep it. In the early manuscript phase of *Lost Son,* the second-person was simply a matter of process. In a way, there's nothing more natural for the novelist-researcher than the epistolary address, so my instinct was to write to this bygone poet directly. My first notebook drafts of the novel were entirely in that form. I didn't really plan to keep the book in second-person, but it soon became clear to me that the story called for it—that the form could achieve a number of things. Bringing readers into the "skin" of this strange character who is almost absurdly vulnerable and yet relentlessly committed was the core challenge in writing *Lost Son,* and the use of second-person narration seemed the most natural way to handle that task. In the literary world, using this point-of-view is some kind of no-no. I don't understand that. To me the second-person is intuitive—we're all so used to it in correspondence, poetry, popular song. In this case, with Rilke being one of the world's greatest letter-writers, the second-person was particularly natural.

Lackey: It is also a blending of subjectivity because it could be you addressing the reader, or you addressing Rilke.

Cunningham: Yes, absolutely. It's a manner of address that can work on many levels at once. It can highlight the presence of an interpretive imagination at work, which I felt was important in *Lost Son*. It can tear down barriers, being an intimate form. It can also be formal, a delicate means of approach, like a flattering letter. The second-person is kind of wonderful. It should not only be defended, but more frequently explored. Again, let's not proscribe artistic boundaries before the journey has even begun!

Lackey: In *Lost Son* you see that blending of subjectivity, also, through Rilke's relationship with Rodin. You discuss Rodin's work *Man and His Thought,* which is a sculpture that pictures a man giving birth to a thought as if it were a person.

Cunningham: Yes. In that moment, that particular Rodin sculpture could be an image of what's happening in the writing of *Lost Son*. What do we have, in building a connection to the artists before us, but our imaginations? Even given an abundant body of fact, use of the imagination is imperative. As readers and artists, how can we know past figures except by, on some level, *recreating* them?

Lackey: And in *Lost Son* when Rodin finally reads Rilke's book about him, he says that the book is as much about Rilke as it is about Rodin, which merges the two artists. Again, this blending of subjectivity. And, if I understand what you are doing in *Lost Son*, some of Rilke's poetic technique, which you adopt in your novel, derives from his relationship with Rodin.

Cunningham: Yes, and this is where *Lost Son* is very much a *Künstlerroman*— and also, in some important ways, necessarily autobiographical. Rilke's development as a poet during the years depicted in the novel was very much a matter of reckoning with Rodin's influence. The driving questions for Rilke during this time are: How does one finally master one's material? Can the physicality of sculpture be applied to the intangible matters of poetry? And how does one live? The novel follows Rilke as he lives these questions, but they were also my own questions during the writing, so *Lost Son* inevitably documents my explorations as well. Admittedly, where Rilke is a protégé to Rodin in the novel, I was a kind of protégé to Rilke in writing it.

Lackey: *Lost Son* uses a quote from an early Rilke journal: "We must become human beings. We need eternity, because it alone gives our gestures room; and yet we know ourselves to be bounded in by tight borders. We must, therefore, create an infinity within these limits—even here, where we no longer believe in boundlessness." Can you explain how Rilke's philosophy about locating infinity within tight borders works in relation to the form of this biographical novel?

Cunningham: I think this goes back to that dual dimensionality of *Lost Son*, the novel as a story of *then* and of *now*. Eliot's "Tradition and the Individual Talent" comes to mind here, being an essay about the "pastness" and the "presentness" of the past. The artist's responsibility is to live within that awareness constantly, to recognize that a work of art created today is not just its own thing, but that it depends upon, and inevitably changes, every work that preceded it. In that sense, the "infinity within tight borders" here is the power of artistic tradition, the communicability between a *then* and a *now*, the aliveness of an artistic communion that transcends time. Annie Dillard has a wonderful phrase about the nature of artists' identity and about the way an artist is formed by virtue of a relation to his or her artistic tradition. Using the example of a painter, she says, "The self is the servant who bears the paint-box and its inherited contents." So *Lost Son* is about that kind of infinity, the ghostly inheritance that is central to any artist's work. Like any artist of today, I am stuck in this *now*, in this present, and yet, there is a part of me that is quintessentially tied to an earlier time.

Lackey: The year 1998 marks a decisive turning point with regard to the biographical novel, as two were nominated for the Pulitzer, and Michael Cunningham's *The Hours* won it. Can you explain what has changed in the literary establishment that has made it now recognize this art form?

Cunningham: In recent years there's been a recognition of what I would call the "data fallacy." We realize on a deep human, creative level that there is more to know than the surface-level data that is supplied to us through, say, a search engine. We have an intuitive wish for a more creative and humane way of understanding history and bygone figures, and I believe we can see a new sensibility emerging in reaction against this info-centric Google mentality. There's an epigraph at the beginning of *Lost Son* from Lee Siegel which I love: "We must understand one another or die, and we will never understand one another if we cannot understand the famous dead." This is ultimately what the biographical novel is about. It's about imaginative understanding rather than an accumulation of facts. It's about penetrating to something deeper, a human core at the heart of these historical and biographical stories that we all inherit. This art form, I think, answers to a desire we all have, living amid a sea of information and yet oftentimes finding true understanding to be conspicuously absent. There's also something to be said about sheer aesthetic joy—as Updike described it, the pleasure we experience when looking at a painting rather than looking through a window. That's why we look at art: We yearn to see things through a human veil. We long for an aesthetically shaped interpretation of our human story.

5

The Biographical Novel and the Complexity of Postmodern Interiors

Michael Cunningham

Lackey: Let me briefly tell you about this project. My objective is to define the nature of the American biographical novel. It is also to clarify why this genre of fiction has become so popular in recent years. That it would become popular is stunning since so many prominent writers condemned it. For instance, in the mid-thirties, Georg Lukács published *The Historical Novel*, which explicitly condemns the biographical form of the novel because it distorts and misrepresents history. Can you explain why, starting in the eighties, the biographical novel has become so popular?

Cunningham: I feel that Lukács had, shall we say, an interesting and perhaps questionable faith in the accuracy of history as written. Is a biography categorically *fact*? However pure the biographer's intentions, I don't think 100 percent accuracy is possible. It's not really within the human range to get everything exactly right. We're subjective, by nature. I'm not talking about intentional distortion. I just mean, we're not video cameras. We're not tape recorders. We bring ourselves into what we see. For instance, years ago, a friend of mine did a profile of me for *Out* magazine. He came over to my apartment, and we talked for a few hours. When the piece was published, all the quotes were fine, but I was surprised to read that my apartment contained a black leather sofa, and an apparently much-prized collection of onyx eggs. I didn't have a black leather sofa. I've never owned, and wouldn't own, an onyx egg. I wasn't all that upset about it, but I did mention it to my friend. Who was astonished. He'd *seen* a black leather sofa, and a collection of onyx eggs. I actually had him come over, just to prove to him that neither such thing was, or had ever been, on the premises. It became clear that my friend had assumed that a gay man of a certain age would have a black leather sofa. And that, for him, an onyx egg was, well, just the sort of useless aesthetic object he'd want to collect. And so, the reliability factor, even on the part of someone who's determined to be as accurate as is humanly possible…

Lackey: For Virginia Woolf, who is a figure in your novel, there is a distinction between fact and fiction, between biography and the novel, which is why Woolf claims that the two cannot mix. In essence, Woolf could not see her way towards the biographical novel. But you could. Why?

Cunningham: I don't see a particularly clear or easily-drawn line between fact and fiction. As I've just said, no one gets the facts entirely right. We can't. We see leather sofas and onyx eggs, because we're convinced, by the context, that such objects simply have to be there. And, really, there's no such thing as fiction, not in the absolute sense. Fiction writers work from our experience of the world and the people who inhabit it, I mean, that's our only source of material. Some of us go to greater lengths than others to disguise that which we've seen and heard, but still, fiction can only arise out of what a writer has seen and heard. And so, it's really a question of degree. The mother in a novel may be more like the writer's actual mother, or less like her, but she pretty much inevitably comes from the writer's relationship with a mother. I don't think it's such an enormous leap, then, really, from writing about a mother who's got to be, to some extent, based on an actual mother, and writing, with a similar sense of license, about a historical figure one has come to know intimately.

Lackey: One argument has been that the rise of postmodernism made the biographical novel possible. In the age of Woolf and Lukács, there was a tendency to question the boundaries between fact and fiction. But postmodernists took the argument one step further by claiming that fact is fiction. Do you think that this contributed to the making of the biographical novel?

Cunningham: Yes absolutely. By 2013, we have as many as seven or eight different biographies of certain key figures in history, and they differ fairly dramatically. We can see that anyone from Keats to Harry S. Truman is a slightly different person, as portrayed by different biographers.

Lackey: Getting back to the question of origins, why are so many contemporary American writers doing biographical novels?

Cunningham: That's a tough one. I think it's in the Zeitgeist, really. Some mysterious urge seems to grip a certain number of writers at around the same time. Why are so many "serious writers" suddenly doing science fiction? I don't know. Maybe I was a little early in writing a biographical novel, but I certainly didn't look around and say, "Hmm, a novel based on a historical figure. That seems like a good idea." It was just a book I wanted to write, because Woolf mattered so much to me. *Mrs. Dalloway* was the first great novel I ever read when I was in high school. It was very important to me, it really changed my thinking about literature and language and what you could do with language. So really, the spawning impulse was not so much writing about Virginia Woolf as it was trying to write a book about reading a book. About how a book could matter to someone as much as a love affair, or any of the other experiences that are more generally considered grist for the novelist's mill. My first idea for *The Hours* was simply to write a contemporary version of *Mrs. Dalloway*. I had no intention of including Virginia Woolf.

Lackey: It was going to be about Clarissa and Sally in the 1990s. Were Mrs. Brown and Richard already in there?

Cunningham: No. None of that was in there. I was going to appropriate Woolf's fictional characters and set them in New York today and see what would be different and what would be the same about their natures in a world very different from London in the twenties.

Lackey: One of the differences is the freedom to understand and express homosexual desire. One gets the sense that Woolf and her Clarissa Dalloway had such desire but couldn't act on it. Is that one of the central differences between the twenties and the nineties?

Cunningham: That was one of my ideas: what if my Clarissa was free to live as a lesbian?

Lackey: And Mrs. Dalloway, who probably had those impulses but couldn't really acknowledge them or act on them, what happens to her psychologically?

Cunningham: What happens to her psychologically? How is she different, and how is she the same? But that question began to feel a little … small. More like a conceit than a subject for a novel. It didn't feel like an interesting enough book to write. I thought about just dumping it, but then I thought, "you know, what if I worked Woolf into it in some way? What if Woolf rose up off the page sometimes and upbraided me for getting everything wrong?" And over time I settled on the idea of this contemporary version of *Mrs. Dalloway* contrasted with the day in Woolf's life where she started writing the book. But it still didn't feel like enough. And then I added the Laura Brown story. And, as a triptych, it began to work.

Lackey: Where did Richard fit in?

Cunningham: There was a Richard figure. It was a woman for a while, a great woman poet. She was vaguely Woolf-esque.

Lackey: For Septimus? Because he's the Septimus figure, right?

Cunningham: Yes.

Lackey: So it would have been a female Septimus.

Cunningham: A novel in my hands goes through tremendous changes from the day I sit down to start it, to the day I'm forced to admit that it's finished. But I think maybe what is most important, for our purposes, is that I didn't sit down to write a biographical novel. What I was writing turned into a partial biographical novel.

Lackey: Did you ever consider using a different name for your Virginia Woolf character? Ralph Ellison strongly encourages writers to do that, and he condemns writers for naming their characters after the original figures.

Cunningham: That seems like such a small and menial distinction. I mean, a great writer who lives in England in the 1920s, named Mable Woodcutty? It just seems pointless.

Lackey: I think in your case it's because it's so obvious that this was based on Virginia Woolf and *Mrs. Dalloway* that it was impossible to change the name.

Cunningham: Right, and I think it's important to say too that I always thought of myself writing a fictional character named "Virginia Woolf," whose life was as close to Virginia Woolf's life as I could make it. But it wasn't, could never have been, Woolf herself. I did do tremendous research. There are few lives as well documented as hers. Between her letters and her diaries, you can pretty much tune into every single day of her life. But there was a difference in my mind between actively trying to portray Woolf, and trying to invent a character who would resemble Virginia Woolf. I think there's a certain analogy between what novelists are doing when we use real historical figures, and twentieth-century portraiture. Think of Picasso's portraits. They're not precise renditions of those people, and yet his portrait of Gertrude Stein, for instance, gives us more about Gertrude Stein than any of the photographs of her.

Lackey: This is directly relevant to what might be the cover of this book. I was recently working with the design team for the cover, and I told them that I want a photograph of Virginia Woolf on one side and I want a painting of Virginia Woolf on the other side, and I want them to be placed in the position of a book so that on the cover it looks like an open book with a photograph and a painting on the two open pages. It would be great were the cover to feature Virginia Woolf, partly because we're already dealing with *The Hours*, but also because Virginia Woolf was one of the writers to blur the distinctions between fact and fiction, as she does so brilliantly in *Orlando*.

She set into motion so much, and I don't think she quite understood how radical some of her own ideas were. In a sense, I think she contradicts herself because her novels are far beyond some of her criticism.

Cunningham: She did make what I think is a meaningful distinction between her fiction and her essays. She insisted that the political had no place in fiction, that her characters were all the heroes of their own stories. There's not much social critique in the novels. She reserved that for essays like *A Room of One's Own*. That distinction makes sense to me.

Lackey: Here's an uncomfortable question for you. You write a novel, which is based on Woolf and *Mrs. Dalloway*. And yet, if I understand Woolf's claim about the impossibility of mixing fact and fiction, I think she would say your novel couldn't work. How would you respond to that?

Cunningham: I'd never imagine that Virginia Woolf would be pleased with my novel. I think she'd be pleased that she was played by Nicole Kidman. If I fantasize about Virginia coming back to life, and I hand her a copy of *The Hours*, I do *not* picture her pleased by my homage.

Lackey: But what would be her objections?

Cunningham: I think she would feel violated. Despite all of her copious letter writing and diary keeping, she was somewhat private. And I think she would find the writing not up to snuff. You know, she was very critical. I hope she would be pleased to know that a book that incorporates her was a huge popular success, because she died thinking of herself, essentially, as a failure. I think that would please her, but I don't imagine the book itself would. But let's get back to the question of fiction versus biography. One of the main powers of fiction is, a novelist can go deeper than a biographer can.

Lackey: In what sense?

Cunningham: As a novelist, I can go all the way into my characters, down to their very hearts and souls. A biographer is restricted to what the subject is able to tell him or her, and there are limits to what we can articulate about ourselves. So on one hand, I probably wasn't dead accurate about Virginia Woolf, but I think I had the freedom to imagine entering her mind in a way that Hermione Lee, great as her biography of Woolf is, wasn't able to do.

Lackey: Can we specify what it is that you can access or represent? Is it the subconscious? Is it an aura? Is it a certain kind of motivation? As a scholar, I'm trying to specify what distinguishes the biographical novel from other novels.

Cunningham: The contemporary biographical novel treats characters based on real people the way Tolstoy created Anna Karenina and Flaubert created Emma Bovary. The biography of Emma Bovary would be of very little use if it were simply the story of a silly, bourgeois woman who wanted to go to better parties. It was Flaubert's access to her mind and her heart that makes it a great book. And we seem to have collectively decided that we have the right to enter the minds, hearts, and souls of people who actually lived, in the way novelists have traditionally entered the minds, hearts, and souls of invented characters.

Lackey: Are you primarily interested only in the biography of the person? Or, does history play a role in your work?

Cunningham: Oh sure, *The Hours* is a novel about three different women, at three different times in history, and at each of those different times, women's lives were differently constrained. When Woolf wrote *Mrs. Dalloway*, a woman could be a wife, a teacher, or a nurse. That was pretty much it. By the time Laura Brown comes around, she has elected to be a housewife, though even in the fifties, she did have other choices. Not of course a huge range of choices, but it's not as if Laura was forced to be a wife and mother because nothing else was acceptable. By the time my Clarissa comes around, a woman can have a career just as a man does.

Lackey: Getting back to Lukács, he criticizes the biographical novel because it centers the novel within the consciousness of a character, which necessarily limits and distorts our understanding of history. But as far as I can tell, the biographical novelists don't agree with this. In fact, they think that the biographical novel can give us something new and much richer.

Cunningham: Exactly.

Lackey: But what is it? Can you explain what it is?

Cunningham: As a novelist, you do your research. I don't think I would have tried something like *The Hours* with a historical figure whose life and thoughts were not as thoroughly documented as Woolf's. You learn as much as you can—and, in Woolf's case, it's quite a bit—and then you take a leap and attempt your own version of the Picasso portrait of Gertrude Stein. Which, as I've said, doesn't exactly resemble the person, but gives you a sense of the person that's different from what you get from a photograph. I think if Lukács were here, I would ask: "what's the problem with these novels, in *addition* to the biographies?" If we novelists were saying, take all the biographies off the shelf, this will be everyone's *only* access to information about this person, then Lukács would have an argument. But why not be part of a larger effort to create a richer, more varied portrait?

Lackey: I think his argument is that the biographical novel necessarily distorts our understanding of the historical period.

Cunningham: I don't agree with that. For one thing, novelists are part of the historical record. Novelists are witnesses to their time. The biographer can tell us about Napoleon laying siege to Moscow. But the novelist can tell us what it was like to live in Moscow then. The novelist records the sights and smells, the novelist records the life of one of the anonymous soldiers who froze to death during the siege. The novelist adds texture and grain and nuance to the historical record.

Lackey: There is a sense in which your novel is quite different from other biographical novels. Bruce Duffy creates Max Einer in order to illuminate Ludwig Wittgenstein's character in *The World as I Found It*, while Jay Parini creates Masha in order to illuminate Valentin Bulgakov's character in *The Last Station*. These are characters set in the same time as the protagonists. Your novel is different in that you project your characters into the future. Can you explain what you were trying to accomplish by moving into the future rather than just simply staying in the time period of Virginia Woolf? Are these characters supposed to illuminate something about Virginia Woolf? Or, are they supposed to illuminate something about *Mrs. Dalloway*?

Cunningham: Well, sure. Laura Brown is reading *Mrs. Dalloway*. Laura Brown finds her only consolation in *Mrs. Dalloway*. Clarissa finds herself essentially living Mrs. Dalloway's life. If we leave it at Virginia Woolf, she thinks of herself as having produced tinselly little experiments that will be stored away in attics. And quite central to *The Hours* is the ongoing life of that book. If it's just Virginia thinking, "well, another silly little experiment," what have we got?

Lackey: There was one change in particular that stood out. The original title of *Mrs. Dalloway* was *The Hours*.

Cunningham: Yes, and I appropriated the title. I ripped off Virginia Woolf in so many ways.

Lackey: When writing *The Hours/Mrs. Dalloway*, Woolf says that she wanted to criticize the social system and show it at work at its most intense.

Cunningham: It originally starts off with soldiers marching to lay the wreath at Trafalgar Square.

Lackey: Right, so Woolf created characters that would represent the kind of coercion implicit in the social system. We see this with Miss Kilman, Dr. Holmes, Sir William Bradshaw, and we see how their coercive and oppressive systems function to destroy somebody like Septimus, who is a visionary, poet, and former soldier. For the most part, you do not have these characters in your novel. In fact, you shift the focus from the external to the internal. It is something inside the characters that functions to oppress. If we see *The Hours* as a contemporary version of *Mrs. Dalloway*, how does the novel function to criticize the social system and to show it at work at its most intense?

Cunningham: I think in this way *The Hours* echoes *Mrs. Dalloway*, because Woolf decided not to open with the soldiers going to lay the wreath at Trafalgar Square after all, but with Mrs. Dalloway going out to buy the flowers herself. *Mrs. Dalloway* is very much a book about the aftermath of World War One, but it's entirely centered on the effects of World War One, just as my character, Richard, in *The Hours*, is destroyed by AIDS. It's about the effects that AIDS had on this particular person. It's not about the epidemic in a larger sense.

Lackey: Your critique is very different from Woolf's because you focus more on good and decent people rather than oppressive figures. Laura's husband is a kind and loving husband. You do not demonize him. There is a radically different kind of oppression that nearly destroys Laura Brown. In *Mrs. Dalloway* we get the Bradshaws and the Holmses. They are clearly trying to coerce the soul, and in the process they are destroying people. You made a different decision by creating Dan Brown as a decent guy. What prompted you to do this?

Cunningham: It's very simple. I just didn't want to write another story of a good woman beaten down by a bad oppressive fifties husband. We've seen that story so many times. Dan, Laura's husband, loves her, and he has taken the rather remarkable step of marrying a woman who is not the great vivacious beauty he is technically entitled to. The irony is, in taking her to live in a castle, he's taking her out of the life that was right for her. His very act of loving rescue turns out to be her undoing.

Lackey: The freedom to discuss homosexual desire in recent years has really enabled us to open up so many new lines of interpretation about the past, to understand the nature of certain types of problems that were a mystery to us until only recently. This is an idea that dominates the contemporary American biographical novel. Here I'm thinking of Bruce Duffy's *The World As I Found It* and *Disaster Was my God*, Jay Parini's *The Last Station* and *The Passages of H.M.*, Russell Banks' *Cloudsplitter*, and Edmund White's *Hotel de Dream*, just to name a notable few. Now that we can talk intelligently, honestly, and without judgment about homosexual desire, this opens up new ways of thinking about the past. Is this one way of explaining the rise of the biographical novel? And where does your novel fit within this tradition?

Cunningham: I'd say that we are not merely free, in an unprecedented way, to write about homosexual desire, we're free to write about sexual desire of all kinds. I suspect Flaubert might have loved to do a couple of sex scenes for Emma Bovary, but he couldn't. I mean, he got taken to court for the supposed immorality of *Madame Bovary* even without any sex scenes. I'm not sure if it's specifically about the freedom to write about homosexuality, so much as it is of a relatively new freedom on the part of novelists to write about sexual desire of all kinds.

Lackey: But isn't one of the problems with Laura that she probably has a desire for women, but she can't really acknowledge that? There seems to be a kind of compulsive heterosexual ideology determining her behavior and she doesn't have the vocabulary to think about her own sexual desires, is that correct?

Cunningham: Now that we're free to write about sexuality of all kinds, I feel that it's incumbent upon a novelist to acknowledge the considerable individual differences in various people's sexuality. The three women in *The Hours* cannot accurately be called "straight" or "gay." That was intentional. For instance, as a gay man, I do have a certain affinity with other gay men, but only up to a point. There are gay men who are married, and monogamous. There are gay men who have sex with four or five different guys every week. There are gay men who have a certain interest in women, and there are gay men to whom the very idea of sex with a woman is repugnant. So, really, the term "gay" gives us some information about the sexuality of the person at hand, but not really all that much.

Lackey: Is that why you included Mary Krull, the dogmatic queer theorist who is very critical of Clarissa?

Cunningham: I don't write many villains, nor did Woolf. However, you'll never find a sympathetic doctor in Virginia Woolf because she was so badly treated by doctors. You probably know this. There was a period when it was actually believed that an infected tooth somehow transmitted toxins into the brain, and so, according to certain doctors, Woolf's problem was bad teeth. They actually pulled some of her teeth in order to cure her madness. And, guess what? It didn't work. Nothing worked. As to "dogmatic queer theorists"… Woolf scholars tend to feel unusually possessive of her. They tend to insist on one single aspect of her life as explaining the whole thing: Woolf as incest survivor, Woolf as repressed lesbian, Woolf as this, Woolf as that. And yes, I did let Mary Krull stand in for a kind of miniaturizing, overly-focused approach to Woolf that I'm aware of in some academics.

Lackey: Jay Parini has discussed the prefaces and epilogues that biographical novelists frequently include in their novels. In these, the authors make the following disclaimer: this is fiction, and it is not to be confused with history, biography, or fact. Parini recommends that biographical novelists stop doing this. He recommends that biographical novelists say something like: "this is the truth as I understand it and I'm telling it to the best of my ability. Take it or leave it." How would you respond to that?

Cunningham: I have come to agree with him. I did add a little preface to *Specimen Days*, because I was fucking with history. I was, for instance, clearly depicting the Triangle Shirtwaist Company fire, which in my novel happens thirty years before it actually occurred. I hope Lukács would at least grudgingly appreciate that. In *Specimen Days*, I rearranged history. I'm honestly not sure if I'd do that again.

Lackey: Lukács thinks that novelists can take liberties with historical fact in order to get to a deeper truth about history. Historical facts don't always suit the novelist's purpose, so the novelist has to rearrange them.

Cunningham: Almost always, yes.

Lackey: But this still begs the question: What kind of truth are you biographical novelists trying to access or represent? The traditional historical novel is trying to get to some sort of universal truth about the nature of the period, whereas the biographical novelists seem to have shifted the focus from the nature of the historical period to something about the nature of consciousness itself.

Cunningham: Yes, again, I think the biographical novelist is trying to record what it was like to *be* that person at that time in history, which is what novelists have always done. It's just now that some of us are doing it with real people.

Lackey: E. M. Forster claims that starting in the modernist period what distinguishes the novelist is the fact that the novelist can chart the subconscious short-circuiting into political action and it was only in that period, when they started to have a more sophisticated understanding of the subconscious, that they could start thinking about the novel in those terms.

Cunningham: Well sure. As much as we love Jane Austen, for instance, she didn't really have a sense of psychology. The concept didn't exist when she was alive. Woolf wrote an interesting essay about Austen. She claimed that

Austen seemed to be moving toward a more complicated understanding of the inner workings of her characters, toward the end of her career. But Freud and Winnicott and all these people have come along since Jane Austen and Charles Dickens. We simply know more than we did about the inner complexities of the human mind.

Lackey: So that could be one of the defining features of the biographical novel, a deeper understanding of the complexity of human interiority?

Cunningham: I think that's a good point, I think we who are writing now are writing with an expanded understanding of the complexities of the inner workings of the human organism. Believe me, I'm not trying to diminish the greatness of writers like Austen and Dickens. But all writers use whatever knowledge is available to them during their lifetimes. Austen and Dickens wrote great novels, they're just not "psychological" novels. Writing now, in the twenty-first century, it would be silly to write as if the study of psychology didn't exist. Woolf, by the way, had just started reading Freud. The Hogarth Press, which was the press she and Leonard ran, was the first to publish Freud in English. Woolf found Freud both interesting, and exasperating. She couldn't deny the originality and radicalism of his thinking. But she also considered much of his thinking to be, well, mere *thinking*. She wasn't convinced about the effects of childhood trauma, or the existence of the ego, the super-ego, and the id. Which is interesting, considering how traumatic her own childhood was. I hope the spirit of Woolf will forgive me if I speculate that some of what Freud was saying actually hit a little too close to home.

Lackey: It seems that two separate strands came together to make the contemporary biographical novel possible. One is an expanded understanding of the inner complexity of the human. The other is the collapse of the distinction between fact and fiction. Do you agree with this? And, if so, can you explain how this might shed light on *The Hours* and the biographical novel more generally?

Cunningham: That's what I was trying to say earlier. Facts are entirely dependent on who's relating them. Objectivity is literally impossible. We see a black leather sofa and a collection of onyx eggs, because we're convinced that those objects simply have to be there. We insist that the key to Woolf's nature resides in the fact that she was an incest survivor, because we (some of us, not me) can't imagine a Woolf who was in fact an incest survivor but was also so much else. For my own conscience's sake, please permit me to say, one last time, that I don't dismiss biography, and the work biographers do. We need a historical record, made up of facts, or at least the facts as best we're able to recognize them.

Okay, I know this is a bit of a generality. But let's just say, for argument's sake, that it's the biographer's job to make sense out of what seems like reams of unrelated and random material. To confer a certain degree of order onto a subject's life. Because we, I mean we humans, as a species, like order. We prefer it to chaos. But then it's the novelist's job to insist, essentially, on the opposite. That, yes, there are patterns, but we, I mean, again, we humans, are impossibly complex. Our contradictions matter as much as our consistencies. I think it is part of a novelist's obligation to insist that our lives don't always make sense, that we are on one hand cogent, recognizable entities and, on the other, we're also living, breathing mysteries that can't really be solved. We do need to know the facts. And we need, as well, to be reminded that the facts don't always add up to what could necessarily be called an explanation.

6

Imagining a Matrilineal History in the Biographical Novel

Anita Diamant

Lackey: Let me start by telling you about this project. For many years, I have been interested in historical fiction. More specifically, I am interested in the biographical form of the historical novel, which has become so popular in recent years and led me to your novel. In *Pitching My Tent*, you say that when you wrote *The Red Tent*, you were writing historical fiction. But if you were writing historical fiction, can you explain what motivated you to center your novel in the consciousness of a specific character? Why didn't you use primarily an omniscient narrator, who would have given us a seemingly more objective perspective of the period?

Diamant: I always worry that my answer to this question will be disappointing. *The Red Tent* was my first novel; I had never tried writing fiction at all. I was a journalist, a columnist and a writer of nonfiction books. When I turned forty, I decided that I wanted a new challenge in my work, so I thought I'd try writing a novel. I didn't have a story of my own that had been sitting in a drawer or rattling around in my head, so I raided the Bible, one of the great sources of stories for us in the west, and told a lesser-known part of the familiar saga of Jacob from the point of view of a minor character. This is a fairly common device, of course, and it can be successful because it can shed new light on an old story. The women in the Bible are, for the most part, tangential figures, some of whom, like Dinah, never say a word. Using the first person was not part of a "plan." As a first-time novelist, I landed on the idea of telling the story from Dinah's point of view because it enabled me to narrow the focus of the story. As a young girl, Dinah would not have had access to the world of her father and brothers; her universe was female. The boys would learn shepherding and trading from their father, the girls would learn spinning and agriculture from their mother. The lives of men and women were integrated in important ways—emotionally, economically, romantically—but I do think men and women inhabited separate cultures until sometime in the nineteenth century.

Lackey: Did you start with the idea of the red tent and this sacred space for women? Or, did you start with Dinah's consciousness?

Diamant: I started looking for a story to tell and at first thought I would explore the story of Rachel and Leah, sisters who shared a husband. I wondered what that life might have been like. But I got stuck; I wasn't coming up with a plot to illuminate that conflict. I kept reading Genesis, and the Dinah story felt like a plot on a platter in that it offered up a mystery, because we don't really know what happened between her and the prince in Shechem. We don't "see" it. Their encounter is told to us in the third person, after the fact, by two of her brothers who are unreliable narrators. Simon and Levy carry some heavy familial grudges and it is they who call what happened to Dinah a rape.

Lackey: Since the 1980s, there have been many novels that have blended fiction and biography, thus using the creative imagination to fill in gaps in our understanding of history and to illuminate human motivation. Here I'm thinking of Irvin Yalom's work on Nietzsche and Spinoza, Jay Parini's work on Leo Tolstoy and Walter Benjamin, and Sherry Jones's work on A'isha. Can you explain what set you on track to write *The Red Tent*? What authors, if any, inspired you to write *The Red Tent*?

Diamant: I wasn't particularly a reader of historical fiction or of biblical fiction and I don't think of *The Red Tent* as biblical fiction. As for inspiration, I would credit Virginia Woolf's *A Room of One's Own* for the first-person voice and for my focus on an invisible woman. Another source—which might seem unrelated—was seeing the original Broadway production of *Angels in America* and having the top of my head blown off, *pace* Emily Dickinson. I thought, "If Tony Kushner could be that audacious and successful, I can risk writing a novel." I get a lot of inspiration for my work from different forms of art, theater and modern dance in particular. The poet Billy Collins wrote a terrific essay in which he credits Loony Tunes cartoons as an important influence on his work.

Lackey: You say you don't think of *The Red Tent* as biblical fiction. But it is fiction. And it's based on the Bible.

Diamant: I guess I'm talking about the genre of biblical fiction. While I have only the most glancing relationship with those novels, I believe they tend to be faithful to the text as it has come down, and that wasn't my intention. I put the text aside early on in the writing, because I didn't want to feel obliged to tell the story as it was codified. So I made the name "Gera" into a girl's name; Leah has twins, which was a way to avoid yet another birth scene. There are many changes, big and small, most of them made consciously. The story as it unfolds in Egypt, for example, is my own invention.

Lackey: The issue of the time period is one reason why *The Red Tent* is so different from many contemporary biographical novels. Joanna Scott wrote *Arrogance*, a novel about the artist Egon Schiele, while Bruce Duffy wrote *Disaster Was My God*, which is about the poet Arthur Rimbaud. Your main character is taken from a sacred text, which is generally considered inviolable. Is it right to assume that taking a character from the Hebrew text imposes different types of restrictions on you than taking a mere historical character? If so, can you discuss the kind of liberties you can take with the character? And can you discuss the kind of liberties that you believe you cannot take? Or are there liberties you can't take?

Diamant: I don't consider the text inviolable. For one thing, I don't believe God wrote the Bible. The Bible was made by human hands. For me, what makes it sacred is that so many people have been reading and arguing about it for the past 2,000 years. That it remains alive is what's miraculous about it; but again, it owes its life to our engagement with it. For Jews, in particular, argument is central. There's a line from the Talmud that says we can turn Torah, which means all sacred text, on its head in order to make sense of it. Jewish tradition offers a lot of freedom for students to approach the text from all directions and then, audaciously, to attribute our interpretations to the divine mind, to God. As a Jew, I felt great permission to tell these stories as I wished.

Lackey: Since the publication of *The Red Tent*, there have been many who have asked if your novel is a contemporary form of Midrash, a rabbinical form of commentary and storytelling that seeks to resolve inconsistencies and illuminate mysteries within sacred texts. You insist that *The Red Tent* is a novel, that you did not intend to write Midrash. However, if we accept the view that feminism is a spiritual perspective rooted in social justice, *The Red Tent* would certainly qualify as a form of Midrash in that it functions to recover a matrilineal history that is conspicuously absent from the sacred text. Given your novel, the sacred text no longer pictures just the God of Abraham, Isaac, and Jacob, but also the God of Sarah, Rebecca, Leah, and Dinah, among others. Can you talk about feminism in Midrash and feminist Midrash, if such a thing exists or could exist?

Diamant: Midrash is about putting imagination into the service of biblical commentary. Midrash was created within the context of the sermon, as a teaching tool for the masses who couldn't read. It is a form of sacred story-telling but when these stories got written down, they were treated as religious texts, too. Midrash gave the rabbis great freedom to explain the usually terse and sometimes contradictory stories in the Bible to make a point, to teach a lesson. For modern readers in liberal traditions, by which I mean those who do not assume there is a single literal way to understand anything in scripture, Midrash is a way for us to place ourselves inside the Bible's stories. The idea and practice of Midrash has been embraced by liberal Christians, and Christian feminists in particular, because it provides new windows and doors into the text. Some readers have taken great exception to my telling of the Dinah story; they see it as a violation, as blasphemy. That notion didn't concern me when I was writing and I stopped looking at the biblical text fairly early in the writing process in order to find my own story, to avoid feeling bound by what I found on the page. There is a great deal of feminist Midrash now, some is written *as* biblical commentary, some written by rabbis as part of sermons. Much of it is quite faithful to the text. There are also Midrashic poems and dances.

Lackey: Does that operate differently according to different traditions? I know that you made a distinction between Orthodox, Conservative, and Reform Jews in one of your essays. So in the Orthodox tradition, would there be feminist Midrash?

Diamant: There is no such thing as Orthodox Judaism; there are Orthodox Judaisms, with differences and variations that currently include one American Orthodox seminary that ordains women. So I don't doubt that there is Orthodox feminist Midrash. Today, I think people make a distinction between modern Midrash and classical Midrash, so anything written after the Rabbinic Period and certainly anything in the twentieth and twenty-first century would be modern Midrash. And some modern Midrash seeks to recover a matrilineal history in a self-consciously feminist way. Allow me to define feminism as the radical notion that women are human beings. That's the whole shooting match and the rest follows: as human beings, women are entitled to the same freedoms and rights as men. I like your definition that feminist Midrash supplies "a spiritual perspective rooted in social justice," but it's not *only* a spiritual perspective. I wasn't out to recover a matrilineal history so much as to imagine one. I tried to make *The Red Tent* as historically accurate as I could, which wasn't all that easy given the vast silence that surrounds that era especially as regards women. But we do have these names, and we do have the outlines of these stories. It's not the job of fiction to recover history, but to imagine it. I don't claim that my book is historically valid.

Lackey: What kind of validity does it have?

Diamant: It has, I hope, the validity of human truth, though it cannot be read as a true story. This is not "ripped from the headlines." I have had readers tell me that they wish what happened in *The Red Tent* was what really happened. But I made this world up out of my imagination, stitching together the bits and pieces of facts that I dug up during my idiosyncratic research. It is part of a much larger transformation in Judaism. Over the past forty years at least, there has been a deepening and broadening understanding that our ancestral mothers left us a legacy as well, and that their memory needs to be honored. This inclusion has changed even common prayer book language for liberal Jews around the world. *The Red Tent* partakes of a larger cultural shift.

Lackey: Christa Wolf wrote a novel called *Medea* about fifteen years ago, and she changed the ending. In Wolf's ending, Medea doesn't kill her children. There is something that is allowing many writers to take liberties with myths and stories. They feel that not only are they entitled, but also somewhat obligated to take this liberty. Maybe I mis-spoke by saying "recover." I like the way you're saying this: you are trying to "imagine" a history. So it's not so much interested in what happened as much as it is a service that we're performing today. Is that correct?

Diamant: I don't think of this as providing a service and I certainly don't feel obligated to make changes. As a result of my approach, people who read through a religious lens may find new ways into the rest of scripture as well as Dinah's story. By going inside the head of a biblical character, the reader might wonder, "Was that what Sarah was thinking?" It might encourage other questions about motivation or the story behind the story. The Genesis stories are especially rich because they are so complicated, sometimes contradictory, and very often family sagas, which are humanly recognizable once you get past thinking of the characters as icons. But I never thought of that while writing; again, it was about telling a good story.

Lackey: So you insist that this is not Midrash; this is not history; that this is a novel and that this is fiction. But you seem to be really committed to getting things right in so far as you can.

Diamant: Some readers see my book as a recovered history, but it isn't, because I'm not a historian. That said, any historical novel should be as accurate as possible. I tried to find out who these women were, how they were, how many children they had. Those questions can be answered, to a limited extent, by looking into the historical record. Since very little is written about women's lives 3,000 years ago I had a lot of latitude. I joke that nobody knows whether I got the goat stew recipe wrong or not. On the one hand, I tried to make sure that the ingredients *in* the goat stew would have been available at the time. But the recipe? I could make it up. And, by the way, my stew mixes milk and meat, which makes it unkosher, reflecting the fact that this story takes place pre-Sinai, when rules about food, among everything else, got handed down.

Lackey: In addition to feminism, would it be right to say that postmodernism also contributed to the making of *The Red Tent*? One of the central claims of postmodernism is that all forms of writing involve the fictionalization of reality, a shaping of our worldview through language. Within this framework, narrative in a patriarchal context presupposes and furthers a patriarchal agenda. You have said that the Bible is incomplete and, on occasion, contradictory. Would it be correct to say that feminist Midrash—*The Red Tent* in this case, if you accept that—implies or presupposes that the Bible is historical fiction?

Diamant: For me, the Bible is not fiction; it is sacred myth. "Myth" doesn't mean it's false but that it addresses the big human questions in a larger-than-life story. What makes it sacred for me, as I've said, is not who wrote it, or Who wrote it, but how the text has informed and shaped the people who have read it and argued over it for the last two and a half millennia. The Bible is not, by the way, one story or one sacred myth, but many hundreds of stories; some horrifying, some inspiring. And these myths were, undeniably, shaped by language and a patriarchal culture, and the fact that it was written in a patriarchal world shaped the way the stories are told.

Lackey: But it seems like there is a tension in what you are saying. You say that you are leveling the text. It was written by humans. It has contradictions in it. God did not write it. It is only sacred because people take it that way. But a lot of people would say that your treatment of the Bible as a text with biases and contradictions lacks reverence, that you in fact do not consider it sacred. Some would charge that you treat it as if it has no more legitimacy than Shakespeare's works.

Diamant: I locate the sacred not in the way "people take it," as a given, but in the human endeavor of trying to make sense of it. Maybe this is a particularly Jewish view, but the argument transcends time, since Jews today are arguing with Jews who died 1,000 years ago. And by the way, I wouldn't call Shakespeare's works sacred myth. They are part of a great "canon," which sounds mythic. But I think there's a difference.

Lackey: So you do make a distinction not because of something intrinsic to the nature of the work, but because of people's attitude? But if that's the case, then something changed between, let us say, the 1890s and 1990s, and something's going to change someday in the future. It's very possible that in 100 years, the whole notion of sacred myth is not going to make sense anymore.

Diamant: My hunch is that there will always be sacred myth. Every culture that I know of has some kind of a sacred myth. The fact that we continue to spin stories and poems and children's books and everything else out of old sacred myth proves its power and perhaps our need. We don't have many sacred myths that bind us together. To be literate, you need to know both the Bible and Shakespeare, at least a little. They both give us language, common references, cultural touchstones, intellectual currency. Whether you were born speaking English or if you're Hindu, it's still important to know who Abraham and Hamlet are.

Lackey: I have seen a lot of things on the Internet complaining about the changes you made to the Dinah story. So it seems to me that, while you want to say that this a sacred myth and that you respect it, some people have a very different notion of what constitutes a sacred myth, and they think that you've taken an unjust liberty.

Diamant: That's the big difference between orthodox/literal and liberal readings. People who read the Bible as literal truth have a hard time with anyone who does not.

Lackey: Do you think if you had written and published this novel in the 1940s, the response would have been much different?

Diamant: I doubt it would have been written in this way or published then. This is very much a novel of its time, published in 1997 as part of a larger cultural conversation. One of the things that inspired the book was Bill Moyers' talk show *Genesis* on PBS. Moyers invited clergy from all the traditions that reference Genesis: rabbis, priests, ministers and preachers from a variety of Protestant churches, and at least one representative of Islam. They sat around talking about the stories in Genesis from their perspectives. It was fascinating and pretty well received; the book based on it did well, too, I think. I was intrigued by the idea that there was an audience for such a conversation, that the Bible could be a springboard for public conversation across religious traditions.

Lackey: In 1939, Zora Neale Hurston published *Moses, Man of the Mountain*, which charts the inner life of Moses as he came to terms with his mission to lead the ancient Hebrews out of Egypt and into the Promised Land. In the preface to that work, Hurston claims that she wants to clarify that there are many versions of Moses, not just the one of the Judeo-Christian tradition. In the 1950s and the 1960s, when Hurston was working on a Herod novel, she considered the story about Herod, from the Gospel of Matthew, not just anti-Semitic, but also the beginning of what would become a virulent form of Christian anti-Semitism. Part of the problem as Hurston understood it was that people accepted the sacred text as inviolable and infallible. If the Bible says that Jews are children of the devil, then believers have no choice but to believe that. To create the conditions for social justice, Hurston believed that it is important to challenge the sacred text, to expose it as potentially flawed and even politically dangerous. Is *The Red Tent* in the same tradition as Hurston's novel? Could you clarify how you are working within the same tradition as Hurston and how you are not?

Diamant: I did not write a book "to create the conditions for social justice" but *The Red Tent* certainly reflects my background and my beliefs, which include a commitment to *tikkum olam*, the repair of the world. I write in English. I'm a woman. I had a pretty decent education. I am Jewish. I am a feminist. I'm a twentieth/twenty-first century American. All these things inform everything I do. Also, I grew up with a lot of opportunity that I don't take for granted. I have watched as women's lives and minds were given freer range and I am well aware of what women weren't allowed to do even in my own lifetime; that understanding informs the way I think and write. Certainly, this explains why I wanted to give Dinah agency and not having her be just a victim. Her life did not end with the murder of her husband; she was strong enough to cope and continue and find meaning and love. People often ask if *The Red Tent* is a feminist novel. While I didn't have an agenda and I wasn't out to redress wrongs, there is no way it can't be feminist because that's who I am—and proudly. But that label is not all-inclusive, is it?

Lackey: Can I ask a question about your choice with regard to Dinah and the rape? In your prologue, Dinah insists that she is frequently remembered as just a victim. Your Dinah wants to be remembered as more than just that. Is getting beyond the reductive view of Dinah and women more generally as victims what led you to reimagine what happened with Shechem, whether it was a rape or not?

Diamant: The prologue was the last thing I wrote. But as soon as I decided to tell Dinah's story, I decided what happened was not a rape. And I was not the first person to see it that way. Others have pointed out that Shechem, the prince, doesn't act like a rapist. He falls in love with Dinah, and he agrees to be circumcised and orders all the men of the community to undergo the knife as well. Pretty remarkable terms to marry someone, and not consistent with the action of a rapist. There is a rape in the Hebrew Bible. King David's son, Amnon, rapes Tamar, David's daughter. He lures her to his room and attacks her. She begs him to stop but he ignores her plea, and throws her out of his rooms when he's done with her. Tamar then goes to Absalom, another brother, and asks for justice. There is nothing like that in the story of Dinah and a careful reading of the text has to make you ask, "How is this a rape?" One answer, which transcends time and culture, is that it was unthinkable that a "decent" woman might engage in consensual sex outside of her tribe or race or religion; that meant any pre-marital sex that involved say, your sister, had to be considered rape.

Lackey: At this point, let me take the conversation in a slightly different direction. In the postscript of *In the Time of the Butterflies*, Julia Alvarez claims that her novel about the Mirabal sisters was an attempt to use the imagination in order to redeem the lives of the violated women in that novel. There is a difference between your work and Alvarez's. Her characters died in 1960, whereas your characters lived more than 3,000 years ago. Were you trying to imagine a life that could have been? Or was it an attempt to recover the condition of women at a particular time in history? Whatever the case, can you talk about the redemptive role such creative work of memory and the imagination can perform for us today? Also, can you explain why the biographical novel is uniquely capable of doing this kind of redemptive work?

Diamant: "Redemptive" is not a word or even an idea I'm comfortable with, although it seems to work that way for some of my readers. Young women— high school and college students—write to tell me that they see the book as an affirmation of femaleness. Not femininity or feminism, but the simple dignity of living in a female body, and doing work that has been traditionally defined and denigrated as women's work. *The Red Tent* honors the life of the body seriously and tenderly, and honors the life and work of the community of women. A lot of people seem to feel that sort of community is absent from modern life, which sometimes leads to expressions of nostalgia for this era, which I try to debunk. I'm not nostalgic for any time prior to antibiotics or anesthesia or caffeine or reading. Readers project a lot onto this book, finding what they wish was in the Bible and what they wish for their own lives. I don't know if that's redemptive, but I think for some, it allows them to feel respect for themselves as women and as human beings.

Lackey: But as someone who teaches a lot of feminist literature, I frequently teach Virginia Woolf, Adrienne Rich, Sylvia Plath, Eavan Boland, and many others, I find that many people recognize the importance of going back and recovering these lost stories of women because there is a narrative rupture in female history. For female empowerment, there seems to be a need for narrative coherence. When I talk to people about *The Red Tent*, this is one thing they find so empowering: that there are these stories, and if we can develop a methodology for reading these sacred texts, we can recover some of those stories. And this would function to empower women. When I say "redemptive," and when Julia Alvarez uses the word redemption, I think that is what is meant.

Diamant: The work of recovering or redeeming the stories of women is not limited to fiction. It is very much in the purview of women's history, which is like social history and labor history, in that they recover stories that were missing from the official canon. The more we know about the silent majorities, the richer the experience of humanity. Of course, since the stories of half of humanity were untold and under-told for so long, there's lots to tell and there will be for a very long time. My book tries to answer the questions Virginia Woolf posed in *A Room of One's Own*. What was life like for her? How many children? Did she have a room of her own, which is to say, time and space to reflect? Those questions are still being answered in many disciplines: fiction, history, theater, anthropology, film, dance, and the visual arts.

Lackey: But your book resonated, I think, partly because it was a scriptural story. I think that's one of the reasons it had such an enormous impact: because it validates in a different way, because it participates in the sacred myth. It captures the sacred myth as people understand it, whereas if your protagonist would have just been somebody from the Renaissance period, it might not have resonated as much.

Diamant: I did not invent this way of looking at the Bible. *The Last Temptation of Christ* by Nikos Kazantzis is an example. I may have written the first novel that gave the whole narrative to one biblical woman; I'm not sure about that. There might have been others. In any case, for women who read the Hebrew Bible as scripture, *The Red Tent* was eye opening, door opening, for some, spiritually opening. But I've also heard from women, and men, who are not Christian or Jewish or Muslim, and they tell me the book moved them as well. To them, it's a book about women's lives, less rooted in a sacred tradition and more rooted in culture. I've gotten some emails from people who grew up in countries where harems were once common, who report that *The Red Tent* seemed in line with what they knew about that all-female world.

Lackey: With respect to the liberties you take, after the rape virtually nothing is disclosed about Dinah in Genesis. There is certainly nothing in Genesis to suggest that she went to Egypt, bore a son, became a midwife, and remarried.

What primarily governed your aesthetic choices as you composed the Egypt section of the novel? Was it the internal logic of Dinah's character? Was it your research about women from the time period? Was it a desire to give her a better ending than the one we see in Genesis? Or was it something totally different?

Diamant: In the Thomas Mann cycle, *Joseph and his Brothers*, Dinah dies. She has a baby who dies and then she dies. That seemed like the most logical ending for her if she stayed with the family. She would have been damaged goods and a reminder of a terrible blot on the family name. I gave her a new beginning in a foreign culture where she doesn't speak the language and everything is different. Not only does it make for a better story, it created an opportunity for her to be happy. I did a fair amount of research about Egypt, which was interesting for me as a Jew because, in our narrative, Egyptians have been the bad guys. Every year at Passover, we retell and rehearse the evil of Egypt where the Hebrews were enslaved. But I learned that Egypt was, in the ancient world, a relatively progressive place for women. Egyptian women could inherit property; they sat at the same table as their husbands and sons. People took baths. The Nile was a source of diverse, good food. I discovered that Egypt produced some of the first medical textbooks; they are full of "prescriptions" like crouching over burning dung, but they also speak of herbs that had medicinal value. What was consistent in Dinah's two worlds was the relative freedom she had as a midwife.

Lackey: Why connect her back with her brother in Egypt at the end of the novel?

Diamant: This opportunity to close a circle is pretty irresistible, isn't it? The Jacob story cycle ends in Egypt when the old patriarch of the family bestows his blessing on Joseph, his youngest son. The whole family is there as well, so it seemed logical to engineer an encounter with them. But again, Dinah is watching it from the sidelines. She can only get secondhand reports about what happens between father and son because the news comes from women. *The Red Tent* is limited and reveals the ways stories are passed down and in what version they are retold.

Lackey: So the Gera encounter is important because it unifies the work by clarifying how the stories told can preserve a matrilineal history. Can you talk about your construction of the character of Gera? And I'm curious here, because in Genesis, Benjamin has children and Gera is a son.

Diamant: I believe Gera is a name that could be used for men or women. Stories of women were told by women, to women, which is why they weren't written down. Dinah was part of an oral tradition that I imagined as mostly lost, but with echoes of what had been. The fact that Dinah's name appears in the Bible suggests to me (as a novelist) that somebody—maybe even a woman—preserved this story and passed it on until it was included and codified.

Lackey: To conclude, I want to briefly discuss the proliferation of biographical novels. There have been many written over the past thirty years. Can you talk about that? And how do you fit within this tradition?

Diamant: I don't have an answer but I can speculate about some of the reasons. One might be the advent of identity politics in the sixties and seventies: the black power movement, renewed Jewish pride, feminism. People reclaimed their own stories, once considered trivial, as important and as valid as the stories of white men. The oral history movement honored the stories of the poorest of the poor: sharecroppers, Appalachian banjo players and the like. The unheard got a hearing and it was pretty thrilling.

The run on biographical fiction may also share something with the passion for the memoir, which may owe something to the popularization of psychology. We are psychologically literate now; we have a language to describe the internal life. We encourage people to talk about their pain, their joy and it's not considered weak or wrong. Not being in touch with one's feelings is seen as a problem; men are constantly being encouraged to get in touch with their feelings. This makes for an interesting problem when writing about people in the past. I don't think people were ever as open and confessional as they are today. Even in my most recent novel, *Day After Night*, which is set in Palestine in 1945, Holocaust survivors did not talk about what happened to them during the war years. It was considered unhealthy to dwell on the past.

Lackey: So what you're saying is that if Dinah's story would have been written in the mid-nineteenth century, nobody would have cared.

Diamant: I doubt it could have been written in the nineteenth century. Certainly not in the way I wrote it. It simply wouldn't have occurred to anyone to ask the first question about the life of a female biblical footnote. She was invisible.

7

In the Fog of the Biographical Novel's History

Bruce Duffy

Lackey: Let me start with a question about Georg Lukács's book, *The Historical Novel*. One of his central claims is that the biographical form of the novel is doomed to failure, because the focus on "the *biography of the hero*" necessarily leads authors to overlook or misrepresent significant historical events and truths. Given the nature of his claim, he would say both of your novels, *Disaster Was My God* and *The World As I Found It*, were not just failures, but that they were doomed to failure. How would you respond to that claim?

Duffy: Well, I guess I'd say Lukács has it backwards. The hero of the novel should be the foreground, and the history should be background. I think the point of a novel, any novel, is really to get inside some human beings—into their world in a way that history or biography can't duplicate, or rather in a way that delivers a different kind of authority and a different kind of pleasure. For me, very few biographers ever really take me inside someone's being in the masterful way a Richard Ellman does with Oscar Wilde, or Robert Caro does with LBJ. To that end, history may play a part, but it can't be the main focus. Facts will only take you so far. So, if you don't penetrate somebody, if you don't fully understand that character, if you don't really understand the political and social context of that world—meaning *your* fictional world—well, the history won't matter.

To me, Lukács has a very totalitarian, Soviet-style view of history, very out of step with the times. Just think of the Web in which ordinary people directly participate in the news process, with immediate access to almost any facts. True, they may be less scholarly in a classical sense, but they are also more savvy and cynical about the news and received history than they were in Lukács' day. That said, I am in no way saying that facts and history do not matter. I am just saying that in a post-Lukács world the novelist has a lot more leeway. And should take it, too.

Lackey: So is your critique that Lukács disengages history from human characters, from humans? That he makes history some sort of objective process that stands outside of humans? Is that what you're trying to say?

Duffy: He demands this imposed, matrix-like system, this historical overlay over the characters—a vast and an inflexible theater in which, I guess, he gets to sit as the judge. It's just so numbing—so *Darkness at Noon*. Honestly, I read Lukács and I feel numb, when I'm not bored. And what's really telling, the fact that I learn almost nothing from him. Read Walter Benjamin—also of that world—and I am *always* learning things and endlessly interested. Why? Because he is so much more alive than Lukács.

Lackey: So you think his view of history is too big, too overstated?

Duffy: Well, obviously, I like big concepts. But I think you can never lose sight of the *scale* of your characters, even the major ones. Most of us live in the fog of the day to day. We're not aware of giant sweeps of history around us in which we are the cogs. As a novelist, I want to put my characters into this fog of the day to day—into what is really going on right around them, the odd and even silly things. This to me is much more engaging and realistic to readers. Imagine a man fighting in the trenches during World War One, as Wittgenstein did. Wittgenstein is stuck in his small part of the war—in his part of the trench, his fear. He doesn't have some synoptic, God-like view from above. That is how people see things—at ground level. And this is what grabs readers, I think. Characters don't have the view of God. None of us does.

Lackey: While characters in the novel may not have a God's eye perspective of history, the historical novelist, coming years after the events in the novel, should—isn't that Lukács' point?

Duffy: As a novelist, I am not here to produce creaky newsreels or serve as some kind of handmaiden to history—you know, the dumb historical bee who can be relied upon to produce honey. But here is what is telling to me: It is very hard to artfully include a lot of history in a novel and not sound dumb or preachy. It really is. If you are not careful it can seem like a dramatic rendering of Wikipedia, or Michener throwing in all his packing crates of research, or Dos Passos with his self-conscious newsreel pauses.

The point for me is, the novelist is not here to *teach* anybody anything. And really, if somebody wrote something comparable to the painstaking history of *War & Peace*—well, would it even work today? I'm not so sure. This is not to in any way criticize the greatness of Tolstoy—written in Tolstoy's time. I just think Tolstoy's mode would feel very clunky in our time.

As we know, for example, we live in a time of profound self-consciousness and irony—meaning, that heavy, humorless use of history can seem earnestly dumb or just cheesy. In this sense, Lukács has not aged well. He is preaching to the wrong time in a church that no longer exists.

Lackey: What is your process of accessing the day-to-day consciousness of a character in the fog?

Duffy: A quick example. At the time I wrote *The World As I Found It*, I had never been to Europe, first because I was poor, and later because I thought my lack of exposure would make the book that much more fictional. And so I stared for days at period picture books. I pored over period letters and diaries. When possible I spoke to people who had been in Vienna, or knew what it was like to be a Jew in Poland in 1916. But what I realized finally was that I couldn't get bogged down in guide-book type detail. What I needed were the two or three killer details. Again, what really mattered was what the character was feeling walking down that foggy, cobbled street—the inner weather. Kafka doesn't have to paint Prague. He *leaks* Prague.

Lackey: Well, apropos of this, one of the things you insist on is that your work is fiction, that it's not history or biography. To my mind, this claim establishes a tidy division between fiction and history, fiction and biography, as if fiction could not be used to shed significant light on an historical period or a biographical figure. But when I read your work, I feel like you give me an inside perspective of history at a particular time or an inside perspective of these characters. Were you strategically dispensing with the overarching histories of the traditional historical novel? Or were you so immersed in the characters' lives that you simply considered the meta-historical perspective irrelevant?

Duffy: With *The World As I Found It* thirty years ago, I definitely arrived with a chip on my shoulder. I hated historical novels—they felt like the life-size talking Lincoln at Disneyland, way back when. Bodice rippers. History made nice.

But here suddenly was Wittgenstein. At that time, no one had written a biography on Wittgenstein. What I generally found were memoirs essentially painting Wittgenstein as this insane twentieth-century saint beyond the ken of mere mortals. Correctly or not, I felt these acolytes seemed to feel they owned his memory. At the same time, I was wildly unqualified for the task. I don't speak German, am not musically trained or a mathematician—and I could go on. And several writers I knew thought I was being insane, wrecking my career before I even had one, writing about some nut, and not even an American nut at that. So from the start, I felt I was doing something new and daring, if not begging for punishment. And I knew I was very consciously engaged in an act of provocation, like those Julian Schnabel pieces made of broken crockery, or Ezra Pound wanting to break the pentameter. I knew I had to break things. All my heroes—Wittgenstein and Rimbaud included— broke things. So I guess I started hurling.

I had no name for what I wanted to do, and no example, nothing I admired. What I was trying to do was draw some big lines around what I was doing to give myself some space—space in which to write about Wittgenstein not as some God but as a tortured, visionary, ridiculous, brave, flesh-and-blood man. To do this, I could not, and would not, be captive to the facts. Did anyone ever manage Wittgenstein? No way. So I came at it in that spirit.

Equally important, I had to invent a language, American and European, now and then, German and British, slang, passive, aggressive, poetic. With a lot of humor—to show the author was in control even when terrible things are occurring. For me the language and style were everything then, and always are, for each particular book. This is why my books are all stylistically different, the new one included. Style is the real hero, and it has to change constantly, especially in a book using history. Nimble—or dead. Funny—or boring. Otherwise, language is just this grey matrix holding stones of fact, like cement.

You know, I have great respect for history and biography—I couldn't do what I do without them. But yes, these are fundamentally different forms. As with anything, there is no clear, unambiguous division between them. Here the advantage that the fiction writer holds over the biographer or the historian is that he or she is not, as I said, so captive to the facts. Forced to color inside the lines. As a result, there are just things you can *say* as a novelist that a biographer or a historian might not feel empowered to say because the known facts won't safely support them. So the novel gives you tremendous power to go to where you really *imagine* these characters are; to *imagine* how they came to be, and who they are. And, like Aesop, how their ideas came to be—to create intellectual myths, as it were.

One thing that was hugely important to me in both these novels, *World* and *Disaster,* was to imagine: *Why* did these people think the things that they did? *What* was it about their life that caused them to think these things—that caused them to be so invested in these ideas, matters of life or death, some of them. I wanted this to be of the highest moral and human urgency. Not merely reporting the facts, as a researcher might. My goal is to put the reader inside the eye of the tornado.

In one of his journals, Wittgenstein wrote of his life, "I destroy, I destroy, I destroy." Similarly, Rimbaud as a teenager painted slanders on the wall of the church—a demon. Name me one writer or poet in the nineteenth century who writes and thinks like a twentieth-century being. Whitman, Dickinson, great as they are, they are all nineteenth-century creatures. All except one—Arthur Rimbaud. A teenager who produces modernism, like some kind of cold fusion, in his room on a dairy farm in the Ardennes. Then proceeds to attack Paris and the complacency of his time. Really, the first punk.

The point is, this kid was writing in the 1870s things that you wouldn't see until the teens or the twenties! I mean, *nobody* thought like that. Well, today, it's still hard to imagine how somebody—a schoolboy!—could be that far in advance of his time. Or how Wittgenstein, in the same way, could reinvent philosophy, or write *The Tractatus*, which for me is almost a severe, logical poem of high modernism. I want readers to feel that risk—that sheer recklessness—and this in part is what changing the facts does—it's dangerous, you bet it is. It unsettles readers. Jangles them. And again, that demands the overaching spirit of a style: poetic and visionary in the case of Rimbaud, formally logical in the case of Wittgenstein—then different, in an interior way, for every character. Style conveys facts not even named. Really, the history of what is *not* said.

Lackey: So you want people to understand the radical nature of the thinking of your characters. But do you offer an answer, and how confident are you in the answer that you supply in the novels? And why should we trust your judgment about these figures and their times more than, let's say, some biographer or some historian?

Duffy: I don't think these things come down to *an* answer—there are many different answers and many points of view, different forms of authority. Yes, I want you to believe the fiction, but otherwise, I'm not trying to convince you of anything—in fact, some conspiracy theory or something. It's various and nefarious, I guess. In fact, Wittgenstein makes the same point when he talks of "language games" in which different disciplines unwittingly play different kinds of language games. And this is how Wittgenstein himself changes the game, relentlessly looking for new things or things to break. "The avant garde is the history of people bored with other people's ideas." The point is, history is not sacred. Getting it right is not the mere facts. It's thinking deeply about these characters—about what they really thought, and why. All in a style that suggests how they might have thought, the way their stomach gurgled with fear, the processes of life.

Lackey: But tell me more about "getting it right." What does that mean to you?

Duffy: With both books I did a tremendous amount of research—and I was tremendously invested in getting a lot of facts right, even consulting authorities on the matter. At the same time, I was careful not to *over*-research to the point of becoming paralyzed in summoning the fiction. The other thing to acknowledge is my principal characters were, and are, damaged people, and without going into the particulars, I come from a very damaged background from the time my mother died when I was eleven. I've also very consciously had a tremendous amount of experience, including being in world danger spots. Meaning, a lot of possibilities as I create these characters, and a deep, first-hand understanding of danger and screwing up.

In the case of the Rimbaud book, I went to Ethiopia, to his town, Harar, then beyond into the tribal no-man's land near the Somali border. This was a smuggler-route, "Road Warrior" landscape littered with wrecked cars and tractor trailers. It's also a place in which every male over the age of fourteen is carrying an automatic weapon and a giant knife. But intense as this is, it is *nothing* compared to what Rimbaud knew in the 1880s. The point is, my trip made me realize—viscerally—the level of France-loathing and sheer alienation that kept Rimbaud penned up for ten years in what now is Ethiopia. Book knowledge won't convey something like that—that electrical charge, half fear and half thrill. I didn't want to over-focus, as usual, on Rimbaud's hashish-smoking teenage antics. I wanted to look at the terrible back half of his life, I mean when he abandons poetry and never once looks back on literature, bitter as an old gunslinger. Again, the point is not to be faithfully factual. It's to be authentic and compelling, even ruthless, in penetrating the impenetrable.

Lackey: Would you say that your strength, as a novelist, is that you've done all this research in order to understand the time period of the character? Or, would you say that your strength is that you understand the logical consistency of character itself, which enables you *ipso facto* to portray the time period of your protagonist?

Duffy: There is a term in symbolic logic called—I believe—"the truth sign." Well, Wittgenstein objected to the truth sign. Wittgenstein thought, "This is ridiculous, that any equation could declare itself true." In much the same way, as a writer, I can't be walking around with a giant truth sign over my head, claiming to know who the true Wittgenstein was. I don't.

Both these books took around seven years. Don't ask me why seven years. Prison sentences. But honestly I must have spent those first four or five years writing all the time and doing extensive research, while not really knowing *what* the hell I am doing. But then all of a sudden, with both books—just when I was about ready to throw in the towel—something clicked in, and I knew *absolutely* what I was doing: I knew absolutely who these characters were, much with a core of anger.

Lackey: Let's look more deeply at Rimbaud. How did you get inside of him and his world?

Duffy: Well, again, for going on five years, I wrote and wrote, hoping—stupidly—that I might make a prick palatable. Finally, I gave half of the manuscript to two close friends—both psychiatrists. And these two readers said, basically; "Hey, Bruce, nice writing. But honestly we can't feel or understand *who* this guy is or *what* he feels." It was crushing to hear—I was in London, on my way to Ethiopia to track him down, but I saw they were right. And why? Because unconsciously—as I think they realized as therapists—I was resisting the reality of Rimbaud, trying to dress up a snake.

Lackey: So what did you do then?

Duffy: Thank god I was on my way to Ethiopia. As I said earlier, Ethiopia was a huge help. It helped me mentally abandon what I had done, and it made me realize how alienated Rimbaud was to spend ten years there. Here's how it hit me. We're in the tribal areas. The heat was around 120 degrees. I'm dazed. We're stopped in the road. It's just me and my guide, and here we are surrounded by all these armed men. No law, no order, no ambulance, when I thought in this almost pleasant dream, *I wonder why they don't kill me?* And that was it. I was inside Rimbaud, a man numb to danger, floating in his own juice. I'd cracked the safe.

There was something else that helped me catch the scent. Something I had forgotten, and that was the fact that about ten years after Rimbaud's death, his mother, a tough old French farm woman of eighty or so, well, she had him exhumed. In fact, she sat in a carriage watching this man dig up her dreaded son and his beloved sister, who had died at age fourteen—really, the only thing she ever adored. Madame Rimbaud is awful, giving the gravedigger a hard time, loathing the gawkers now that her son is so famous. I thought, *this woman is a bitch,* and I was thrilled. So let her be a bitch! Let him be a prick! *Fuck'em.* The two most liberating words any writer should know. I thought, *he's not likable.* Amazing, visionary, many things, but not likable. And then it hit me: *This is the story of a monster raised by a witch.* Further concussions followed, one of the biggest being to treat him as the outlaw he was, rather than some fancy poet. What I loved was the idea of Rimbaud as a *poet with a gun.*

Lackey: Isn't there pressure to have likeable characters?

Duffy: Well, the truth is, your characters pick you. It's not about someone you'd like to invite for the weekend. The question is, does that character live or not? Feel real or not? *That's* what people want. Or so I like to believe.

Lackey: Why didn't you follow the lead of someone like Robert Penn Warren, who changes Huey Long's name to Willie Stark in *All the King's Men*? And was there any pressure from the editors for you to change the name? Or, were they okay with you using Wittgenstein's name right from the outset?

Duffy: I had a wonderful experience with my first publisher Ticknor & Fields—then part of Houghton Mifflin. I've actually got a funny story here. Ticknor never once tried to get me to change the name—to come up with some fictional name for Wittgenstein, like Silverstein. But about three or four months after they'd accepted the book, I got a worried call from my editor, who said, "We've got a problem here." Seems the editorial board at Houghton Mifflin had asked to see the book. Then they got greatly concerned, and wanted footnotes in it. Footnotes! Well, I had a fit. I told my editor this was just one of the stupidest things I could possibly imagine. The analogy I used was, "Does a general give away his battle plan?" "No way," I said, "I'm not here to pasteurize this thing for people, I'm not doing it." And my editor said "okay" and that was the end of it.

Lackey: But it makes sense because you were doing something unconventional in 1987. Most people would think of your book as a biography, but you're saying it's a novel. You can see that from an editor's perspective, they're confused.

Duffy: True. But you see confusion was the purpose. A purposeful confusion. The idea was not to create an Easy-Reader Wittgenstein. I wanted people to think, and actually I was hoping it would prompt them to consult other sources. Like the *Tractatus* itself, or Otto Weininger, who is a central figure at the end of the novel. The point for me was that I *wanted the reader to be in a state of anxiety* about what was true and what was not. And, being practical, I wrote a disclaimer explaining the spirit and aesthetic of the book. Besides mollifying the Houghton Mifflin editorial board, I didn't want readers so antagonized that they couldn't get beyond page five—or miss the whole point of the book playing fact detective.

Lackey: By the way, that's one of the key ideas in Wittgenstein's work—to unsettle and challenge the way words mean. This is central to his philosophy. So he becomes the perfect figure to unsettle established boundaries of fiction and thought.

Duffy: Wittgenstein has a great saying that philosophy is "showing the fly the way out of the fly-bottle." Out of common confusions. He was very provocative, and you're right. This is a big part of the spirit of the book. As far as my use of names, another brief anecdote. After the book came out I became good friends with a highly influential novelist who loved the book. But once we knew each other better, one day he told me that he believed my decision to use the real names was, as he put it, "a grievous aesthetic mistake." I'll never forget those words. "Grievous!" Like I should promptly hand over my sword or something. This was a brilliant man of immense sophistication, not some reactionary. We had kind of a fight about it, and of course we got over it. But my point was that, by using the real names—by mixing it up—I believed I was making an otherwise boring, costume-drama form aesthetically interesting.

Lackey: Getting back to the Rimbaud novel, you give readers something unexpected, which is a Rimbaud who becomes an anti-Rimbaud, someone who could no longer write, not even letters...

Duffy: It's as if Rimbaud had taught himself how to un-write. A lyric genius at fifteen years old, by age thirty-five, his letters home are excruciatingly awkward and formal. As if he had suffered a brain injury. And perhaps in a sense he had.

At this point late in his short life, Rimbaud is starting to become famous. His works are being published in Paris. Of course he thinks it's all rubbish. That's what's so frightening, I think. Rimbaud never once veered from his complete contempt for what he had done when he was a teenager, things the world would need another fifty years, at least, to learn. So, on one level, I found this horrifying. And yet on another level, I respected Rimbaud's integrity.

Lackey: And here late in the book he's dying and forced to lose his vanity.

Duffy: A prick gets his come-uppance. At the end of the book, we have to watch Rimbaud's leg get amputated, and we have to watch a man die and come to humanity like everybody else. Even take the sacraments late at the last minute. Everybody dies. Everybody has to go through this death process. For someone as proud—as arrogant—as Rimbaud this was a real comeuppance, to learn to be a mortal, as opposed to an *im*mortal. No happy ending, no change in heart, and a coming to death. It was here I came to like Rimbaud.

Lackey: Shifting to another topic, one of the things that has struck me about the contemporary biographical novel is that so many of you are dealing with both the Holocaust and anti-Semitism. You see the concern with anti-Semitism in David Mamet's *The Old Religion*, but you see the concern with anti-Semitism and the Holocaust in Jay Parini's *Benjamin's Crossing*, Ron Hansen's *Hitler's Niece*, Lance Olsen's *Nietzsche's Kisses*, and Irvin Yalom's most recent book, *The Spinoza Problem*. Why is there this obsessive concern about anti-Semitism and the Holocaust in so many of these novels? We certainly see this concern in *The World As I Found It*, especially in the character of Max, who is contradictory and complicated. That he becomes an S.S. member is really a stunning development within that narrative. Could you talk about the role of anti-Semitism in your novel?

Duffy: The Holocaust looms over my generation. I was born in 1951, just six years after the war. My father, an ex-naval officer, liked to watch *Victory at Sea* and World War Two TV documentaries. It was frightening to see little boys in short pants standing under Nazi guns. How could such a thing occur? How could you participate and return to normal life later? I'm not claiming I thought about it in any deep way as a child—it was just there. And so in the case of Max, the character you mentioned, I was struck by how a man could be so charming and also so frightening, and such a racist: how could all these temperaments be present in the same person? How could such a person be blind to these alter egos? Forgive himself, in effect.

I think I also saw this—obviously, on a smaller scale—when I was growing up in the D.C. area. Maryland was a pretty redneck place in the sixties and seventies, or at least around where I was living. So I had several friends who were racist and free with the N-word. People like to forget it but this was common. I just grew up with it. So in writing, I was trying to come through that mess. Racism, unconscious racism, whether it's black people or Jews or whomever—it's all part of it. My second novel, *Last Comes the Egg*, is full of racism. And I had a shift. My best friend in High School was Jewish. Both my wives are Jewish. But in the case of *The World As I Found It*, my first wife's grandmother was from Poland, and she spoke Yiddish. Nannie lived in this apartment in the Bronx where there were a number of old ladies, many concentration camp survivors with the tattoos inside their arms. And Nannie was just the sweetest old lady. I thought, "Well, I want to interview her." After all, Warsaw was close to where Wittgenstein was fighting in World War One. Nannie left in 1921, before the Holocaust, but she lost family to the Nazis. Well, Nannie started to talk about her memories. I have never seen such power and horror as in her rage against the Poles who routinely beat her family. One time Polish soldiers scalped off her grandfather's beard. Terrible things and not uncommon in many parts of Europe. Well, for me, that power, that anger was like being hit with an electric charge. It gave me a certain power, an inside privilege to speak these things, or so I thought. I should add that my first wife had a cousin, a man in his seventies very close to her grandmother, and a real tough guy. Moniek was an electrician in New York City, Brooklyn. But he had been in a Russian concentration camp, a

German concentration camp, and had fought in the 1948 Arab-Israeli War. I have never seen a darker, angrier person in my life. Moniek even had a coiled way of standing that you could imagine inside the barbed wire, always looking behind his back. To talk to someone like him, well, that told me—beyond what any book could convey—about all these terrible emotions. The point is, with varying success, I was always looking for the shock of real experience. Not just the physical details, but the emotions. The emotions tell you everything—radar. They are your guide.

Lackey: So where did you get your conflicted Wittgenstein from, then? What sense did you have that he was so conflicted about his Jewishness?

Duffy: That was more made up. I can't really point offhand—this was more than twenty-five years ago—to some ready archival source. What astounded me was this whole Jewish dream of assimilation at the turn of the century, this lie that if the Jews converted to Christianity they would be accepted. And they believed: In Austria and Germany there was a period before the twenties when it was very common for Jewish families to assimilate and become Christians. Saying, if you become Catholic, things will be okay for you. And of course when Hitler takes power, things were not okay. The stain is ineradicable. And this is not just true over in Austria. To a lesser extent it was true in the US as well. Essentially, it was the same story of families trying somehow to purge themselves of their Jewishness or change their name. Or grandly overlooking the whole thing, say, as Robert Oppenheimer did pretty much. Many painful strategies and few successful.

Lackey: But getting back to the Wittgenstein character. In the novel, we get hints of him grappling with his Jewish heritage, the assimilation, becoming Catholic. But it's all leading up to the scene with G. E. Moore, when Wittgenstein goes to his house. It's a planned confession and Wittgenstein's going to finally tell him and several others that he's guilty—among other sins—of having denied his own Jewish heritage.

Duffy: And that *is* true, by the way.

Lackey: How did you approach Wittgenstein's confession, which is one of the last things one would expect him to do?

Duffy: In this scene, it was very hard for me to witness an incredibly proud man just scalding himself, just laying himself naked before other people. And who else would ever do such a thing? Tough as he could be on others, Wittgenstein was even harder on himself, to the point that friends feared him committing suicide if he failed in his own eyes. A sort of intellectual samurai. But I was very drawn to this, the idea that real thinking is a code with very real dangers—risks to the soul. That's the kind of world I wanted to capture. Ideas that carry real consequences. Integrity that will not be compromised.

Lackey: Is that part of what drew you to Otto Weininger? At age twenty-three in 1903, he made that sacrifice when the world rejected his book *Sex and Character*. Can you explain what led you to include the Weininger section in the novel?

Duffy: Looking back, I think on some level Weininger reminded me of Rimbaud. Not as a racist. I've never seen any evidence that Rimbaud was an active racist, or cared. Like Rimbaud, Weininger was a young genius with an intellect of an order that verges on insanity, even the demonic. For a certain kind of personality, such brilliance, so young, has to verge on insanity—10,000 volts pumped into a small fuse. Of course it blows. Few, if any, can withstand such power, such insanity. Rimbaud stopped writing forever. Weininger committed suicide. This is the kind of raw, seductive power than Weininger has, and I shrunk from it at first. It's like reading *Mein Kampf* or talking with the devil. But see, for a writer, the trick is not to open *Sex and Character* or *Mein Kampf* with contempt. The trick is to clear your mind and read *Mein Kampf*, say, as an out-of-work carpenter with a hungry family might have in 1929. That is my job as a fiction writer. Never to be superior to the material, but to use it, rather, like an Ouija board to find strange new places.

Lackey: But were there some specific ideas that drew you to Weininger?

Duffy: Well, Weininger had to have been the first, or one of the very first, to realize that none of us is purely male or female—that we fall somewhere on a continuum of sexual identity. Today, we can accept or at least uncomfortably entertain such an idea. But in 1903, this was frightening and revolting—terrifying. In short, like a nightmare, Weininger expresses many of the pathologies and nightmares of his time, from race to sex. Novelistically, Weininger's funeral—after his suicide—was a very dramatic and concrete way to show the toxic ideas that the young Wittgenstein was exposed to, again, in a time in which ideas could literally be a matter of life or death. Weininger's funeral made all these conflicts stand out.

Lackey: So if we think of *World* as illuminating the conditions under which Wittgenstein's philosophy came into being—specifically in the time period in which he lived—what does Wittgenstein's experience tell us? Why did you write about him in particular?

Duffy: Well, as far as why I wrote about him, I'd encountered a magazine article about this modernist house in Vienna that he had helped design and build for his sister. This was in the middle of the 1920s, when Wittgenstein had actually stopped being a philosopher. I think in that time, what attracted me was I had reached a point where my fiction wasn't going anywhere. At the same time, I was not very happy with what I saw being published in the so-called age of minimalism. So I think—I mean after the fact—that I felt a certain kinship with Wittgenstein, I mean as two displaced persons. Here I was, a writer hiding out as a Sunday painter, and here was Wittgenstein, a philosopher hiding out as an architect. So the book actually began as an idea for a painting. I was going to do this kind of collage with various prose poems in it.

So I did some drawings only to quickly realize that I didn't know much, or anything, about Wittgenstein. Worse, I'd minored in philosophy only to realize how meager my understanding really was, especially of symbolic logic. So I started to read about Wittgenstein, and here I soon had a revelation: At that time in the early eighties *there was no biography of Wittgenstein.* None. What an amazing situation! It was as if I had blundered into a treasure room. In other words, I could project my own story of Wittgenstein's life in advance of the inevitable biography. Scoop the story. So that was what led me—pure beginner's luck. I'm sorry, what was the second part of the question?

Lackey: It's about how Wittgenstein's personal life inflected his philosophy. I'm thinking here about the Golem scene, when he's at the theater. This turns out to be a very powerful scene—it resonates deeply.

Duffy: That was totally made up.

Lackey: But tell me, how can we use that to understand Wittgenstein or his philosophy? Or should we?

Duffy: In the Golem scene, he goes—with great arrogance—to a Jewish theater, to him a very grubby, ignorant thing. Here he confronts his true past, so upset by a seemingly garish simple-minded scene—and so unconscious of his deeper emotions—that he passes out. Anyhow, I can't make a direct connection to his Jewishness, or suppressed Jewishness, and his philosophy. I think the thing that quickly stunned me about Wittgenstein was the three brothers who had committed suicide. How do you come back from that, the sheer damage? But honestly, I didn't really know much about his family, and in a way I didn't want to. So I created characters. Knowing only the basics, I created Karl Wittgenstein. I created the other siblings that we have here. The trick was Wittgenstein, creating a character living on an edge in which *he* had to be perfect, with a sense of terrible peril if he wasn't absolutely perfect. A man on a tightrope. I wanted readers to feel that danger.

Lackey: It seems that he associated Jewishness with imperfection, and that's one of the reasons why he was constantly denying his Jewish heritage. Leading to that night when he made his confession to G. E. Moore.

Duffy: And I think you're right.

Lackey: So something happens there. Something happens that changes him when he's going to finally accept his Jewishness. Do we see that as a positive moment in his development? Is it a moment of self-acceptance?

Duffy: Well, there is a sense of self-acceptance—relief, I guess. But this is not a guy who then immigrated to Israel. But during World War Two—to acknowledge who he really was, to acknowledge his shame, even if he is too hard on himself—we all have a few of these secret griefs. But what I admire, for Wittgenstein it was always about what's right—about life as an obligation. Above all, Wittgenstein did not want to be a liar—ever. Or superior in a class way. As he said once, "All men are the same distance from God." There's a thought you can think about for a long, long time.

Lackey: Let's shift to the connections between Wittgenstein and Rimbaud, because these are two very different types of figures. Can you explain the logical connections between these two figures, and can you explain what makes these men in your novels so radically different from each other?

Duffy: At one point in Wittgenstein's journals, he says essentially, "If I have to describe my career, it's 'I destroy. I destroy.'" And Rimbaud had the same ruthless aesthetic. Rimbaud had very little respect for what he saw being published in his time, or for the thinking of his time. He, too, came to destroy. Both were also great writers, and so that was also the stylistic battle, to reflect in the writing Wittgenstein's precision, and Rimbaud's wildness and precision. For me in this sense, the writing is itself a character in these two books. Well, that was the aim, at least.

Lackey: Yet it seems that your Rimbaud was actually trying to build a better world in those early stages. He was destroying, but he also had this vision of rebuilding—maybe even the concept of love, reimagining it.

Duffy: Absolutely. In *The Illuminations,* Rimbaud's visionary prose poems, he invented a phantasmagoria of worlds colliding. Illogic. Events out of sequence. Dada and Surrealism long before they arrive. Even the montage style of early films that threw early movie audiences into fits with their different, jarring images. Nobody even dimly thought this way in 1872. This is how revolutionary Rimbaud was, and that is not a term I use lightly.

Lackey: Did he realize that it didn't work—that it was a utopic fantasy?

Because he just gave up. Here I see a difference with the Rimbaud character—giving up in disgust.

Duffy: That's a really good distinction. Early on, when he's sixteen, Rimbaud is extremely idealistic. But by twenty, what I believe killed the poetry was the inevitable end of childhood. Still, Rimbaud's reaction was extreme. Poetry is barren, a lie. Every last word of it. And being the extreme person he is, Rimbaud never veers from that course, even at the very end of his life when his work is being discovered. For him the fruit is still rotten. And this is very modern, like Marcel Duchamp when he gave up painting for chess. Painting is like wallpaper—the pointlessness of painting in an age of mechanical reproduction. This is very much like Rimbaud, and it's disturbing. But welcome to our time.

Lackey: What else is modern about Rimbaud?

Duffy: He wants to create this brave new place in the world for women, in which woman also would be a Poet. In those days, so far as I know, nobody thought about the place of woman! Except to have children.

Lackey: That's why when I think about the Rimbaud character, one of the most intriguing parts of the novel is your analysis of the rational derangement of the senses, this intentional disordering of the mind. When I read the Wittgenstein novel, I feel like, "Wittgenstein's tearing things down—everything, including himself—but I rarely see him trying to build something up." Whereas the Rimbaud character thinks—and this is very Nietzschean—"I'm going to have this rational derangement of the senses. I'm going to disrupt all these comfortable, stable categories so that we can start to reimagine the world in a new way." But he gets so *terribly* disillusioned. It seems to me that, in his post-poetry world, he ultimately subscribes to a kind of corporate business mentality. Am I reading it right?

Duffy: I agree. I think the thing that is so touching about him is here he is, sixteen years old, and he's going to revolutionize love and have a systematic derangement of the senses. And by twenty, he gives it up, all of it forever, after doing some of the most—in my opinion—stupendous poems ever written, poems utterly unlike anything else. To have such an amazing body of work, to have such amazing integrity in what he did, then to just cast it aside—for me that was the story.

Lackey: Where are you going next? What book is on the horizon? Do you have one?

Duffy: It is still early in the game—less than a year into writing it. But the title is *A Towering Brilliance*, and it's built around the design, the dropping, and the aftermath of the first atomic bomb. It's really built around the physicists who built the bomb, mostly Jews, and many refugees from Hitler. It will have quite a cast of characters, very varied: Oppenheimer, the main character, as well as Einstein, Niels Bohr, Leo Szilard, and the rare woman in that world—Lise Meitner who coined the word "fission." We'll also be with General Curis LeMay, operationally in charge of the Enola Gay, the B-29 that dropped the bomb. And the Japanese writer Mishima, who dodged the war at twenty and then became an ultra-nationalist when Japan by then was a country of pacifists. In 1970 Mishima had his own private army and to protest the new Japan, he publically committed *seppuku*, had himself beheaded. Believe it or not, though, there will be a lot of humor in the book!

Quite aside from building the bomb, I want to look at the morality of the bomb. Robert Oppenheimer ran the Manhattan Project to build the first atomic bomb in World War Two. Oppenheimer was one of the most cosmopolitan scientists, ever, almost a pacifist in disposition. Yet before they drop the first atomic bomb, here he is giving precise instructions on how the bomb should be armed for maximum destructiveness. And he knows it's going to trigger an arms race. They all know it, some of the smartest people on the planet, yet they go ahead.

8

Sensualizing and Contextualizing Historical "Truth" in the Biographical Novel

Ron Hansen

Lackey: Let me begin by telling you about the nature of this project. I'm trying to figure out why, starting in the 1980s, so many prominent writers began to author biographical novels. I'm also trying to define the nature of this genre of fiction. Can you start by explaining why you have written novels about Gerard Manley Hopkins and Hitler's niece?

Hansen: I'm always looking for lively stories to tell and I'm not much interested in writing about myself. And I read a lot of history and biography and often find myself so captivated by the narratives that I begin seeing the unfolding events as cinematic scenes. There's a "Wow!" factor that makes me wonder why nobody else has written the story with all its possibilities as fiction. I was especially struck by Geli Raubal, Hitler's niece, a little-known girl in the Weimar Republic. But Hitler always said that she was the only woman he ever loved or would ever consider marrying. After her death, he had all-night vigils before her portrait each Christmas Eve. Everybody knows that Hitler had a Thanatos complex in that he was only really interested in people after they were dead. Some say it was partly because of the trauma he experienced in watching his mother die. Eva Braun only excited him after she attempted suicide, and they both successfully completed the act after their wedding in the Führerbunker. In *Hitler's Niece*, I saw myself as a prosecuting attorney building a case to demonstrate that Hitler either had murdered Geli or had ordered her done away with. And I was fascinated that so many historians simply accepted the fact that she had killed herself with her uncle's pistol when there was no evidence that she was suicidal. She was even in the midst of writing a hopeful letter to a girlfriend in Vienna. But Geli knew too much; she was dangerous. Had she left Adolf's purview and control she might have given away secrets that would have destroyed his political career. In the novel I felt I was developing my case for a jury of readers.

Lackey: I suspect that you had a different orientation and approach in your first biographical novel, *Desperadoes*.

Hansen: I happened upon *The Dalton Gang*, a biographical study by Harold Preece, and immediately saw it as a fascinating story. Emmett Dalton was the sole survivor of the gang's failed attempt to rob two banks simultaneously in their hometown of Coffeyville, Kansas. That was in 1892 and in some ways represented the end of the Wild West. He did time in prison, married his childhood sweetheart, lived into the late 1930s as a tee-totaling real estate broker and building contractor in Los Angeles, and saw his own memoir, *When the Daltons Rode*, turned into a movie. When, in old age, he returned to Coffeyville, he was celebrated by the very defenders who'd killed his brothers. *Desperadoes* is about wild youths and reckless ambition and the transition from the Old West to the new.

Lackey: And you followed that with another biographical novel, *The Assassination of Jesse James by the Coward Robert Ford*.

Hansen: William Kittredge read *Desperadoes* and asked me to write a short story about the Old West for a special issue of *TriQuarterly*. Because I had written about the Dalton Gang, who'd strived to imitate the misdeeds of the James-Younger Gang, I ended up knowing an awful lot about Jesse James. It seemed to me nobody had ever told the full and accurate story of how and why Bob Ford killed Jesse James, so I began writing that as a short story. After about thirty pages, I realized I had just scratched the surface, so I apologized to Bill Kittredge but told him I thought I'd found my next novel.

Lackey: Did you have any models for doing this kind of fiction?

Hansen: Not novels, but Shakespeare's plays. So many of them were biographical. He took the rough facts of history but then supplied further context, invented romance and drama, and presented it all in wonderfully poetic dialogue. But the characters, incidents, and rough shape of his plays would have been very familiar to his initial audiences. His plays were a way of giving new and enriched life to recognizable figures while also giving his imagination room to play with his fictional interpretation of events.

Lackey: Did you ever read Styron's *The Confessions of Nat Turner*?

Hansen: Yes I did.

Lackey: Do you see that as a successful biographical novel?

Hansen: I read it, but I didn't like it as much as others have.

Lackey: Why?

Hansen: I thought it was overwrought and I didn't believe that this was the real Nat Turner.

Lackey: That was Russell Banks's critique. He thought it was a failed novel because it didn't accurately reflect who Turner probably was.

Hansen: I agree. However, Styron's novel provided the inspiration and freedom to write a biographical novel back in the late seventies. The same thing with E. L. Doctorow's *Ragtime*. Doctorow took real characters, such as Harry Houdini and J. P. Morgan, and put them in actual historical situations, but through irony, comedy, and the sheer zest of his writing made nineteenth-century America seem fabulous in both senses of the word. Earlier Doctorow had written the Western *Welcome to Hard Times*. With that and *Ragtime* I felt I was given permission to write biographical novels about the Old West. And that led to later examples.

Lackey: Let me turn to *Exiles,* which is your biographical novel about Hopkins. Hopkins was a Catholic priest and a first-rate poet. What can you communicate about Hopkins through the biographical novel that you couldn't through a traditional biography or scholarly study?

Hansen: In the novel I was trying to explain the origins of inspiration and the process of poetry writing for readers who don't know very much about the craft, and to deal with our conceptions of evil, theodicy, and failure. I was educated by the Jesuits and still have good friends in the Society of Jesus, so I felt I knew something of Gerard's religious yearnings, and I could analogize a poet's life from my experiences as a prose writer. I knew the exaltations and frustrations of teaching, I thought I had a good handle on his bipolar personality, and I was wild about his poems. But unlike a historian or biographer I could speculate and make educated guesses about Fr. Hopkins and his rather tortured but ultimately successful career as a poet and priest. With his biographer, my old friend Paul Mariani, I visited Hopkins's theologate of St. Beuno's in Wales so I could give readers an accurate description of the room he slept in, the hallways he walked, the faces of sheep chewing grass in the meadow. Those are the things historians have to overlook but that have meaning for readers. The accumulation of details enables readers to share the experiences of the fictional characters and situations.

Lackey: Can you briefly make some distinctions between your earlier biographical novels and your later ones, such as *Hitler's Niece* and *Exiles*? You do something very different with each one of them and I am starting to notice that there are subgenres of the biographical novel. For instance, Zora Neale Hurston, Anita Diamant, and Rebecca Kanner have done biographical novels based on the Bible. Would you say that your novels are in different subgenres?

Hansen: There is a difference based on the amount of available information, which enables some to have more fidelity to the historical record. There was not much known about the Dalton gang. I knew about their robberies and how they died, and I knew what they looked like because there were photographs available. But almost none of their dialogue was available. Emmett Dalton's memoir was playing fast and loose with the truth, and the journalism of the day was full of misrepresentations and hyperbole. So my writing and invention could be more pliable. As for Jesse James and Robert Ford, there was greater fame. A lot more was known about them and I carefully researched them. I visited the places they lived, stood inside the room where Jesse was killed, read the same *Kansas City Star* he would have been reading. Eighty-nine books had been written about Gerard Manley Hopkins when *Exiles* was published so I knew an awful lot about him, but very little about the nuns who died in the shipwreck of the *Deutschland*, and half the book is about them. There seemed to me different obligations in terms of fidelity to the truth for each of those novels, but I'm not sure that constitutes a subgenre. Some biographical novelists have a very elastic view of the truth, and some are much more faithful. The fiction writers I really admire, like my friend Jim Shepard, are always very scrupulous about the facts. But what a novelist is expected to provide are things that are not recorded by history: private moments, intimate conversations, gestures, weather, and the smell of food. But that's what gives vitality to long over with events.

Lackey: The literary critic Georg Lukács condemned the biographical novel in his work *The Historical Novel* and he did so because he believed it necessarily distorts and misrepresents history. In *Exiles*, you engage history by mentioning the laws that led to the persecution of Catholics in Germany, England, and Ireland, but you focus mainly on the ways those anti-Catholic laws destroy the lives of people such as Hopkins and the five nuns he wrote about in his poem "The Wreck of the Deutschland." Can you talk about the role the biographical novel plays in accessing and picturing a particular dimension of history?

Hansen: But Lukács admired the historical realism in Balzac and Tolstoy and Sir Walter Scott, so we're not that far apart. I think the biographical novel provides much-needed context for historical events and functions like those connect-the-dots pictures in which you only see the hidden face or object after you have drawn all the lines. Historians usually focus on a few of those dots, generally the economic or political. But other cultural, physical, or metaphysical dots really hit people where they live. For instance, when I was writing about Jesse James hiding out in St. Joseph, Missouri the daily front page news in the *Kansas City Star* was about Charles Guiteau, who'd been convicted of assassinating President James A. Garfield and was about to be executed. Wouldn't the idea of assassination of a public figure and the fame that followed be very influential to Bob Ford? Yet earlier historians and biographers never brought it up because it wouldn't have seemed pertinent given the shape and expectations for their books. The biographical novelist tells the truth about the events but also gives the reader a sense of what the glimpsed human beings must have been like and how they were nudged and determined by the circumstances around them. Jesse James was killed not on a Saturday night as song and legend has it, but on the Monday morning of Holy Week, and on the day after Palm Sunday when there probably was a sermon on the crucifixion of Jesus that would come with Good Friday. Some historians would not find that important to include, but it would have been part of the collective unconscious of the time. The effect that had on Southern sympathizers was monumental as they perhaps unwittingly linked Jesse's death with the crucifixion of Jesus, linked the Missouri governor with Pontius Pilate, and envisioned Bob Ford as a latter-day Judas.

Lackey: Do you think the limitation with historians is their method of analysis? Or, do you think that there is something in the skillset of the novelists that enables them to access something about history, character, and motivation that is significantly different from historians?

Hansen: I think historians are interested in the consequences or *doings* of a character and novelists are interested in the *being*, the motivations. What governs their psychology? What are the existential facts of their life? Are they resentful? Hungry? Do they have ailments? Historians have a thesis or argument they buttress with established facts. Novelists have similar opinions but they personify them and act them out. It's precisely how debate and drama differ.

Lackey: In the author's note to *Hitler's Niece* you describe your novel as a work of fiction that is based on fact, but you make an important qualification: "most consequential moments of any person's life go unglimpsed by either historians or journalists, and those intimate moments are where fiction finds its force and interest." Therefore, you claim that you "felt free to invent in those instances, but always in the spirit of likelihood and fidelity to the record." Can you talk about your strategies and techniques for representing one of those consequential moments in your Hopkins novel?

Hansen: When Hopkins first starts writing the poem "The Wreck of the Deutschland" he shows it to one of his friends—a fellow scholastic who is also studying theology in Wales—and Hopkins at once wants to show off the new meter in his poetry. Hopkins says he doubts that an editor will ever publish the poem, or as he said in a letter, "The journals will think it barbarous." And his classmate asks, "Why write it, then?" And Hopkins replies in puzzlement, "Why pray?" As far as I know Hopkins never likened his poetry to prayer; that's a self-revelation concerning my feelings about writing fiction that I'm guessing Gerard would agree with. There are moments of inspiration in fiction writing, moments where you feel you are in a waking dream that you're not fully responsible for. And the feeling is very similar to prayer, when you make yourself vulnerable, permeable, an instrument of God's will. In each case you hope that there is some kind of consequence that is useful to yourself and to others.

Lackey: But why should we trust your depiction of such a consequential moment?

Hansen: Well, that's for readers to judge. The novel will be a success if it persuades the reader to say: "Oh yeah, it must have happened that way." Yet there's also a dichotomy. Readers, for example, might look at a dinner table conversation among the five nuns in *Exiles* and realize that it is funnier or more modern than it probably could have been, and even while they realize that the author is putting words in the five women's mouths they would begin recognizing the usefulness and enjoyment of getting a sense of five separate personalities. And as I say in the note to *Exiles*, we know so little about these women. I looked into biographies of nineteenth-century European foundresses with the objective of recognizing and capturing the stirrings that motivate a girl to go into religious life. So there was a factual basis for my characterizations that I hoped would provide a convincing verisimilitude to my recreated people. You try to persuade readers of the logic and fidelity of your truth.

Lackey: In *Exiles* you give readers individual sections about each nun's background. When reading, I was wondering: are these your representations of the nuns? Or, are they supposed to be your Hopkins's representations as he is doing research in preparation for writing the poem?

Hansen: No, it's all mine. He never even mentions the names of the nuns in "The Wreck of the Deutschland." At most you get him describing Sister Barbara Hültenschmidt as "a lioness," "a prophetess," and "a tall one." He just knows those five sisters died.

Lackey: Did he do much research?

Hansen: No, there was almost nothing available to him then. The newspaper accounts that he would have had access to were just the *London Times* and even then he was in the midst of his theological studies and had very little opportunity to do further research. Once he asked his mother to send him information, and she sent him the wrong newspaper clipping. In his exasperation he just worked with his own experiences of conversion, what he spottily knew about the shipwreck, and with general principles of Catholic teaching, particularly as they have to do with human suffering. I invented the scene where Gerard goes to the cemetery and finds their names on the headstone. As far as I know he never did that, though the cemetery was close to his boyhood home.

Lackey: There's an author's note in both *Hitler's Niece* and *Exiles* and they both start with the same sentence: "This is a work of fiction based on fact." However, there is a major discrepancy in the length of the two notes. In the 1999 novel about Hitler's niece the note is almost three pages long, while in the 2008 novel about Hopkins the note is a short paragraph that is less than a page long. Can you explain why there is such a difference in the length of these two notes?

Hansen: The difference in *Exiles* is that the notation is divided into two parts. There's the first part, an Author's Note about how I went about creating the novel, and then at the end there is "A Note on My Sources." *Hitler's Niece* puts those explanations, or justifications, together in the same note.

Lackey: But in *Hitler's Niece* you have about five paragraphs defending your approach and clarifying your method, whereas in *Exiles* there is only one short paragraph.

Hansen: I wonder if that's because by 2008 there seemed to be more of an acceptance of the biographical novel. I remember that when *Hitler's Niece* was published in 1999 an Australian review considered such a handling of historical characters a "newfangled" idea. I heard none of that with *Exiles*. And of course fictional representations of real lives is actually a very old idea. Even Homer's *Iliad* is based on real people.

Lackey: But a lot of those works changed the characters' names. For instance, in *All the King's Men* Robert Penn Warren changes Huey Long's name to Willie Stark. Why don't contemporary novelists do this as much anymore?

Hansen: Perhaps it's because libel laws have loosened up. You have to justify that your privacy has been invaded or you have actually been wounded by someone's account. Early on novelists hid behind the guise of the *roman à clef* so they'd have more freedom with the basic material. But perhaps they noticed that biographical films were depicting real people with impunity and decided if movies could get away with it, fiction could get away with it, too. But once you use a real person's name, you have to be faithful to the events and what he or she was like unless your characterization is so outlandish—as in Robert Coover's portrayal of Richard Nixon in *The Public Burning*—that the public would recognize it as a cartoon.

Lackey: Ralph Ellison argues that the moment you become historically specific, you limit your character's possibility for having universal significance. For instance, he was very critical of William Styron for naming the character Nat Turner. Ellison adopted this view because he wants to portray more universal meanings. For instance, in *Invisible Man* he refers to the Brotherhood, which clearly represents the Communist Party. But he never explicitly says that the Brotherhood is the Communist Party. The reason why is he wanted it to be not just the Communist Party but any kind of political organization. Calling it the Brotherhood gives him more freedom to signify in a universal way, whereas the moment you become historically specific you lose that kind of universalizing capacity. Would you agree with that?

Hansen: I disagree totally. We work by analogy. If I talk about a real person and real events, the reader can still make the connection to something that is going on now. One of my problems with *Invisible Man*, which I've taught many times, is that the book is *too* allegorical. I knew Ellison was referring to the Communist Party, even my dullest students did, and it didn't enlarge the narrative at all to think of the Brotherhood in a more vague and general way.

Lackey: Biographical novelists consistently invent scenes in order to communicate something about a biographical figure or an historical event. For instance in *Hitler's Niece* you skillfully build up to the scene when Geli meets the Catholic priest Rupert Mayer for the second time. This scene resonates powerfully. However you mention in your author's note that you have no idea whether Geli met Rupert Mayer. Why include this scene? And what does it communicate to the reader about Geli's situation? Finally, what does this fictional scene communicate about the history of Nazi Germany?

Hansen: Fr. Rupert Mayer was one of the first to discover how dangerous Hitler was. He spied on many of Hitler's early speeches, recorded what was going on, and warned his congregation about him. Geli Raubal was Catholic and probably still regularly went to Masses despite her uncle's antagonism to any religion not centered on himself. He and Geli were living in a posh Munich apartment not far from St. Michael's Parish where the Jesuit priest was assigned, so it's entirely likely that she could have happened into a Mass where he preached. She was certainly in need of somebody outside of Hitler's Nazi circle to talk to as she gradually came to realize what the uncle she formerly adored was really like. And that set in motion her ultimate fate.

Lackey: Do you think that biographical novelists can access certain kinds of truths, historical truths if you will, that can expand the borders of knowledge in ways that other intellectual professionals cannot? And why should we trust the findings of biographical novelists?

Hansen: Our first chore is to make history accessible. There are people who read biographical novels who would never dream of reading straight biography. And as I said, we supply the flavor and context of the times. A friend of mine, when reading *Desperadoes* in our Stanford workshop, said whenever his telephone rang he had to shake himself out of the nineteenth century to answer it. Ideally that is what you want to force readers to do with historical or biographical fiction. I was at an American history convention, and the historians were debating these very issues, noting there was a fierce division within the history camp as some remained obedient to the rigid rules of evidence while others sought to become more popular and more compelling by adopting the practices of fiction writers.

Lackey: The compelling nature of fiction to illuminate history?

Hansen: Yes.

Lackey: In 1968 there was a famous debate on this topic. The historian C. Vann Woodward moderated a round-table conversation with Ellison, Warren, and Styron. He started by making a distinction between history and fiction. But both Ellison and Warren insisted that history is fiction. Their claim goes like this: historians think that they are doing something that is nonfiction but because they frame the material in a particular way and because the information is mediated through a specific consciousness, it is naïve for historians to think that they stand above or outside fiction. Would you agree with that?

Hansen: Oh totally. I point out to my classes that fiction comes from the past participle of the Latin *fingere*, which means to shape or to mold. History is already shaped by the very selection of the material that historians choose to write about. As soon as they have a focus, they also have an agenda. They ignore some things and highlight others. I have a world of respect for historians and honor their important efforts, but I think most would agree that they shape information in order to make their points. Otherwise they would end up with a profuse and unwieldy mess.

Lackey: Do you think that this postmodern breakdown of the distinction between fact and fiction has contributed significantly to the rise of the biographical novel?

Hansen: Postmodernism certainly makes people feel freer to invent and distort. But the finest biographical novelists still feel that they have to obey certain rules, that there are boundaries. Take, for instance, Jay Parini's *The Last Station*. Relying on authentic historical incidents, Jay felt free to invent scenes and conversations but within the realm of likelihood. And because of that his novel is persuasive and seemingly true to Tolstoy's life.

Lackey: So when you call your work a novel, you are implicitly saying that you have the freedom to take more liberties than an historian. But when you call a work history, or a memoir, or a biography, you have less freedom. Can you specify the kind of freedoms you can take as a novelist but that you cannot take as an historian?

Hansen: When I was working on *Hitler's Niece*, my wife and I stopped off at an Austrian inn for dinner and ate at a lakeside picnic table. At another table were four Austrian men with two bawdy women who could only have been prostitutes. They seemed to have been having a wild old weekend. When I imagined Hitler and Geli vacationing on a similar lake in 1930, I introduced those Austrians into the surroundings to make visual the kind of renegade cultural values of the time.

Lackey: So you take an episode from the contemporary world and extract from it a mentality or an aura that you then incorporate into your novel.

Hansen: That's right, because you are trying to capture the sensuality of an event. And you have to do that with visual stimuli or sounds or tastes that the historian is denied. But once you start playing with such things, incorporating too much from another world, the narrative can become confused and pointless.

Lackey: So can you specify what liberty you cannot take?

Hansen: When I was adapting *Desperadoes* for film, there was a scene in which the Dalton Gang rides into Coffeyville and gets wiped out while trying to hold up two banks at the same time. A movie producer, thinking of box office, asked, "Why do we have to have them die? Why couldn't they live through it?" Well, I'd heard that the producer of Robert Altman's classic Western *McCabe & Mrs. Miller* had been upset in a similar way when his star Warren Beatty was killed in the ending so I realized that our producer, like him, was thinking it was too much of a bummer for audiences to see their idols die on screen. But I thought that alteration would have been such a significant violation of fact that I would have found it impossible to script in that way. The Dalton family was large but I neglected those who were not criminals. I have no problem with that. But shifting too far from the history seems wrong to me, and an insult to the memory of the people who are my focus. Just as poets obey the meter and rhyme of their form, I feel constrained to get across what must have happened and what the protagonists actually did. When Jesse James is shot in the back of the head, his wife rushed in from the kitchen and saw Bob Ford standing there in the gunsmoke, and as she knelt to her husband she screamed, "Bob, have you done this?" He said, "The gun went off accidentally," and she replied, "Yes, accidentally on purpose." Most journals of the period carried that contemporary-sounding account, but it probably seemed like an anachronistic off-note in my novel. Yet I felt I could not get rid of it and was stuck with having to make the sentences work because they were on record.

Lackey: Could we say that you have two separate approaches as a biographical novelist? On the one hand, your job is to make a story realistic and enjoyable so that it is accessible for contemporary readers. On the other hand, your job is to dig into the archives and the logic of character and narrative in order to get to a more accurate assessment of what happened historically. You do this in order to give us a more realistic and accurate picture of history. Is that correct?

Hansen: Exactly. You approach these things with a sense of wonder. How is it possible that this event happened in this way? Why haven't other people talked about it? You've come to a conclusion yourself and then you go back and try to connect the prompts and reactions. And you ask yourself: in my experience of humanity, do people act this way? If they don't, then I know there's something wrong with the narrative. You use the history to justify each step you take, but you also use your own sense of psychology and human nature to make all those things authoritative. If one element doesn't add up to another, then you know you're on the wrong track.

Lackey: Why did you center *Hitler's Niece* within the consciousness of Geli? And what could you communicate about history through this focus on the relationship between Hitler and Geli?

Hansen: Geli was my stand-in for Germany, illustrating how Hitler was able to woo an entire nation by telling the people what they wanted to hear, offering blandishments and scapegoats, exciting some of their worst impulses, promising revenge for injuries, all while seeming an honorable leader. And Geli was an intimate who was at first captivated by and in love with Hitler. But she gradually came to understand his satanic nature. Likewise, but only after the war, Germany finally became fully aware of his evil and perversity and even now succeeding generations feel the shame of their forebears for having followed him. Had the Germans only known what Geli tragically knew, Hitler could not have run against von Hindenburg in the 1932 presidential elections, nor been appointed Chancellor by von Hindenburg a year later. Geli became for me a personification of the Germany that did not know what they were getting in Adolf and of those who correctly read the signs of the times and fled.

Lackey: To conclude, can you tell me other biographical novels that you consider outstanding? And can you explain why you consider them outstanding?

Hansen: Along with those novels I've already mentioned there are those of my co-interviewees: Julia Alvarez and *In the Time of the Butterflies*, about the vibrant, valiant Mirabal sisters and their challenge to Trujillo's dictatorship, and *Blonde* by Joyce Carol Oates, a novel I recommended for the National Book Award because of its sad, haunting, evocative representation of the life of Marilyn Monroe. Raymond Carver has a surprising and lovely last story, "Errand," about the final days of Anton Chekov. My favorite book by Norman Mailer is his "true life novel" *The Executioner's Song*, an overwhelming and perfectly-pitched account in both "Western" and "Eastern" voices of the crimes, court trials, and final execution in Utah of Gary Gilmore. My friend Jim Shepard's novel *Nosferatu* is a stunning, sympathetic fictional biography of F. W. Murnau, which captures the life of the German film director by glimpsing the man in various crises of development. Happily there are many biographical novels out there, and more are surely coming as fiction writers recognize the genre's fascination and power.

9

The Art of Claiming Power in the Biographical Novel

Sherry Jones

Lackey: Let me start by telling you about the nature of this project. I'm trying to figure out why, starting in the 1980s, so many prominent writers began to author biographical novels. I'm also trying to define the nature of this genre of fiction. Can you start by explaining what led you to write a novel about A'isha?

Jones: In the winter of 2002, I was finishing my degree at the University of Montana, where I was studying creative writing. For my honors thesis, I decided to produce a creative work, as I'd always wanted to write fiction. By that point, I had been a journalist for twenty-two years. In the wake of 9/11, the Western world was discovering how women were being treated in Afghanistan, under the Taliban. As a feminist, I was shocked and also embarrassed that I hadn't known about this. I was deeply moved by an essay I heard on NPR by an American Muslim woman in which she said: "because of how Islam treats women I've had to drop my religion." I'd had similar experiences with Christianity. I read about how the women in Afghanistan were Westernized. They were involved in all aspects of public life, and then it was all taken away from them. I started researching women in Islam, and I read two or three books, including *Nine Parts of Desire* by Geraldine Brooks. These books all mentioned A'isha, the nine year-old wife of the prophet Muhammad. They also mentioned that Muhammad had twelve wives and concubines. I thought this was amazing, because Christian culture is completely desexualized. Christianity completely detaches sexuality from spirituality, but in Muslim culture, their Prophet actually had a very active sex life. I was really intrigued, and I thought, why don't we know this? I decided I wanted to learn more about these women, especially A'isha. She was a nine year-old girl who married a fifty-four year-old man. She grew up in this misogynistic culture in which women and girls were chattel, the property of men—and this pre-dated Islam—but she became this extremely empowered and influential woman. I wanted to explore how that could happen to a woman who was married to a supposedly patriarchal, misogynist, religious leader. I didn't realize it at the time, of course, but women's self-empowerment would become the recurrent theme in my books.

Lackey: One of the things I've noticed about a number of biographical novelists is that, while they are writing about the past, they are also writing about the present. Would you say that's true about you? And if so, can you explain why?

Jones: That is true. I've been struck, as I've researched, by how little we've evolved. That's something that good biographical fiction addresses and makes us think about. We are still struggling with the same dilemmas and struggles people faced in seventh-century Arabia, and in twelfth- and thirteenth-century Europe, and, probably, for time immemorial. Power, greed, violence, male-female dynamics, women's struggle for empowerment—it continues today. I think that we can use events of the past to shed light on the present and to make us think about how far we haven't come in all these years. For instance, in *Four Sisters, All Queens*, which is my most recent novel, immigration is a big issue. There was a huge outcry in England at the time against immigrants. The barons, led by Simon de Montfort, banished non-English people from the country, although de Montfort was French! So-called Christians committed horrible atrocities against Jews, and, during the Crusades, against Muslims. Patriarchy privileged men and deprived women of rights and opportunities. That's all still happening today. We can look at the events of the past in order to understand the present, and perhaps to guide us to a more humane future.

Lackey: If one of your objectives was to tell A'isha's story, why didn't you write a biography about her? What is it that you could achieve through the novel that you could not through a biography?

Jones: Initially, Random House was going to publish *The Jewel of Medina* and *The Sword of Medina*. But because of fears of terrorist attacks, Random House decided not to publish them. The editor said that the situation would be different if these were non-fiction books. I found this interesting, that a fictionalized portrait of A'isha could be more dangerous than a non-fiction, biographical book about her. Perhaps that's because fiction takes us into the hearts and minds of people and helps us develop empathy.

Lackey: So are you saying that fiction can bring about a bigger transformation than a historical work?

Jones: I think for the reader, yes. Fiction can be transformative. It helps us to see how others who aren't like us, or so we think, really are very much like us. Fiction explores the greater truths of what it means to be human in ways that I don't think non-fiction can really do. Non-fiction looks at historical figures from the outside, whereas fiction explores their inner lives. As writers we become our characters, and we hope that our readers will, as well.

Lackey: *The Jewel of Medina* and *The Sword of Medina* are different from most contemporary biographical novels because you take as your subject a major figure from a religious tradition. Is it right to assume that writing about such a figure imposes different types of restrictions on you than taking on mere historical figures, as you do in your most recent novel *Four Sisters, All Queens*? If so, can you discuss the kinds of liberties you can take with religious characters, such as A'isha and Muhammad? And can you discuss the kind of liberties you believe you could not take?

Jones: I approached my research to *The Jewel of the Medina* and *The Sword of the Medina* as a journalist, that is, objectively. I didn't know anything and I had no preconceived notions. I wanted to discover the facts and maybe some truths about Islam and its founders. So when I wrote my book I wasn't consciously trying to paint a prettier picture of Muhammad. I wasn't trying to "rosy up" the consummation of A'isha by making her older than nine, as some accused me of doing. I tried to figure out what these characters are like, who they were as people. I had to choose from all the many versions of history, not the versions that made these people look the best, but the ones most true to my characters. For example, someone could say (and people did), "She didn't portray Muhammad raping his nine-year old wife, because she didn't want to offend Muslims." But if I had thought that Muhammad did that, if it were true to his character, then I would have written it that way. There was nothing that I thought I couldn't do. My main objective was to portray these characters as real people, to bring out their humanity and to show them as people who struggle the struggles and fight the fights that we all do as human beings.

Lackey: What I'm looking for here is not necessarily the things that he did, the things that happened. My question is about the kinds of liberties that you can take with the facts in order to get to the interiors. You claim that your objective is to get to these internal realities; that is what a biographical novelist does. What kind of creative license do you have? What facts can you alter and still respect the reality that you are trying to represent? For example, you say that you have no evidence that A'isha ever wielded a sword. But you wanted to represent something inside of her, so in your novel, she wields a sword. What kind of things could you invent in order to access A'isha's inner world? And what kinds of liberties are unacceptable?

Jones: There is the "affair of the necklace," which is also called the "affair of the lie" if you're a Sunni. The story is that A'isha was left by the caravan at a desert oasis, and that she came into Medina with a young warrior named Safwan the next morning. Some accused them of adultery. We don't really know what happened between them. Were they intimate? A'isha wouldn't say. When I originally wrote the book, I wasn't going to say, either. I was going to let the reader decide, because I felt that was territory I couldn't venture into, as it is part of the sacred religious history. But my advisor, Kate Gadbow at the University of Montana, said, "The reader wants to know what happened in the desert. You have to take a stand," and so I did. Ultimately that turned out to be a good thing, because it helped me to portray A'isha as a young woman who had experienced temptation but overcame it. And if my whole story is about her finding and claiming her strength, then I was able to do that by filling in that scene.

However, I want to make one point about religious figures. By their very nature, they are larger than life. So when you're writing biographical fiction about religious figures, everything you write is about something else, something greater than they are. Even though I wanted to portray their humanity, they weren't mere human beings. Muhammad said, "I am a mortal man," but he was not just any man. In *The Jewel of Medina,* he's lustful, but not lascivious. He becomes enamored of power, but he's no tyrant. He starts out in *The Jewel of the Medina* as very sincere, even enduring persecution and banishment to the desert for the sake of his visions, but then as his following increases and he becomes the leader of a growing community of faithful Muslims, he starts envisioning the spread of Islam throughout the world. He starts to believe his own press releases. He takes more and more wives as a symbol of his prestige. So power goes to his head, but he has to resist the temptation to abuse that power. Also, he can marry A'isha when she's nine years old, but he's no pedophile—he would not have maintained his following if he were—so he waits until she becomes a woman before consummating the marriage. As a spiritual leader, he has to have something that the rest of us don't, an inner goodness or an inner light. The same is true of A'isha, who later became the revered "Mother of the Believers." She was very jealous, but not malicious; she was sexual, but not adulterous; she could be tempted, but she couldn't really succumb to temptation, because, like Muhammad, she is a sacred figure. They were larger than life. *The Jewel of the Medina* is about them, but by extension it's also about the nature of God, the nature of humanity, the way we should live our lives today and for all time, because their very lives embodied these questions.

Lackey: Scholars make a distinction between historical and biographical fiction. In your afterword to *The Jewel of the Medina* you refer to your novel as historical fiction, but because the narrative is told primarily from the perspective of A'isha, some would categorize it as a biographical novel. Why did you primarily center the narrative in a particular consciousness? And what could you achieve through this approach that you could not through a seemingly more objective and omniscient narration?

Jones: I wrote my first draft from an omniscient point of view, in third-person, telling the story of Muhammad and the founding of Islam through the eyes of all his wives. But an editor told me that I needed to have a protagonist, that the book really didn't have a narrative arc but was just a series of vignettes. Eventually, A'isha rose to the top as the natural voice, because she was the wife who lived with him the longest and she was his favorite. He died in her arms. She was also one of his advisors. She would have been privy to many of the inner workings of Islam and the decisions its leaders made. So I decided to have her tell the story, and to do so from the first person, a more intimate viewpoint that enabled me to portray her inner life as well as that of Muhammad and Islam from her perspective as I imagined it.

Lackey: You have taken some liberties with the facts in order to access the inner world of A'isha. This act of combining fact and fiction in order to represent the interiority of a historical figure is something writers would not have done 100 years ago. What has happened in literary history that has given you the freedom to write this kind of novel?

Jones: History books written even in the first half of the twentieth century tend to be very chatty, filled with the historian's own personal observations and even speculations. They read like novels. Modern history is very fact-oriented, almost journalistic in style. It gives "just the facts, ma'am," and can seem pretty dry in comparison. Maybe biographical fiction has arisen to fill the narrative void that resulted. Nancy Goldstone's history *Four Queens* inspired me to write *Four Sisters, All Queens*. After I read that book I thought, I want to know more about these women. I want to know how they felt about the things happening in their lives. I want to understand more fully their relationships with each other, and what they were really like. The only way I could do that was to invent and conjecture. People who like history also want a good story, so a lot of them now turn to biographical fiction.

I think I can get away with this now largely because of postmodernism. The relatively new idea that truth doesn't exist in an absolute form but is subjective allows writers to portray real-life people from a viewpoint that is, admittedly, subjective. We realize now that, even in our own lives, we often have no idea what's really going on. Feelings and perceptions differ from day to day, if not moment to moment. That's why we can have novel after novel about the Tudors, and each of them different. Hilary Mantel's version of Anne Boleyn differs from Philippa Gregory's, although both authors adhere to historical fact. They're probably both partly right about her, and partly wrong, but it doesn't matter. The reader understands that each Anne is part fact and part subjective invention, a product of the author's own projections, manipulated in service to the story.

Lackey: There has been a lot of controversy surrounding the publication of *The Jewel of the Medina*. Random House was initially slated to publish the novel, but the publisher abandoned the project out of fear of terrorist attacks by radical Muslims. Do you think that your positive representation of a female, such as A'isha, is the source of the controversy? Or, do you think it is the imaginative representation of the inner life of Muhammad that caused so much concern? Or is it something totally different?

Jones: You would think people would be outraged by my portrayal of Muhammad as a real human being and taking the liberty of putting words in his mouth. But I haven't had too many complaints about my book along those lines. The book's feminist overtones seem to rankle people the most. Some have complained that I've made A'isha too feminist. Two Canadian Muslim women wrote to me complaining that I'd written A'isha as resisting the veil. They said that everyone who knows the *ahadith*, the sayings of the prophet Muhammad, knows that A'isha cherished the veil. She loved the veil so much that even after Muhammad, Umar, and her father were all buried in her bedroom, she wore the veil even when she was alone in her room. To me, this is ridiculous. How do we know that she wore her veil when she was alone? There was nobody there to verify it. But this kind of thinking helps women to justify their own veiling, which patriarchy has imposed either overtly or hegemonically.

Ironically, *The Jewel of Medina*, like *The Satanic Verses*, has caused the greatest uproar among people who have not read the book. I've had death threats and calls for my assassination, all from men, using misogynistic language. I've been called every bad word in the book, including "feminist." So I must draw the conclusion that the feminist aspects of my book, in which I portray Muhammad's egalitarian attitudes toward women and how he helped women, threatens the oppressive, patriarchal goals of radical Islamists.

Lackey: Something in the nature of the biographical novel poses an implicit challenge to the authority of sacred figures and texts, and I wonder if this is part of the problem here. Take, for instance, Muhammad's decision to marry the wife of his son. This is considered unthinkable, for it is strictly forbidden by Al-Lah. But in *The Jewel of Medina* you clarify how he was able to circumvent this prohibition. In a conversation A'isha notes that Muhammad's son is adopted. This leads Muhammad to claim that Al-Lah has given him permission to marry his son's wife because his son was not a blood relation. Your A'isha snidely remarks that "Al-Lah hastens to do Muhammad's bidding." The general view is that God dictates truth to humans, but within the context of a biographical novel, which pictures the evolution of characters in relation to one another, one gets the sense that divine revelations are actually the products of human desire or political realities. To what degree does the very form of the biographical novel pose a challenge to the authority of sacred religious traditions by illustrating how religious truths are likely to be the products of human desires and political concerns?

Jones: We are taking the sacred and imbuing it with humanity, which is where it began, where it started out.

Lackey: But wouldn't most religious people say that it didn't begin with humanity, that it emanated from a heaven of ideas, that God imparted it to humanity? The whole point is that the divine Truth stands outside of humanity, isn't that the view?

Jones: That religion stands outside humanity?

Lackey: Yes, and the truths of the religion. One of the key claims among some religious thinkers is that divine truth is not a product of human desire. God has revealed truth to humanity. Of course, a lot of people have challenged this view, especially in the West, such as Thomas Paine, Friedrich Nietzsche, and Sigmund Freud. So we in the West are very comfortable saying that divine truths are really just human inventions. But I think you have done to Islam what many have done to Christianity, which has been to expose the humanization of its divine truths.

Jones: Muhammad himself said, "I am a mortal man." He cautioned his followers not to worship him, not to make of him this sacred figure. He was a human being, just like them. He was given these revelations from God, but he was only the mouthpiece. He did not see himself, at least so he said, as being anything more than that. I think what happens with religion in general is that there's a visionary who has this direct connection to something larger outside of ourselves and is uniquely able to impart that vision in a way that others find appealing. This results in a following. When that leader passes, those who remain do not necessarily perceive that vision. These are just ordinary people trying their best to carry on the tradition of the visionary founder. But then power struggles happen. Religion becomes corrupted by humanity. So it may have started with a truth that was revealed, but humans, being flawed, botch it up. In a way, I think it would have been better if after Muhammad had died, that Islam had died. If after Christ had died, that Christianity had died. We writers challenge religion and religious authority because we approach the world with more skepticism. We do what writers ought to do, which is to analyze, think, question, and challenge. Our job is to think and to make others think, to raise the big questions—not even necessarily to provide the answers—but to raise the questions, and to stimulate others to ask questions also. I'm not interested in putting forth the popular perception of the prophet Muhammad among Muslims. I couldn't possibly do that anyway, as it's all so subjective; everyone has a different idea of how he was and who he was. What I can do is offer my own personal vision or my own personal interpretation of his life. To people who criticize my portrayal of A'isha, I say, write your own book! I think we should have more books about her. And they are all going to be different. None of us knew her personally; we can only interpret through our own individual lens.

Lackey: There is a subgenre of the biographical novel, which fictionalizes the lives of figures from religious texts and traditions. Here I'm thinking of Anita Diamant's *The Red Tent*, Rebecca Kanner's *Sinners and the Sea*, and Colm Tóibín's *The Testament of Mary*. All of these texts focus on the inner lives of women from sacred texts and traditions. Can you discuss your work within the context of this subgenre?

Jones: What we are doing is giving these women their humanity back. I used to say after *The Jewel of Medina* that next I was going to write a novel about the Virgin Mary. Colm Tóibín did it and I love his book. I read it as soon as I found out about it. I was so curious to see what he would have come up with, how it would be different from mine. My book would have had Mary raped by a Roman soldier because that's another theory, advanced not long after his death, that Jesus's father was a Roman soldier. My reason for doing that would be to give Mary her humanity back. I think the sacralization of women, the putting of women on a pedestal, actually does them a disservice. There's no greater empowerment for women than to face temptations and obstacles, to struggle and to overcome those struggles, to recognize one's own strengths, and to claim one's own personal power. This is especially difficult in a patriarchal society, because we are second-class citizens. In any culture in which God is male, woman is automatically secondary. My goal is to give these women their humanity back, to show their doubts and struggles, their fears and their obstacles, and their questioning. It is to show

how they dealt with their lives in a real way. Seeing them engage in the nitty-gritty of life honors these women much more than portraying them as virgins or as being submissive and subservient to a religious ideal.

Lackey: You claim that you are giving women their humanity back. But is it also true that you are trying to take away the sacredness of males? If I understand your argument, it is that men have put themselves up as a divine being. God is a male. Therefore, males are divine. This explains, in some ways, why you have this passage where A'isha says to Muhammad: "God certainly hastens to do your bidding." It's not just that you're giving women their humanity back, but you have to bring men down a little bit in order to make this humanization of women possible. Am I getting that right?

Jones: When you give women back their humanity and you show the men through women's eyes, that's going to happen automatically. Just because men want to be worshipped and they want to portray themselves in history as being closest to God, it doesn't necessarily mean that women believe that. The women I think we want to read about, or that I want to write about, are the women who have that unique ability to hold on to their center, to believe in themselves, and to claim their own power. That's what I liked about A'isha. If she had been just this nine year-old girl who married the Prophet, I would have felt bad for her. If that had been the end of her story, I might not have made her the protagonist of this book. But that story about Muhammad marrying his son's wife is actually in the *hadith*. I didn't make that up. I dramatize it a little, but that's what supposedly happened. She didn't always buy into Muhammad's personal mythology.

Lackey: But dramatizing that *hadith* within the context of a biographical novel calls into question the legitimacy of the truth. As readers, we see that this truth is coming from a human motivation rather than some sort of divine dictate. This is the very nature of the biographical novel. Something inherent to it undermines traditional views of divine truth.

Jones: That's right because, as novelists, our first and foremost loyalty is to our characters. That's what I'm trying to do. I'm trying to be true to my character. I don't really care that much if my readers like the character. I don't really care if they like my book. I'm not really writing for them; I'm writing for the character. I want to get inside the heart and mind of another person. I wanted to show Islam as being founded by real people. Of course, Muhammad was a visionary who had an especially strong spiritual connection and was blessed by the divine, so he believed. But on the other hand, he was a mortal man, and I want to show that. For me, I get my inspiration from ordinary humans who overcome obstacles and claim their power. What inspiration is there for me in a Jesus who never sinned, who was perfect his whole life? Why should I admire thirty-three years of sin-free living? He was obviously hard-wired not to sin. So how hard was it for him not to sin? And why should I be inspired by that? For me, my inspiration comes from learning how other people have struggled with and overcome temptation so that I can find out how to do that myself. How can I claim my own strength in the world? How can I overcome temptation? How can I become a fully empowered woman in a patriarchal society? And how can I be a supposedly equal citizen when God is male?

Lackey: To conclude, can you talk about some biographical novels that you consider outstanding? And can you explain why you consider them outstanding?

Jones: *The Red Tent* was one of the first biographical novels I read. I thought it was ground-breaking because it took a story from the Bible and fleshed it out with real people. And there was a lot of invention there. The Bible stories are only sketches. There is so much room to fill in the blanks. *The Red Tent* made me think about a book that I read a long time ago called *Ariadne*. In that book, the author takes the figures in Greek mythology and writes about them as real people. *Ariadne* was my first exposure to the idea that Greek mythology grew out of real life events. *The Red Tent* did the same thing for me. I also love *Sinners and the Sea*. It is such a powerful tale of a nameless woman. It's so symbolic of women's situation in the patriarchal world, that they don't even have a name. It also explores the deeper issues of man's inhumanity to man and religious zeal. It brilliantly portrays the justification for violence that religion provides, especially extreme religion. Tóibín's *The Testament of Mary* is powerful because it gives Mary her humanity and takes her off the pedestal. It also explores motherhood, the pain inherent in motherhood, and maybe the disappointment. It doesn't matter if your child is a prophet of God or a chimney sweep. You connect with that child and that's where it hits you, and hurts you. So it explores the deeper significance of parenthood, the pain and struggle that it brings. What makes these books outstanding is that they not only tell the story of a person, but that they use the story as a springboard from which to explore the deeper meaning of what it means to be human, the struggle inherent in humanity. My favorite biographical novel is *Wolf Hall* by Hilary Mantel. It gives us a fully rounded character in Thomas Cromwell. We get to see his good points and his bad points, his ambivalences, his shadow and light. We feel sympathy for him, we admire his intelligence, we see how he grew up as an abused butcher's son to become this great advisor to the king. It is subtle and complex, and a very moving tale. Mantel does what great novelists are supposed to do;

she explores what it means to be human: our search for love, our struggle to survive, our grappling with the realization of our own mortality. And those things are true throughout human history. It is fascinating that we still haven't figured it out, how to be human gracefully. We are still like awkward chicks just hatched from the shell.

10

Feminist Naming in the
Biographical Novel

Rebecca Kanner

Lackey: Let me start by telling you about the nature of this project. For the last couple years I have been trying to figure out why, starting in the 1980s, so many prominent writers began to author biographical novels. I am also trying to define the nature of this particular genre of fiction. Can you start by explaining what led you to write a novel about Noah's unnamed wife?

Kanner: I went to Talmud Torah, which is a Jewish school in St. Paul. We studied the Torah and each morning we said a prayer called the Amidah. This prayer mentions Abraham, Isaac, and Jacob. My teachers, who were mostly women, added the patriarchs' wives, Sarah, Rebekah, Rachel, and Leah. So the women of the Bible were very present for me, which made it odd later in my life when I thought about Noah's wife. I wondered, "Why don't I remember her at all? Why isn't she present for me in the way that these other women are?" I went back to Genesis and saw that she wasn't named. She's just mentioned in passing five times as "Noah's wife." When I saw this, I understood why I couldn't remember her. The fact that she didn't have a name made it hard for us to talk about her. It also made it more difficult for me to think about her. I was hoping that by naming her I would bring her into my consciousness and also give us a way to talk about her.

Lackey: This fact about the name is one reason why your novel is different from Anita Diamant's *The Red Tent*. As a novelist, you are working in the same tradition as Diamant in that you take a female figure from the Old Testament and breathe life into her character. But your novel is different because your biblical character doesn't have a name. Can you talk about how you were influenced by Diamant? And can you also discuss how your work and approach differs from hers?

Kanner: I embrace the idea that you can give someone power by giving her a voice. What I most admired about *The Red Tent* is that it gave voice to a woman who didn't have one in the Old Testament, in this case a woman who is typically seen as a victim. Like the protagonist in *The Red Tent,* my character is also voiceless in the Old Testament. But not only is she voiceless, she's nameless. Without a name, Noah's wife is only able to be identified by her relationships to other people—wife, mother. There is a point in *Sinners and the Sea* where Noah's wife asks him for a name, and he tells her he's already given her one—he's given her the name "wife." Later, when they are on the ark, and she considers the possibility that Noah and her sons might die, she wonders, *"if they die, who will I be?"*

In addition to *The Red Tent* I was inspired by a book by David Maine called *The Preservationist* in which Noah's wife wasn't named. I loved the book but wanted to explore a different role for Noah's wife than the one she played in Maine's book—that of the long-suffering wife who has accepted her lowly status. I wanted to flesh her out differently, and let her tell the story from her perspective. Once I started writing and found her voice it was really easy to tell the story because she took over. She was dying to be heard. And so my task then as a writer was to step back and let her lead the way.

Lackey: You say that Maine treated her as a long-suffering wife who has accepted her lowly status but you did not want that. What would be the alternative to that version of the story of Noah's wife?

Kanner: The alternative version is for her to find strength as the story evolves. In *Sinners and the Sea,* because of a birthmark she's born with, and the way she is reviled in her village, she's very timid as a young woman. As the story unfolds her troubles multiply. She becomes the wife of a very old man who most people think is crazy. Daily, she has to deal with this aloof husband who speaks more to God than to her. Once her sons are born she struggles to keep them from being sinful in a town full of sinners. Then she has to hold her family together on the ark. Noah loses faith and thinks that God has abandoned them—he's not sure they'll survive. The sons are at war with each other. Life is very hard at this point on the ark. Imagine being on a car trip with your family and a bunch of animals for a year. Now imagine you don't know if you'll ever be able to get out of the car. Noah's wife gains power from successfully handling these struggles. It's she, more than Noah, who ends up leading the family to the New World in *Sinners and the Sea.* She's not going to end her life as the same person she was when it began. She's going to be changed by what happens and through that she's going to find her voice and come into her own. And so that's what I wanted to do differently than David Maine.

Another part of her growth as a character in my novel involves her realizing that her birthmark, which she has hated her whole life, has saved her. Without it, she wouldn't have made it onto the ark. This plot point was important to me, because I wanted to convey that our struggles and those things we hate most about ourselves can end up being assets and perhaps even saving us in the end.

Lackey: Here I want to shift focus for a moment. *Sinners and the Sea* differs from many contemporary biographical novels. Most biographical novels focus on relatively recent figures. For instance, Joanna Scott's *Arrogance* is about the artist Egon Schiele and Bruce Duffy's *Disaster Was My God* is about the poet Arthur Rimbaud. Your main character is taken from a sacred text which is generally considered inviolable. Is it right to assume that taking a character from the Hebrew text imposes different types of restrictions on you than taking a mere historical figure? If so, can you discuss the kind of liberties you can take with these characters and the text? And can you discuss the kind of liberties you believe you cannot take?

Kanner: I tried to remain true to what's in Genesis about the flood and that wasn't hard as it is only chapters six through nine, just a matter of pages. While I didn't drastically alter what is in Genesis, I took a liberty in adding a large plot element. I think most people's reaction upon seeing that Noah's wife isn't named in Genesis is to assume that she probably had a name but because she was unimportant her name isn't mentioned. I wanted to come up with a different explanation for why Mrs. Noah wasn't named in Genesis, one that didn't involve her being unimportant. In my novel, she's born with a birthmark, and in this time before science, it's seen as a demon's mark. Her father thinks that without a name people won't be able to talk about her. And so, in the hopes of protecting her, he doesn't give her one.

Lackey: There's an interesting parallel between your work and Diamant's. At the end of *The Red Tent* we get a character named Gera who is in the Old Testament but who is a boy. In *The Red Tent* Gera is a girl, which is important, because this is how Dinah learns that her name and story have been kept alive. We figure all this out through Gera when she tells the story to Dinah at the end of the novel. You do something similar. There is a Javan in Genesis, and it is a male character. But you make Javan into a female. Can you talk about your decision to make this male character into a female character?

Kanner: Javan is in charge of the town. She's a harsh ruler, but Shahar is very happy that there's some sense of order in the town. I think it would be unusual for people to see a female as being the overlord of a town. But in this case Javan is. This woman is so important that a *male* child is named after her, but later her influence is hidden, as no one knows the name originates with her. Because oftentimes women's influence is hidden or women aren't given credit for their achievements and contributions, I thought it appropriate to add a plot point that demonstrates this.

Lackey: In my interview with Anita, we talked a lot about feminist Midrash. She said that she did not think of *The Red Tent* as Midrash. However, many people read the novel in this way. Midrash, as you know, is a rabbinical technique of writing and interpretation that fills in gaps in biblical stories. But the tradition itself has been very patriarchal. Would you consider your work a version of feminist Midrash? And is feminist Midrash legitimate?

Kanner: I hadn't thought of *Sinners and the Sea* as Midrash until my rabbi endorsed it, calling it "an excellent example of the traditional Jewish method of Midrash meeting the modern writer's pen." Then the *Publishers Weekly* review came out. It begins, "Debut novelist Kanner brings to life the nameless wife of Noah in a deeply imagined midrashic interpretation of the biblical story of the flood." I think the act of engaging in midrashic interpretation, whether you call it Midrash or not, is feminist for the reason you cited, that Midrash along with most of the other literature about the bible has mostly been written by men. The biggest midrashic element in my novel is the explanation of why Noah's wife doesn't have a name in Genesis, which is that because of her birthmark her father doesn't name her so people can't easily talk about her. This rejection of the simplest explanation for her being unnamed in Genesis, that she has a name but is so unimportant it isn't mentioned, could certainly be considered feminist. The other midrashic element in *Sinners and the Sea* is the plotline with the nephil (a giant). I had to find a way to allow a nephil into the New World because there are nephilim (giants) before and after the flood. They are actually at the beginning of the story of the flood in Genesis Chapter 6 and then they're not mentioned again until Numbers, the fourth book of the Old Testament. I asked myself how they could have somehow survived the flood. I offer my explanation in *Sinners and the Sea*. And yes, a woman is involved in getting a nephil to the New World.

Lackey: Your decision to include the nephilim is significant. Everything in *The Red Tent* is comprehensible through the lens of realism, the natural laws of psychology, sociology, and anthropology. Your novel is different because you include scenes that defy the laws of nature and psychology. For instance, even though Jank strikes Noah with a spear, it never penetrates; Shahar has an encounter with a nephil; and Ona gives birth to a nephil. How do the references to the miraculous and the supernatural function in your novel?

Kanner: I think that a belief in miracles and inclusion of the supernatural or things of a mythical nature broadens the world for the characters and gives a biblical feel to the novel. It seemed only natural to me to include these elements. The Bible is full of supernatural occurrences which are of great significance to both Jews and Christians. Passover is my favorite holiday. It's a commemoration of the Jews' exodus from Egypt, which is one big supernatural story: Moses seeing the burning bush, ten plagues including the one that Passover is named after in which the Angel of Death flies over the houses of the Egyptians and kills the first born, and the parting of the Red Sea.

In *Sinners and the Sea* the supernatural element creates tension for Noah's wife and I hope also for the reader. When Noah tells her that God talks to him she isn't able to write Noah off as completely crazy because there are supernatural signs that some large invisible force is indeed watching over him. And yet, Mrs. Noah never gets to hear what God says, and she's skeptical when Noah tells her God has declared that there will be a great flood. I can't say how the supernatural elements will function for the reader, but personally, I like to read stories that have some sort of mystery, supernatural element or magical realism. It opens the world for me.

Lackey: This brings us to an important question about the development of this subgenre of the biographical novel, which focuses on sacred stories and texts. Colm Tóibín recently published *The Testament of Mary*, which, unlike *The Red Tent*, addresses biblical miracles. He includes the miracle of Jesus raising Lazarus but he offers as a possibility a secular explanation for the miracle. It might have been a medical fluke of some sort, so it is possible that Lazarus wasn't really dead. In *The Red Tent* Anita got rid of all of the supernatural references. But you and Tóibín, at roughly the same time as his novel was released just a few months ago, have published biographical novels that include miracles. Can you explain why that's the case?

Kanner: It sounds like his book is different from mine because he suggests that Lazarus wasn't really dead.

Lackey: He leaves it open. It's just not clear in *The Testament of Mary*. In the novel, we are in the psyche of Mary and there are hints and suggestions that it can go either way. What I find interesting is how Anita *strategically avoided* any references to miracles or supernatural events in the Bible, whereas you do not avoid them. In fact, you incorporate them into your novel. Why legitimize the supernatural in your novel?

Kanner: I don't interpret the Bible literally, but I am a spiritual person. I leave myself open to miracles, and I enjoy the feeling I get when I think about things taking place in the universe that I don't fully understand. That's one reason I include the supernatural in *Sinners and the Sea*. The other reason it's included is that I can't think of the Bible without immediately thinking of the supernatural. I wanted my novel to have a biblical flavor.

Lackey: Another significant difference between *The Red Tent* and *Sinners and the Sea* is the source for the story of your novel. There is little information in Genesis about Dinah but there is certainly more about her than there is of Noah's wife. In my interview with Anita she said that she spent considerable time working through the logic of the rape scene in the Genesis story. Shechem apparently rapes Dinah but after the seeming rape Shechem's father offers Jacob a substantial dowry and then agrees to have every male in his kingdom circumcised in order to get Jacob's approval for a marriage. Anita says that this is not the behavior of a rapist. Given the logic of the story, she gives an alternative way of thinking about Dinah's relationship with Shechem who was named Shalem in *The Red Tent*. In Genesis there is virtually nothing about the women in Noah's life. Not even their names. When it comes to the representation of women, your work is almost pure invention. Can you talk about your strategies to access and represent female characters such as Javan, Shahar, and Zilpha? Here I'm thinking about the kind of research you did in order to help you fill in those characters.

Kanner: There is not a written history of 3000 B.C. for me to work with. I reread the Bible and then wrote until I found Shahar's voice. My task was to step back and let her tell the story. As for the female characters, I love Javan, the town's most notorious madam. For the reader she might not be immediately likable. She's crude and often violent. In fact she's a mass murderer. But she's also a caring mother who is willing to sacrifice herself for her daughter. There's something deeply satisfying and life-affirming about finding the good in people, especially when it's well hidden. I avoid any black and white depiction of good versus evil. The lines between good and evil are often blurry I think, and certainly that is more interesting to me. I especially dislike the virgin/whore dichotomy, the portrayal of women as either all good or all bad. Allowing for ambiguity in characters humanizes them, and seems the only truly respectful approach to writing about people.

As for Zilpha, I was at first channeling Zilpah who is an actual character in the Bible and is one of the women Anita Diamant writes of so beautifully in *The Red Tent*. It became clear that my Zilpah had taken on a personality of her own, and she differed so much from Anita's Zilpah that I ended up transposing the last two letters of my character's name.

Lackey: One last question about the differences between *The Red Tent* and *Sinners and the Sea*. God does not seem to be an important factor in *The Red*

Tent as characters do not get directives from the divine, but in your novel they do. For instance, God speaks to Noah and what God tells him comes to pass, that there is going to be a flood.

Kanner: Noah's wife wonders about the nature of this God her husband claims is speaking to him, and this creates a lot of tension and uncertainty in the story for her. Initially there is tension because she doesn't know if God is actually speaking to her husband, which makes living amongst sinners and preparing for a flood she's not certain is coming more of a struggle for her than it is for Noah; she is rudderless even before they are in the ark. She doesn't know what to believe or what's going to happen. However, being the one who God speaks to ends up making the end of the story more of a struggle for Noah. Noah feels a great responsibility for what happens. He believes he's the one who could have saved the sinners. He, more than anyone else, is haunted by their deaths.

Lackey: So God speaks to Noah, but your Shahar faults Noah and sometimes God. Noah says that God created the world in seven days, but Shahar corrects him saying that it was done in six days. And Shahar, in defiance of Noah and his God, saves Herai and tries to save Javan. From Shahar's perspective, Javan is not as bad as Noah suggests and there is not a massive divide between her son's sinfulness and the sinfulness of the doomed sinners. While your novel suggests communication between the human and the divine, the divine in your novel does not always appear to be in the right. Can you talk about the nature and the role of the divine in your novel?

Kanner: This is an area that is riling up some conservative Christians. No one in the novel is perfect. Not even God. At the beginning of Genesis God creates the world. Not long after, in Chapter 6, He decides it's corrupt and that He's going to destroy it. Either He made a mistake when He created the earth, or He was not able to control what He had created. So He is imperfect and that is really upsetting to certain Christians who see God as being perfect and perfectly loving. All I can say is that I feel I was true to Genesis chapters six through nine in my portrayal of God. I think I'm more comfortable with thinking about God outside of "God is perfect" or "God is love" because I studied the Old Testament as a child. Jews often have a complicated relationship with God because of our study of the texts and also because of our history. I have a friend whose father was a Holocaust survivor. Considering all that has happened to our people historically, and her father in particular, she describes her belief in God as somewhat masochistic.

Lackey: Do you plan to write another biographical novel?

Kanner: Yes, I'm writing a biographical novel about Queen Esther. It takes place in 485 B.C.E. so there is a wealth of historical material for me to work with. Esther is a Jewish girl who is taken into the harem of King Ahasuerus, a man some scholars believe was King Xerxes. Under the supervision of various eunuchs and female servants Esther and the other virgins go through a year of beauty treatments to ready themselves for the king. Esther hides her true identity as a Jew, even after she's made queen. But once a man who wishes to wipe out the Jews comes to power she has to reveal to the king that she's Jewish in order to save her people. I'm telling a feminist version of that tale. What I dislike about almost all of the novelized renderings of the story is that they are usually written as a romance between Esther and this king who has her and a whole harem of women. Though the harem life may sound glamorous the women are actually just pampered prisoners. In my book Esther is not in love with the king. She is very smart about what she's doing. She knows she has to manipulate the king in order to save her people. I also explore what life would actually be like as a woman who is just kept as a thing for a man. In my book the women of the harem are often drunk and catty. Esther struggles against both of these things with the other women and within herself.

Lackey: In biographical novels, there is a tendency to center the work in the consciousness of a particular character. Why not just give us an omniscient narrator? That would have given us a seemingly more objective perspective of the whole time period. What kind of value is there in centering a narrative in a particular consciousness?

Kanner: Women's stories have often been overlooked, and traditional women's work is often considered less important than men's. When I saw that Noah's wife wasn't named in Genesis I was very struck by that. This woman is too important for us to gloss over or forget. She was married to a prophet, and she is the matriarch of the New World. In *Sinners and the Sea* I wanted to give her the opportunity to share her experience. She tells of being the wife of an aloof man who might be crazy, trying to keep her sons safe in a town full of sinners, being the mother of warring sons, taking over as head of the family when Noah loses faith, and successfully keeping her family together and bringing them to the New World. In my current novel about Esther, I wanted to give voice to a different Esther than I've seen in other fictional accounts of her life. One who is smart and grows savvier as she navigates palace politics.

11

Re-Composing a Life in the Biographical Novel

Kate Moses

Lackey: Let me start by telling you about this project. I'm trying to figure out why, starting in the 1980s, so many prominent writers began to author biographical novels. I am also trying to define the nature of this genre of fiction. There have been many traditional biographies and scholarly studies of Sylvia Plath. Why did you write a novel about Plath? And what can you, as a novelist, communicate about her that a biographer and/or a scholar could not?

Moses: It started when I was rereading Plath's *Collected Poems*. I came across a note by Ted Hughes in the introduction that said Plath assembled her manuscript for *Ariel* in December of 1962, and she had a particular and thoughtful order for the poems. She told Hughes at the time that she intentionally began the book with the word "love" and ended with the word "spring"—the volume started with the poem "Morning Song" and ended with the poem "Wintering." She told several people, including Hughes, that the writing of these poems had "saved" her. Plath was also aware of what she'd accomplished artistically with these poems—she predicted in a letter to her mother that *Ariel* would "make my name." But Hughes rearranged the manuscript after Plath committed suicide in February 1963. They were still legally married and he was her literary executor, and he later wrote that he felt responsible for getting her book out into the world. A number of the most controversial and searing poems from the manuscript had already been published or contracted for publication, so they were known by editors and a few readers. When Hughes approached Plath's publishers about *Ariel* he wanted to leave some of those poems out because he felt they would hurt people she knew, including her mother. Of course, some of the acidic poems that Hughes wanted to delete were directed at him. Plath's American and British publishers wanted those poems. They permitted Hughes to work with the manuscript and so he pulled poems

out and substituted others. He later admitted this in the introduction to
Plath's *Collected Poems,* published in 1982, which also includes the original
order of the *Ariel* manuscript in an appendix. When *Ariel* was published in
1965, it became a huge sensation. Plath was right. It did make her name—
garnering a page-spread review in *Time,* which is huge for any book of
poetry, and selling 40,000 copies in a year, eventually becoming one of
the best-selling books of poetry of the twentieth century. As a coherent
work, *Ariel* as edited by Ted Hughes has a particular trajectory. It seems
to be a narrative of a woman who is intentionally moving toward her self-
destruction. Robert Lowell's foreword claimed "these poems are playing
Russian roulette with six cartridges in the cylinder … they tell that life, even
when disciplined, is simply not worth it." And that became the way people
saw Plath: defiantly suicidal, a lost cause from the start. Years later, with the
publication of *The Birthday Letters* shortly before his own death in 1998,
Hughes reiterated this idea that he was helpless to protect Plath against her
own determined martyrdom.

So when I read Hughes' comments about Plath's manuscript of *Ariel,* I
was dumbfounded. She started with "love" and ended with "spring"? Clearly
Plath had another idea for the shape and narrative of *Ariel,* and that narrative
was largely unknown. Out of the countless writings on Plath, there was only
one scholarly article about her version of *Ariel,* written by Marjorie Perloff,
and no one had ever done a complete study of the *Ariel* manuscript and what
it suggested about Plath as an artist and a human being. As a long time Plath
reader, but without any desire to write about her—I thought everything of
value had already been written—I went back to the *Ariel* poems in Plath's
arrangement, based on the order appended in the *Collected Poems,* and it
was clear that the story she had created in her version of *Ariel* was entirely
different from the published *Ariel.* Like the *Ariel* we all know, it too was
mythic and archetypal and fierce, but it was very much a narrative about a
persona, a woman, who was remaking her life after having it burned down
to the ground, and she was rising to another place of survival and optimism.
This stands in stark contrast to the published *Ariel,* which ended with the
poem "Edge" in which a woman is perfected by her own death, her lifeless
face smiling with accomplishment, and there's an image of her two dead
babies curled on either side of her. "Edge" wasn't even in the original *Ariel*
manuscript. Plath's *Ariel* ended with one of her cycle of bee poems, set in
winter and asking the question, "Will the hive survive … to enter another
year?" The poem, and so the book, ends with an image of rejuvenation, a
declaration of optimism and survival: "The bees are flying. They taste the
spring." As soon as I read Plath's version of *Ariel* I could see the narrative
she'd created. She told a totally different story about her work and herself,

and everything I'd thought about her was wrong. Now that I knew the real story, I felt an overwhelming responsibility to make that story known.

Lackey: So is it an attempt to render justice either to what Plath originally planned in the poems or to Plath herself that compelled you to write this?

Moses: Both. Based on her own statements and the comments of people who knew her, it was clear that she saw those poems as saving her, and the story they told was essential to how they would be read. They were her redemption.

Lackey: But she committed suicide shortly thereafter.

Moses: Right, and that was for me the question that needed to be answered. How could she go from feeling, "I'm a genius of a writer, I have it in me," as she said in a letter to her mother in October, feeling that the work saved her, trusting it to get her to a springtime in her life, to committing suicide only a few months later?

Lackey: So Plath finished *Ariel* in October?

Moses: Most of the poems in Plath's *Ariel* were written between the spring of 1962 and early November of 1962, with a few from 1961. She continued to write poems until the week before her death, but nothing after November 1962 did she include in *Ariel*. She thought the poems that she wrote in December of 1962 and January, February of 1963 had "a different weather," they were part of a different story altogether. So the poems that she wrote in 1962, largely after the breakup of her marriage, were the bulk of the poems in *Ariel*. Most of Plath's poems that have the darkest tone and a sense of futility and loss of faith in herself and in art's ability to save you are poems that Hughes inserted in the volume published in 1965. They weren't included in her version at all. Plath was notoriously shrewd and efficient as a steward of her own work. Her manuscript for *Ariel* was meticulously assembled and dated on her desk at her death. She could have changed it if she wanted to. But she didn't. Her *Ariel* had a specific and intentional narrative trajectory.

Lackey: So there was a puzzle there for you. Plath says that the volume saves, and yet she kills herself only three months later. As a writer, your task is to enter into that psychological space in order to make some sense of what happened in that intervening period. Is this right?

Moses: That's part of it, but I also wanted to understand why her version of *Ariel* was so important to her. At that time, Plath was a mother with two young children, a baby son born in January 1962 and a two-year-old daughter just out of diapers. Her husband had left her and she was suddenly a single mother with no childcare, trying to remake her personal and artistic life. At the time I began my novel, I was also a young mother and wife with a baby and a slightly older child, and I'd been through an earlier end of a marriage with my older child who had been a baby at the time. I wanted to understand how this woman went from feeling optimistic to feeling completely without hope. I wanted to know: Why weren't her children, to whom she was utterly devoted, and her art enough to keep her going? That was the question Plath's *Ariel* raised for me. To me, the *Ariel* she put together was the equivalent of Plath leaving herself a trail of crumbs in a dark forest so she could find her way out. It was as if she had assembled the story that she wanted her life to take, to lead herself to a point of hopefulness and optimism, to rejuvenation in the coming spring. And she put this book together in mid-December of 1962, right before the coldest winter in 200 years hit England, when she would be without electricity, without heat, without a phone, her car snowed in, alone with two little kids who kept getting sick, and she kept getting sick. In January 1963 *The Bell Jar* was published, not with a bang but a whisper. During that time she started writing the really dark, bleak poems, including "Edge." They weren't all bleak—think of the poems "Kindness" and "Balloons," written about a week before her death—but she didn't reshuffle the *Ariel* manuscript to include any of those late poems, dark or light. Looking at just the exterior circumstances of her life in those final weeks, how practically difficult it became, there is an argument for how things started shifting for her, leading her toward despair and suicide. And yet she didn't change *Ariel*, she was doggedly pursuing her solo literary career in London, she was, to my mind, tenaciously hanging on to that impulse toward survival. I never wanted to write the story of Plath's death. It was her life force that I felt pulsing in her version of *Ariel*, that was the story that hadn't been told. I wanted to explore that "moment before," when she was putting this book together, still believing in herself and her work. The artistic process itself, I felt, was essential to a fair and balanced understanding of Plath.

Lackey: You mention Marjorie Perloff's essay, which you acknowledge to be insightful and effective. If you were so committed to getting this story about Plath told, why not write a book about it? Why did you choose to write a novel?

Moses: I felt that a biography or a book of literary criticism was not going to have the expansiveness of imagination that would be required to illuminate Plath's psychology and her emotions at the time that she was putting *Ariel* together. If I were to have written my book on Plath as nonfiction, I would have to write a book in which I was projecting possibilities that I couldn't know for sure. Actually I never considered writing from a nonfictional perspective. I was trying to understand Plath's feelings, her interior landscape, how she responded internally to the circumstances of her life, how she transformed those circumstances into metaphor and image and symbol, not just in her poetry but in her self-concept. A work of nonfiction would have restricted me in revealing interior truths about Plath. For Plath in particular, the facts of her life simply can't tell the whole story, certainly not the story of her art and how that art reveals her complicated humanity, what her art meant to her. I needed fiction's room for nuance and association and possibility rather than a stark declaration of facts. Fiction is much more effective in representing the prismatic shifts of human emotional life than individual facts.

Lackey: So you have more freedom as a novelist than you would as a biographer or as a scholar?

Moses: Absolutely. As a novelist I could make suggestions about who she was at the time and how she was thinking and try to get into her mind in a way that I would have been restricted from expressing in a completely factual book. Plath in particular was a woman of shifting personas and moods— Hughes himself later wrote that he never saw her show her real self to anyone else until the final months of her life. With nonfiction, working only with facts, it's much harder to try to capture an individual who might be arrogant and euphoric one minute, such as the Plath who wrote to her mother "I'm a genius of a writer," but who was also masking her terror and loneliness and anger and vulnerability at the same time.

Lackey: But why should I trust you? Why should I think that you could access and represent Plath's interior world?

Moses: I guess the reason I could be trusted to tell this story is because I never considered "the reader" or whether they might trust me while I wrote. I approached the book first with a sense of deep responsibility to the real Plath, to her work, and to the facts of her life; secondarily I felt a responsibility to living people who had known Plath to not tread on their memories. But I felt from the start that the essential trust was between the real Sylvia Plath and me. In writing this book I became beholden to her. I was committed to researching the facts as thoroughly as I could and to represent them and her as accurately as possible through the lens of a created interior perspective. I don't believe I captured in full the real Plath in my fictional Plath, or that such a thing is even possible. Aspects, facets, glimpses of people are as much as any writer can hope to depict with any degree of accuracy and truth. I never strayed from what I came to believe was the truth of Sylvia Plath, as much as anyone can recognize the truth of another person.

If readers can trust my depiction of Plath's interior world, that's a bonus. It is not that I think a reader's trust is unimportant—it is vital—but with fictional works such as my novel about Plath, the writer's job is to be responsible to her subject. If she succeeds in serving her subject, she will serve the reader as well.

This may make me sound crazy, but it is why I feel I did my best for Sylvia Plath: around the time I began rereading her *Collected Poems*, before I had any idea of writing about her, I started hearing a woman crying in my head. All the time. After I came to understand Plath's version of *Ariel*, the crying continued, a constant keening in the background of my mind, accompanied by the scent of rotting apples. And I began to dream about Plath. Both the crying and the dreams continued through my writing of the novel. In fact I dreamt of specific places and vistas that I had never seen but that I would later recognize during my research travel, for instance that her study window in Devonshire was close enough to her apple orchard so that yes, she'd have smelled the rotting apples. Or fictional descriptions I wrote that prompted people who knew Plath to ask me after the novel was published, how did I get permission to go inside the Devonshire house? How did I get access to the apartments in London or W. S. Merwin's house in France? The answer was, I didn't—I described these places as I saw them in dreams, and the dreams turned out to be pretty accurate, it seems. The rational explanation is that I did such exacting research for so many years that these places put themselves together in my mind in fairly refined ways. And maybe that explains why some of the people who'd been close to Plath in those years, people I assiduously avoided while I wrote my novel, later told me how shocked they were by the precision of my understanding of Plath's psychology. Those comments made me feel I'd done right by the real Sylvia Plath. In my limited way I felt I'd honored my commitment to my subject. The weeping in my head stopped around the time that Plath's version of *Ariel*, titled *Ariel: The Restored Edition*, was published in 2005, two years after my novel.

Lackey: Biographical novelists tend to invent scenes in order to access human interiors. But we have a dilemma here. On the one hand, you respect the facts, and you add a chronology at the end of the novel in order to say here are the facts of her life. On the other hand, you take some liberties. Can you talk about the liberties that you take and can you justify them?

Moses: In order to create a believable character who readers can feel an emotional connection to and an investment in, they need to be able to get as close to that character as possible, which is another reason I needed to write this book as fiction rather than as a biography. I wanted readers to feel as if they were standing in the room with Plath as she was moving through her life. Here I should mention one thing. We don't know exactly what Plath was thinking during the time that she put the *Ariel* poems together because her journals from that time were either destroyed or lost by Hughes. Yet we know that Plath was a pathological chronicler of her own life. So up until this moment when Plath was writing the *Ariel* poems and assembling the manuscript, I could read about her from her own perspective. I could get that close, and readers everywhere can get that close as well, because her complete journals were published in 2000. But for those last few months of her life we don't have her journals. We have other things, like her calendar from 1962, which she used as a kind of journal. For example, I knew she painted hearts on her sewing machine on the same day that she sewed clothes for her daughter, Frieda, on that same sewing machine. I knew the day she took out the garbage or went Christmas shopping for the kids. I knew when she went to the gas board to get heat or the day she baked gingerbread or painted her bedroom. I also read her unpublished correspondence, which is archived in various libraries, and studied all of the biographical writings about Plath and recorded interviews with people who knew her. From all of this information I could build a scene in which Plath goes to the local post office to plead for phone service, or recreate conversations between Plath and her mother or with Dido Merwin. The scene in the book in which she goes to the local post office to beg for a phone is built from the facts of knowing that she actually did go there repeatedly. I don't know exactly what she said, but from the tone in her letters and from a sense of her interior life in her journals, and how she was reported to behave with other people, I could imagine and try to render how she would have gone about the process of getting a phone. The same is true about a scene with her mother, in which Plath's mother sent a telegram saying that there's an emergency, and so Sylvia ran out with the kids to the local phone box to call her mother back. Based on my research, I knew that Plath's mother had an uncanny knack for inserting herself when Plath was feeling most vulnerable, and that she had sent various telegrams of this type not just to Plath but even to Plath's neighbors and acquaintances throughout the fall of 1962, trying to get her daughter's attention or check up on her. They were well meaning efforts, but ultimately not appreciated by Plath. At this particular point in the real Plath's life, her mother was trying to convince her to come back to Wellesley, and Plath was mightily resisting that effort. The poem "Medusa," unquestionably about Plath's relationship with her mother, refers to transatlantic phone calls keeping an unwelcome thread of connection between the two women. So in this case I created a scene in which the conversation between them is not a debate over several letters, or a reference to a previous phone call between them, but the call itself. I knew that the closest phone box was next to an elementary school and what the weather was like that day, and that Plath would have run out in the cold with her children in the pram, fearful about an "emergency" back home in Wellesley, and I imagined that school kids could have been in the yard having recess, squealing and playing in the background, oblivious to the young mother on the telephone trying to both appease her concerned, over-involved mother and shed herself of tentacles of undesired connection. I could create the conversation between them from the reality of documentation on Plath's relationship with her mother, and by rendering the two of them in dialogue get as close to them as I could. So my justification for making up those scenes was to take the facts and then create a moment where I tried to make Plath and sometimes other characters rise up off the page in that moment of direct experience.

Lackey: To clarify my question about the liberties you can and cannot take, let me give you an example from Russell Banks' novel *Cloudsplitter*. Banks describes the Brown family walking in the 1840s along a road next to Lake Champlain on the way to what's going to become their home. A local historian called Banks after the book came out and said that the road wasn't there in the 1840s because it wasn't built until the 1870s. Banks knew that fact, because he had a map from the 1840s. But he put the road there anyway, because he wanted to picture a different kind of symbolic truth through the image and scene. Were there any moments in *Wintering* when you violated the literal, factual or historical truth in order to picture another type of truth or when you created a scene that did not happen?

Moses: My first impulse, my gut response, is to say no, I didn't. I don't feel I violated Plath's essential truth in my novel—but I did put words in my fictional Plath's mouth. I gave her thoughts and opinions and feelings that I can't verify. I placed her in situations at specific moments in time and depicted what transpired as if I'd witnessed those events. I conjured those words and thoughts and opinions and feelings and situations with utmost care, using an elaborate map of facts to locate my fictional coordinates, but in the end I wrote a fiction. My novel is a simulacrum of the real Sylvia Plath's story and her experience in the world. So in a way *Wintering* is in total violation of literal, factual and historical truth. But here I think *Ariel* can be an example of how facts are pliable and subject to manipulation: read one way, those poems seem to be stark evidence of a person who is a danger to herself. Read another way, they're a courageous chronicle of hope. What manipulations and violations I may be guilty of were committed to get at another kind of truth, as you put it—to my mind, that truth is far more fair to Plath, and to others, also, and more even-handed overall than the bald facts.

Lackey: This raises questions of ethics and responsibility. What liberties can you take as a biographical novelist and what liberties can't you take? Would you say that it's unjustified for somebody like Russell to change a historical fact?

Moses: I think it depends on what is changed and I think it depends on the book itself, what the writer is trying to do. I agree with the criticism that some biographical novels just regurgitate biography and then pass themselves off as fiction. But these works would not necessarily qualify as fiction.

Lackey: Because they lack a fictional element?

Moses: Not necessarily because they lack fictional elements. They may have all the craft of fiction. But are they illuminating the subject in a new way through fiction? This is something biography can't do. The biographical novels that are most interesting to me are the ones that use fiction in order to illuminate the character in a new way that facts alone can't. For example, Jerome Charyn published *The Secret Life of Emily Dickinson* a couple years ago. This novel is wildly imaginative, like Virginia Woolf's *Orlando*. It plays with the idea of Emily Dickinson's fantasy life. Charyn created a fantasy life for her that was this wild and far flung thing, but that was his purpose. He was trying to show the enormity of Dickinson's imagination. With a book like that I feel that it's completely justified to stray from the facts and play, because that's the whole point of such a book. For another reason I feel Russell Banks was justified to change that road. When you are working with historical material as opposed to a strictly contemporary situation, there is a subconscious palimpsest of knowledge and experience that comes into the reading of the book. The reader knows what has happened since the story's boundaries of time, and these layers of understanding are laid out on the very experience of reading. For some readers, this might not work. My own example in this kind of vein was a reader who wrote a letter very upset with me because I had people eating popcorn in a theater in 1962 in London. She said, "I was in London in 1962 and nobody ate popcorn in the theatre at that time." I thought, that's fine, but in America in 1962 or in America when Plath was growing up, they would have eaten popcorn. So for my fictional Plath to have been thinking in terms of the idea of eating popcorn in 1962 still works for what her imagination would have brought to the experience of being in a movie theater. Every case is going to be different. What I would resist is writers claiming their fictional works to be biographical, but creating fictional scenes about real people that manipulate those facts purely to further an imposed fictional narrative, rather than to better serve their biographical subject.

Lackey: Some prominent writers have either rejected or condemned the biographical novel. For instance, in a 1939 essay, Virginia Woolf argued that the "novelist is free" to create, while "the biographer is tied" to facts. For Woolf, writers have to choose between the art of representing a person's life accurately, which would lead them to produce a biography, or creating a living and breathing character, which would lead them to produce a work of fiction. Blending the two in the form of the biographical novel is not an option. Given this claim, Woolf would say that your novel *Wintering* is a failure. How would you respond to this?

Moses: I don't entirely agree with Woolf. In that essay she talks about the rise of biography, and since 1939 biographers have expanded what a biography could be, just as they've expanded what fiction can be. Woolf did so herself. Individual writers' works have widened the boundaries of how fact and fiction can come together in the writing about a real person. At the same time I think that writers have to be clear from the start: Are they writing biographical fiction or are they using a real character in order to write a fiction that is doing something else entirely, is about something other than their human subject—say, Michael Ondaatje's use of Count Lazlo Almasy in *The English Patient*? I can't imagine Ondaatje ever claiming his novel to be biographical, and anyone who read it so would be wrongheaded. I never thought of *Wintering* as biographical fiction but thinking about your questions and how Woolf defines biography, my book is a biographical fiction in that it is scrupulous about the facts of Plath's life. Where I have imagined Plath's life it is still tied to the realism of the facts, their existential truth and significance, so that conversations and interior life are imagined, but I haven't tried to make a story that veers away from the facts of her life. In that way I was lucky. The facts of Plath's life in the moment that *Wintering* occurs, two weeks in December of 1962, are themselves an amazing story to tell. That story was revealed to me not only by the manuscript of *Ariel* but also through Hughes's poems about Plath, *The Birthday Letters*. When I looked at *Ariel* versus some of the poems in *The Birthday Letters*, I realized that there was a pivotal moment for Plath that occurred as she was completing the assembly of *Ariel*, and that was the pivot on which her sense of hope shifted to a sense of hopelessness.

Lackey: I'm trying to combine two questions here. It seems to me that Woolf could not see her way towards the biographical novel. Something in her way of thinking about literature prevented her from combining fact and fiction in the form of the biographical novel. Something happened in the way people understand literature today that enabled them to see their way towards this genre of fiction, and the year 1999 is a decisive turning point because two novels were nominated for the Pulitzer: Banks' *Cloudsplitter* and Michael Cunningham's *The Hours*, and Cunningham's novel won the prize. Can you explain what changed in our understanding of literature to make the biographical novel possible and can you explain what has changed in the literary establishment that has made it now recognize this art form?

Moses: The publishing industry runs with what is successful. Without putting a judgment on that, the publishing industry was good at seeing that *The Hours* and *Cloudsplitter* were really successful novels, so that made it more likely they would publish similar novels with the hope that those books too would become popular and successful. Writers realize that the moment seems to be right for publishing this kind of work. Literary trends are always in flux and I'm not sure that there's any magic in it. I think a lot of publishing is about what worked yesterday and what we thus hope will work tomorrow.

Lackey: Biographical novelists usually have two separate focuses and approaches. For instance, in *Blonde*, Joyce Carol Oates uses the life of Marilyn Monroe in order to examine the dysfunctional American culture of the 1950s and 1960s, while in *Lost Son*, Mark Allen Cunningham focuses on the inner life of Rainer Maria Rilke in order to illuminate the poet's work. Is *Wintering* more in the Oates tradition in that it uses Plath and her works to illuminate a key cultural moment in history? Or, is it more in the Cunningham tradition in that it focuses on Plath's inner life in order to illuminate the poet and her work?

Moses: It's much more like Cunningham's *Lost Son*. I see *Wintering* as a novel about the creative process, Plath's creative process in particular, but it's very much about the creative process and an artist's relationship to her work. Not only an artist's experience of her work in the moment, it is also about how a work of art and its creation change the artist, and about anticipating the work's life beyond its creation. So I definitely think that *Wintering* is much more about illuminating Plath from the inside and through her relationship to her own art. At the same time *Ariel* is a work of art in its historical moment and Plath in the early 1960s, when she was rejecting a dominant patriarchal culture that she had been struggling with for all of her adult life. With the writing of *Ariel* she was throwing it off with violence and confidence and disdain. In order to show that accurately I had to take the historical moment into consideration, as Oates did, and show Plath as a woman, as an artist, as a single mother in 1962 in her cultural milieu. It was essential that you understand Sylvia Plath as an American woman at thirty, as a single mother in London in 1962, in order to understand why she made the choices she did, and why she felt what she seemed to feel as expressed in the poems and her letters.

Lackey: As a scholar of Holocaust literature, I have often wondered how the references to the Nazis and the Jews function in Plath's poems "Lady Lazarus" and "Daddy." In your novel, the relationship with Assia, the woman with whom Hughes had an affair, offers a potential explanation of one of Plath's potential sources for such references. Can you discuss how your novel provides some insight into the origin and content of "Lady Lazarus" and "Daddy"?

Moses: As we see in her journals, Plath was a great mythologizer of her own life from the time she was a teenager. You can see her creating personas for herself, trying on different garments of self. In her poetic work she created a personal mythology and attached herself to various kinds of archetypes. She was a follower of Robert Graves' *The White Goddess*, which figures prominently in the *Ariel* imagery and the way she put the manuscript together. And Plath was very aware of her cultural heritage as a child of German immigrants who were educated and striving for the American dream. She was born in 1932 just prior to World War Two, so she was coming to awareness as a little girl as the war was breaking out. There was a lot of negative sentiment towards Germans in the US at the time. Based on letters and memoir writings by her mother, Plath's family attracted some negative responses. She also was acutely aware that when her father died in 1940, he left the family essentially destitute. She went from having this very comfortable life, living along the beach with a mother at home and grandparents nearby and her father a noted professor of German and biology—an expert on bees—at Boston University, to having to sell her house, move inland, and combine households with her grandparents so her mother could work full time to support the whole family. In consequence Plath became an overachieving "scholarship girl." When she went to Smith College, scholarship students had to live in designated housing and they actually had to do service for the students not on scholarship, so class and cultural distinctions were magnified. Plath felt both victimized and guilty for her resentment: She was German and an American but a member of the underclass. She was a brilliant student but achieved academically to prove her worth. Part of that complex psychology is expressed in poems like "Lady Lazarus" and "Daddy." "Lady Lazarus," of course, alludes to the Biblical Lazarus's resurrection after death. Plath recast the story as a myth of herself almost drowning as a child, then attempting suicide at twenty, then rising from the death of her marriage: "I have done it again./One year in every ten/I manage it--". But the early drowning incident didn't happen to Plath—it happened to her brother.

She appropriated it as part of her own myth because she was self-dramatizing and the symbolism worked for the poem. In the same way, when Hughes left in the summer of 1962 and was having an affair with a German Holocaust survivor, Assia Wevill, all this rich archetypal mythological imagery was there for the taking. She could cast herself as a victim of her "daddy" and his replacement, a big brutish man dressed in black with a "Meinkampf" demeanor, and she could even utilize Assia's name, which rhymes with "ash"—the poking and the stirring of ash in "Lady Lazarus" refers to Plath's budding friendship with Wevill, who apparently expressed pointed curiosity about the Hughes-Plath marriage before embarking on an affair with Hughes. There are Plath scholars who make an argument for her political awareness and activity, and she was politically progressive, but I don't think she thought in terms of politics when using Holocaust imagery as a non-Jew. She was using it because it worked for the individual poems.

Lackey: Do you get the sense that she was reading a lot of the newspapers at the time? The Adolf Eichmann trial was going on during the early sixties. Was she thinking about the Holocaust and all the issues that the Eichmann trial raised?

Moses: She was very politically aware, she was a reader of newspapers, she took part in demonstrations against various cold war events that were happening during her adult life, so she was alert to what was going on. But did she write "Thalidomide" because of the politics of a drug that stopped miscarriage but induced birth defects? I don't think so. I think she wrote the poem because it worked to render her poetic ideas about victimhood and disfigurement of self. Everything was fodder for her. I don't believe she was using these kinds of tropes politically. She was using them as an artist. She was using them for their emotional charge as art.

Lackey: You mention that you work more in the Mark Allen Cunningham tradition by focusing on the development of the artistic process. Let's say, just for the sake of argument, that you wrote a biographical novel more in the *Blonde* tradition, which would focus more on history and political critique. Would you have more politically active moments in the novel? For instance, would you have your Plath go to one of these protests? And if you would have had this different focus, how would you have changed the novel? I'm trying to get you to imagine how it would be different so that we can see how these two different traditions of the biographical novel function.

Moses: If I had been writing more of a biographical novel of Sylvia Plath in her historical moment I would not have written from such a close internalized perspective and I would have had more scenes of her out in the world and engaging with other people, engaging with the events of her time. But really, that's one of the reasons that I was glad to focus on her interior life. Given how recent Plath's life was and how many people are still alive who knew her, I really didn't want to venture into the territory of creating fictions out of real experiences that other people were a part of. That goes back to your question about responsibility and what you feel is acceptable to change fictionally and what is off limits. For me it was off limits to involve living people. I know this is veering into a different sort of answer but I hope that's okay. Frieda was a toddler and Plath's son Nicholas was a baby when their mother died, and they were essential to my telling the story of Plath in that moment of her life. She was living fully in the experience of being the mother of young children as well as being a poet who was getting up at four a.m. to write, because otherwise her kids would be awake and needing her full attention. So I had to deal with the fact that the children were necessary to this story but that they are living people, or were at the time when I wrote it. Nicholas has since died. I did not want to appropriate their life experiences, or potentially their memories, and I didn't want to appropriate the experiences of anyone else who was alive who'd known Plath. That was imperative to me as a point of integrity as a human being, beyond being an artist. So I purposely didn't include real people in the novel who were still alive except for Frieda and Nicholas. The way I got around what I felt would be an unfair appropriation of their lives was that all of the depictions of children are taken from my own children and my own experience of motherhood—with my children's permission! Though there are all sorts of wonderful details about Plath's children from her perspective, her letters and journal entries about things her children did, my feeling was, that's all they have left. They can't hold on to anything else from their mother except those letters and whatever stories have been told to them. I couldn't take that from them. It would be so wrong, and I could never have done that. In terms of adults who knew her at the time, I also felt that I didn't want to infringe on their realities and their memories. At the same time, I didn't want their realities to infringe on the fiction I needed to create to tell the story of the real Plath as truthfully as I could.

Lackey: There's been a shift in recent years in our understanding of depression, that it's more biological and chemical. At times, your novel suggests that this is potentially what led to Plath's depression. This is a new way of understanding depression, but it challenges one of the traditional ways of reading Plath. The traditional view is that a dysfunctional patriarchal society contributed significantly to Plath's depression. Does the new approach to depression minimize Plath's critique of patriarchy in works like

Ariel? And can you talk about your approach to Plath in light of these new categories for explaining depression?

Moses: I wouldn't say that this new way of thinking about depression minimizes her critique of the patriarchy. In fact, what we now know about depression and biochemistry actually make her ability to so precisely articulate her feelings about this even more amazing and astonishing. While I was working on *Wintering*, the newly edited Plath journals were just coming out. That was early 1990 and I was eagerly interested in those journals and what they might reveal about Plath. What I found was that a lot of the material that had been cut from the earlier published journals suggested that she suffered not just from clinical depression, but, possibly from other forms of mental illness. There are suggestions that she was bipolar. I did more research and interviewed doctors and I found that Plath had probably been suffering from what her own doctor thought was an extreme form of premenstrual syndrome, called premenstrual tension at the time and which we now know as premenstrual dysphoric disorder, or PMDD. We know that Plath's doctor was trying desperately to get her into a hospital at the end of her life and had prescribed antidepressants to tide her over until she could see a specialist and be hospitalized. In Plath's last letter to her mother she said, "I'm going to see a doctor, a woman doctor recommended to me by my beloved Dr. Horder in a few days." The day of her appointment was Monday February 11, 1963. Plath killed herself earlier that morning. It turns out that the appointment she had was with a doctor named Katharina Dalton, who was a colleague of John Horder, Plath's general practitioner. Dalton was a respected physician and researcher in women's health in London. She was the only doctor in the world in 1962 whose practice and research were devoted to helping women with this disorder. PMDD is basically a psychotic form of PMS and has very specific symptoms. Patients with PMDD are more likely to be bipolar and/or more likely to suffer from depression. I contacted Dalton and she confirmed that Plath had been referred to her by Horder, and she was supposed to see Plath on the morning of her death. Hughes's sister Olwyn confirmed that she understood from Hughes that Plath had very clear cyclical physical indications of this disorder, but as Olwyn Hughes said, "we always just thought she was crazy, just a difficult person." But Plath was actually suffering from a really serious biochemical imbalance. After Plath's death, her mother revealed that she knew relatives had suffered from depression in her husband's family, but she decided not to tell her daughter for fear it would be a burden. So through her whole life, Sylvia Plath never understood that she had a family tendency to serious depression and possibly bipolar disorder, and that her frequent illnesses and mood swings might be caused by a reproductive disorder. She thought she had a personality flaw, a weakness of character.

Lackey: Is it possible that she also thought her depression was a consequence of living in a patriarchal society?

Moses: Yes, exactly. She thought it was all either her fault or it was her external situation, and her job was to muscle through it.

Lackey: But aren't the *Ariel* poems primarily exposing the oppressive structures of patriarchy?

Moses: Absolutely. Not only was she railing against the patriarchy in the poems, but the imagery was unknowingly connecting to her biochemical problems. There are recurring images of being victimized by the moon, as in the poem "The Moon and the Yew Tree," being stuck in the vice-like branches of this tree. She'd been writing about these kinds of oppressive forces since she was a teenager, about being victimized by what we know as archetypal symbols of female chemistry and biochemistry. So she was both actively dealing with her resistance to a dominant patriarchal oppression and she was subconsciously drawing on imagery that reinforced the ideas that she was consciously articulating. What she didn't know was that there was a connection.

Lackey: To conclude, can you talk about some biographical novels that you consider outstanding? And can you explain why you think them outstanding?

Moses: I think first of Edmund White's *Hotel de Dream* about Stephen Crane. One of the reasons I love that book and pick it out in particular is because of the fictional Crane's reaction to the work that he is creating within the novel. It is a story within a story, and Crane is writing a fictional story about this young male prostitute who is iconic in his beauty. At one point the fictional Crane says, "I don't know any longer if the real boy is truly who he was or if my version of him has become my reality." The fictional Crane's artistic version has overtaken the real. I think that expresses a lot about what we're doing with biographical novels. Taking a real person and trying to create a version of them that is not necessarily idealized but comes to life in this full way. When you think from the biographical perspective, a fictional version can't possibly be who the real person really was. My own feeling is that it's impossible to actually capture any human being in their fullness. We are way too complicated. In nonfiction or fiction, we can't possibly fully capture any individual. The best we can do is capture facets of them that are so illuminated that they feel real and fitting and make a reader feel, "yes that must be what that boy was like to Crane, and that must be what Crane was like." The fictional boy prostitute is no more the real boy than the fictional Crane is the real Crane—but can we believe in them, as readers or as writers? If we can, if we do, I think we have succeeded as well as anyone could in writing about the experience of being human.

12

Enhanced Symbolic Interiors in the Biographical Novel

Joyce Carol Oates

Lackey: Let me start by telling you about this project. I'm trying to figure out why, starting in the 1980s, so many prominent writers began to author biographical novels. I'm also trying to define the nature of this genre of fiction. Since the year 2000 you have become increasingly more interested in biographical fiction as you have written creative works about figures such as Edgar Allen Poe, Emily Dickinson, Mark Twain, Robert Frost, and Ernest Hemingway. Can you explain what motivated you to start writing this kind of fiction?

Oates: In terms of *Blonde*, I remember seeing a photograph of Norma Jeane Baker when she was about sixteen years old. I wasn't even sure when I saw the photograph that I knew who it was and then the caption of course said "Norma Jeane Baker." I was so struck by the fact that this girl was in high school at the time. She reminded me of many girls I'd gone to school with and she wasn't particularly glamorous. This made me think about the extraordinary metamorphosis that would transform an anonymous, unknown girl in a short time into this icon, this blonde goddess Marilyn Monroe. The idea came to me in a flash, that I'd like to write a novella, a postmodern treatment of this phenomenon of how a person loses her specific identity, becomes a cultural icon or artifact and loses her soul and identity. I had planned it to be quite postmodernist, an experimental narrative moving very swiftly through the years and ending with her being given her name. So the last line of the novella would be "Marilyn Monroe" with quotes around it.

Lackey: Was that the first time you authored biographical fiction?

Oates: Is there a difference between biographical fiction and fiction that just has historical figures in it? Because I had Mark Twain just briefly in a novel called *A Bloodsmoor Romance*.

Lackey: Biographical novels usually center the novel within the consciousness of a particular character, who is named after a historical figure like Twain, Marilyn Monroe, or Ted Kennedy.

Oates: I hadn't done that before. I didn't think at all of *Black Water* as biographical fiction. It is more like a ballad or an allegory, the elf knight riding in the forest. I wasn't thinking much of Ted Kennedy specifically. This is a very different sort of person, so I wasn't thinking at all that was biographical fiction.

Lackey: The standard view is that a work like *Black Water* would be considered a historical novel because you decided to change the name from Ted Kennedy to The Senator, which gives the character a more symbolic or allegorical significance. Changing the character's name and significant dates gives you more freedom, whereas in the biographical novel the character is named after the original figure, which supposedly limits the author's freedom. A lot of people are asking the question: "Why are so many prominent writers doing this kind of fiction now?" In the past, as is the case with Robert Penn Warren's *All the King's Men*, authors would change the name from Huey Long to Willie Stark. But they are not doing that as much anymore.

Oates: I've read and admired Gore Vidal's *Lincoln*, which is a deftly executed historical novel.

Lackey: That's right. And he also did *Burr*.

Oates: It never really seemed to me that unusual. There must have been many books about Lincoln, both fiction and nonfiction. I haven't read them. As for *Blonde*, I wasn't thinking about the biographical novel. I was thinking about the phenomenon of how the ordinary person grew, loses her name Norma Jeane Baker and becomes Marilyn Monroe. But then, when I got to about page 180, when she's about twenty, it just seemed really exciting to me that I would continue writing through her whole life. So ultimately, the novel is about Marilyn Monroe as she becomes more and more Marilyn Monroe. At first, she's always Norma Jeane. Then there's a certain point in the novel when she starts to be called "Marilyn" and a point when nobody remembers Norma Jeane and she's forgotten Norma Jeane herself. That's what interested me very much, to write about celebrity and fame. I didn't set out to write about Marilyn Monroe. It was more that I'd seen this photograph. I could have written about somebody else if anybody else had had quite that trajectory. You couldn't write about a fictitious person and get the same sort of resonance. Without specifying the name, it wouldn't mean anything. Willie Stark, is that his name?

Lackey: That's right, Willie Stark, who is based on Huey Long.

Oates: The name doesn't mean anything at all, but writing about Huey Long has a real charge, especially decades ago. Let's say you were writing about Shakespeare and inventing a kind of life for him, you'd be writing about Shakespeare as the phenomenon and the historical figure. And so why other people are doing this I don't know.

Lackey: There have been biographical novels, but not many until recently. Arna Bontemps did one in 1936 on Gabriel Prosser called *Black Thunder*, and Zora Neale Hurston did one on Moses in 1939. But before Styron's book about Nat Turner there are very few notable biographical novels. After *The Confessions of Nat Turner*, many prominent writers started authoring biographical novels. In 1968 Styron won the Pulitzer for *The Confessions of Nat Turner*, but in the Pulitzer's jury report, *The Confessions* is characterized as a historical novel. This is interesting because I don't think the committee had a category for making sense of the biographical novel at this time. The year 1999 is of crucial importance, because two were up for the Pulitzer: Michael Cunningham's *The Hours* and Russell Banks' *Cloudsplitter*. To my mind, something happened in the late nineties that made the literary establishment recognize this genre of fiction as legitimate.

Oates: I thought of *Blonde* as a historical novel. It's not that I really thought in these terms at all. It's basically just writing a novel.

Lackey: But when you say you thought of it as a historical novel, what does that mean? What does it disclose to us about history?

Oates: To me a historical novel is something I have to do a fair amount of research for because it may take place before I was born, before I knew anything. It inhabits a world that for me is history. It could be the year 1100 but you have to do research. Whether it's 1949 or 1970, we have to do research. We can't just start writing and remember and put things in. You actually have to go and do some real research. So to me that constitutes a historical novel.

Lackey: Shifting to another question, your character Henry James vows that no biographer would ever be able to plumb the depths of his secret and subterranean soul. Ironically as a novelist, James spent his career refining the technique of accessing the deepest levels of human interiors. What James could not have anticipated was the rise of biographical fiction, specifically biographical fiction about him. What is it that a writer of biographical fiction can give writers that a traditional biographer could not?

Oates: Novelists can speculate and be imaginative. I think of myself as an experimental and postmodern writer, so I can do things with the imagination that James would not have allowed, things that are mythic or parodistic. James was a psychological realist. He had a very rich concept of consciousness that is curiously devoid of the domestic, sensuous, or literal. He seems not to have much of a visual imagination. If you contrast him with somebody who has a strong visual consciousness like Vladimir Nabokov or D. H. Lawrence, there's a profound difference. Virginia Woolf doesn't have much of a visual consciousness either. It's all a shimmer of thought impressions and people don't actually have bodies. For instance, in *The Wings of the Dove* it is mentioned that Milly Theale has red hair. That's about it in this huge, long densely layered novel. You don't know what anybody looks like. All we get are reflections. It's a curious way of looking at life as only thought impressions rather than sense impressions. It's really quite extraordinary what he's trying to do. I thought of *Blonde* as a mythic novel. She's like Moby Dick. She's this figure that people all project onto and have different thoughts about.

Lackey: You mention your postmodern inclinations. Some argue that postmodernism made the biographical novel possible. The argument goes like this: We used to think there was a clear division between history and fiction, between reality and literature, but postmodernists argue that fact is already saturated with fiction. Given the blending of fact and fiction in postmodernism, many contemporary writers say to the historians: "You are not giving me anything that is *non*fiction even though you pretend that it is history and that it is somehow above or outside fiction." Would you say that postmodernism has contributed to the rise of the biographical novel?

Oates: Things start to shift and the bedrock of realism shifts. For instance, in the nineteenth century a reputable portraitist would paint a slightly flattering picture of a subject. It would be completely recognizable, very beautiful. Then something starts to shift and we have the work of Picasso and later in the twentieth century Francis Bacon and many others. They paint portraits of say, Gertrude Stein, but the portraits now are not at all real, not realistic. They have a glimmer of psychological realism. The one of Gertrude Stein is probably the most famous of these iconoclastic, experimental portraits. *Reputedly*, she said she didn't look like that, and Picasso said, "you will look like that." Francis Bacon has his "Screaming Pope" and portraits of his friends. He does portraits of people but in ways that are very disturbing and very private.

Lackey: Would you say that these artists are accessing a different kind of truth?

Oates: It's more a universal truth. When I write about Norma Jeane Baker I'm writing about a lot of people, even men. I'm writing about the biographical subject and smudging it a little to suggest that if you look in that mirror of Marilyn Monroe you will see something like yourself. Rather than her being this unique historical figure all by herself, I sense that there is a bond between us. And as I said before I felt drawn to write about her because she looked so much like girls I had gone to school with and even a little bit like my mother, a certain kind of girl in the 1920s or 1930s in America. She wasn't an "okie," but somebody like an "okie," a displaced American person who doesn't have any roots, who is washed up in California. The continent has shifted and she finds herself there. Monroe stands in stark contrast to someone like Elizabeth Taylor, who is more aristocratic.

Lackey: And the reason why so many men felt free to abuse Monroe was because of her background. They could manipulate and mold her and use her for their own particular purposes.

Oates: Yes, that is true, but she also manipulated and used people. She was one of these irresistibly wounded, infantile women that men are drawn to. They think maybe they might victimize them but then they end up like Arthur Miller and others being pretty much debilitated themselves. It is like being drawn to this beautiful flame, where the moth is drawn to the flame. Some men I'm sure did victimize her, but she also had power, a lot of power. And people like that who are borderline personalities are very deeply narcissistic and wounded. They can really hurt other people tremendously, which I think she did.

Lackey: Some prominent writers have either rejected or condemned the biographical novel. For instance, Virginia Woolf argued in a 1939 essay that the novelist is free to create while the biographer is tied to facts. For Woolf, writers have to choose between the art of representing a person's life accurately, which would lead them to produce a biography, or creating a living, breathing character, which would lead them to produce a work of fiction. Blending the two in the form of the biographical novel is not an option. Given this claim Woolf would say that your novel *Blonde* is a failure. How would you respond to this?

Oates: I just think that's silly. Virginia Woolf had so many misguided and foolish ideas about James Joyce, D. H. Lawrence, Arnold Bennett, and Katherine Mansfield. She thought that *Ulysses* was a failure; she never wrote anything approaching *Ulysses*. She's basically someone who was limited herself and when she saw what Joyce was doing, it is just so overwhelming and brilliant and way beyond anything she could think of, she just had to pronounce it a failure. I don't think that's important at all. But if you look at a novel that's very iconoclastic and experimental like *The Public Burning*, which is supposedly about Nixon and the Rosenbergs, you know that there is no way that that is a biography of Nixon or in fact the Rosenbergs. If Virginia Woolf read a novel like that she would not have been able to comprehend it because she lived at a different time. And I think that was her problem when trying to comprehend Lawrence and Joyce; she seemed to be in the vanguard of new techniques, but I don't think she was anywhere near the level of Joyce. She was basically trapped in her time.

Lackey: But that's the key to the question, isn't it? What was it about her time that made her incapable of imagining the biographical novel?

Oates: I have no idea. Shakespeare was writing great plays and using history and using historical figures and they certainly knew about Shakespeare. I have no idea why it was so limited. I think it was just her. She had very catty and nasty things to say about Katherine Mansfield who in many ways is a better writer than she is. Virginia Woolf couldn't begin to do the sorts of things that Katherine Mansfield did, let alone Lawrence. I don't particularly like her fiction. It is very over-rated I think. She's a great writer, but I think she is very over-rated.

Lackey: Your most recent novel is *The Accursed*, and it engages history.

Oates: Yes, it has lots of historical figures. Woodrow Wilson and Upton Sinclair are the main characters, one twenty-six years old and the other about forty-nine. But I wasn't thinking in terms of biography or history when I wrote that novel. It was more a postmodernist look at America. I was living in Princeton at the time and looking at the place I was living in 100 years ago. I don't really know why writers do what they do and I think most people don't really know the reason. Evolutionary psychology teaches us that people's motives are very obscure. People make war in other countries with the pretense of religion or democracy. But it is basically this Darwinian land-grab. They want the land, the fertile soil, and the waterways, but people never say that. In talking about literature, and that may include Virginia Woolf, they say things that sound plausible or maybe even impressive. But the real reasons that they are saying them may be different. And I think that Virginia Woolf is extremely anxious and envious. She even said something about James Joyce, that it is impossible for a living writer to judge another because it's too raw. That is a wonderful quote. She conceded finally that she couldn't really even read *Ulysses*. She was so put off by what she called the "soiled linen" and his schoolboy vulgarity. She looks down from a higher economic class, just basically not able to see that was a great work of art. Like somebody walking around an enormous mountain who just sees defects in this part of the mountain and just goes on. But I think that's true for most writers. So when I try to answer honestly, I say, "I don't think I really had a motive." I saw an opportunity.

Lackey: A number of the writers I have interviewed say that biographical novelists are unique because they can access and represent an undocumentable interior. According to this view, historians give us mainly externals, the facts. But the biographical novelist can access the motives and sometimes the subconscious. These writers say that they know the story, the external frame of the historical period, but their goal is to access and represent the motives. You as a writer might not be able to access what you are actually trying to do, but is it true that you're trying to get to the interiors of your characters? That you're trying to access them?

Oates: I suppose so, but the characters are fictitious. Trying to get to the inner self of a fictitious character is somewhat paradoxical. The effort of writing any kind of art is something that precludes explanation. I think there are poems of great exquisite beauty that are musical and profound but they can't be paraphrased. You can paraphrase most of Emily Dickinson's poetry, but that doesn't begin to approach it. I feel that I'm trying to express the mystery and the opacity of life. There are certain junctures in *Blonde* that are very raw and bleeding, like something has been broken and the marrow is exposed. Now Monroe is this blonde actress who slowly becomes this archetypal figure, and she wanders into a drugstore because she can't sleep, and she sees these Hollywood magazines. She sees her own picture on the cover and it's a beautiful picture. She is very made up and she's in some fancy dress and the real person standing there, the so-called "real" Marilyn Monroe—here is the image of what she is going to become. What would it be like to be on the eve of your death and you see how you're going to be remembered by posterity. And it's so far from being you. To me that was a poignant moment of great tragedy, but not really expressible in any other terms except as I'm telling you right now. So if the reader's reading that, the reader would have a certain feeling. But I'm not sure that it can be expressed in any other way.

Lackey: I want to discuss one of the approaches a number of biographical novelists use. Marilyn Monroe is an ideal subject for a biographical novel because she does in film what you do in the novel. Let me clarify what I mean. In *Niagara* Monroe plays the character Rose Loomis, and in order to access that character's interiority your Monroe surmises that Rose had a dark secret which in part explains some of the character's behavior. Is this a fictional scene or is this something that Monroe actually did?

Oates: That is fiction.

Lackey: When your Monroe specifies the nature of the secret, that Rose put a baby in a drawer which led to the baby's death, are we supposed to think that she intuits correctly? Or are we supposed to see this as a hypothetical that could serve to illuminate something about Rose's character?

Oates: She is working with an instinctive actress's approach to what she is doing. Monroe had actually been put in a drawer by her crazy mother, and she herself was nearly killed by her mother who was schizophrenic. Now I don't know *literally* in real life if any of this happened, but it might have happened. It is very plausible that that would have happened. It was very thrilling to go through the movies that I saw of Marilyn Monroe that are detailed in the novel and to look at the movie from the point of view of Norma Jeane, from the point of view of posterity. It was like seeing her from some vantage point in the future. She is dead and she is a posthumous voice narrating the movie of her own life.

Lackey: Anita Diamant uses what I think is a similar approach to the material as you in her novel *The Red Tent*. She bases her novel on the story of Dinah's rape from the Old Testament. In my interview with her, she said, if you read the Old Testament story closely and carefully, it doesn't sound like a rape, and the reason why is that the father offers a huge dowry because his son wants so badly to marry Dinah. In fact, the son loved Dinah so much that the father agreed to have the whole tribe circumcised in order to win this woman's love. Anita said she spent hours laboring over the logic of that story. She was concerned with the logic of character, culture, and history, and she ultimately concluded that the Old Testament story of a rape didn't make sense. My whole life I have been given one story about Marilyn Monroe, which is that she was a mindless bimbo, a dumb blonde. But you have given me a very different Marilyn Monroe. I wonder if this is what a lot of biographical novelists do. You all have a keen sense of character and story. Therefore, you can give us new access to history and culture, because you have a unique gift. It's not some sort of mystical, magical intellectual capacity. Rather, it is a hypersensitive awareness to the way character, story, culture, and history function. Is this what many good biographical novelists do?

Oates: That might be the case. Biographies have different interpretations of the same character. For instance, Jay Parini wrote a very positive biography about Robert Frost after Lawrence Thompson published his, which is very negative. And then Jeffrey Meyers has another biography following Jay Parini, which is in the middle. He's unsparingly critical, but he's sympathetic and forgiving. So it's like the three Robert Frosts you know. Frost would have liked Jay Parini's, and he would have been very upset at Lawrence

Thompson's biography. It's basically that Robert Frost is seen doing the same things in all three books but the biographer has put a different light on it. One book is doing it for one reason, another biography is doing it for a malicious, selfish reason, and another biography, Jeffrey Meyers', is doing it because he's deeply unhappy and he can't help himself. So there isn't any sense that there is a fixed personality anywhere.

Lackey: So we could say it's all up for grabs. But the other possibility is that some of these biographies are just wrong.

Oates: Yes, they could be wrong. Or they weighed too much in one direction. That's true. I recently wrote a story about Robert Frost. It is an imagined interview with Frost, and it basically becomes clear that the interviewer is accusatory of Frost. She starts off flattering and fawning, but then she gets more and more personal, interrogating him, and finally accusing him. You realize that she's a fiction of his imagination. He is punishing himself with this sort of self laceration. But he says at the end, "all these things may be true, but I'm a poet and my work is going to endure." He doesn't say it like that but the idea is that even though he's this contemptible person who did all these awful things, which he acknowledges, the fact is that he managed to write some poems that are beautiful and strong and are going to endure, and so the whole thing is justified by that. I didn't really know that I would come to that conclusion but maybe that's the basic bedrock of art. That Shakespeare or Milton or Chaucer and all these people worked out of different motives but what remains ultimately is that they were able to extract something great from their personal selves with all their failings and sorrow and tragedy. These works that are permanent, permanent as long as the language is permanent.

Lackey: So would you say that what leads you to write about certain people is not that you have a particular take on them but that there is some sort of mystery about them?

Oates: Yes, some sort of mystery. The most recent thing that I wrote is inspired by the Tawana Brawley case. But I don't use her name. A character who functions as Reverend Al Sharpton appears in the novel, but this character *is not Al Sharpton* in fact. So the historical individuals are not in the novel. Rather, their historical roles are the subject of the novel. I am very interested in events in our culture, and not much interested in the minutiae of individuals, which is the stuff of tabloids. I am interested in those events that have symbolic, ideally universal significance. This is a good example of changing the name because I wanted to change many things about it and work with different voices. This work becomes a dialogue about race, the confusions and blindness of race, and people seeing their own faces and things that are very subjective. But with that, it never would have interested me to write about Tawana Brawley or Al Sharpton. I'm interested in the symbolic possibilities of people who are *like* them. But my characters are more interesting, elastic and subtle than the real people. From my research, I discovered that these people were not nearly as nuanced or subtle as my fictitious characters. I don't know what the real Marilyn was like, but I don't think it is such a stretch to imagine a very poetic, sensitive, serious and earnest person. She writes little things in my novel, and in real life she did some writing. It wasn't very good. I have seen her writings and I didn't use most of it in the novel. I used maybe one line but I always enhance characters and make them a little more than they might have been in real life because I think that's what art is. King Lear may be a senile old man but he speaks so beautifully, and that's an enhancement of life.

Lackey: I interviewed Russell Banks, who wrote the biographical novel *Cloudsplitter*, and he deals with race in a similar way to what you're describing. His novel is narrated by John Brown's son Owen, and when doing the research for that novel, Russell discovered that, while everyone agreed about the facts of John Brown's life, there were two radically different interpretations of the man. From the perspective of many blacks, Brown is a hero and a saint, but from the perspective of many whites, he is a madman and a criminal. Russell realized that there is something problematic about taking an authoritative stance as is frequently done in biographies. So in *Cloudsplitter* he represents what happened, but he resists the impulse to take an authoritative stance in his fiction. Your task in *Blonde* is different because Monroe has so consistently been characterized as a mindless blonde. You obviously didn't want to make her such a mindless character, as you made her rich and complex. There are two possibilities here. First, art uses an historical event or character to make something much richer, as Lear becomes much more interesting than a senile old man. Second, art can revise our understanding of a biographical figure or a historical event, so your Marilyn Monroe is much richer and more complex than she is generally portrayed within the culture. Was one of your objectives to recover in part a more authentic and complex Monroe?

Oates: Yes, I felt that she was really a good actress. I thought that she was really like a genius. I thought she was much more sensitive and more thoughtful than she has been portrayed, much more playful, alive, and complex. She was always considered a "B" actress and everyone kind of condescended to her. Elizabeth Taylor was on this completely different plateau and Marilyn Monroe never even made much money compared to some of these other actresses. She was also very serious. She was always taking lessons, acting lessons, dance lessons, and other kinds of lessons. She was always trying to improve herself. When the actors were having lessons, acting class, she's the one who shows up in a crisply ironed white blouse and a skirt and they're all wearing jeans, and I think that was actually true. Many of these details are true. Many things I made up because they seemed plausible and insightful, but some things are actually real. She had many love affairs and abortions. I only deal with one of those abortions in *Blonde*. She was obviously a person of some compulsiveness and she had an addict's personality, much more than I gave her. She lived without thinking about the future. She was addicted to barbiturates and she was addicted to other things. She was a desperate person. I made her more an artist, because I think of her as an artist.

Lackey: But you charted very slowly and patiently how she moved towards addiction. At first, she is opposed to drugs, but she is slowly immersed into the Hollywood and drug culture.

Oates: The directors and movie people gave her drugs. The doctors injected her with amphetamines and barbiturates. You and I both teach in university departments. Suppose your English chair calls you in and says, "now it's time for your amphetamine shot." You have the choice of saying "no" and then you get fired or you take the shot and gradually you get addicted to it.

Lackey: Russell made a similar point in my interview with him. He said that when he's writing about something in the past, he is also writing about the present.

Oates: Oh yes, that's true.

Lackey: In the case of *Blonde*, the drug culture that we see in Hollywood is now painfully more apparent with so many young people dying.

Oates: That's right.

Lackey: And what is very useful in your novel is that you give us a way of understanding the dysfunctional psychology at work within this culture.

Oates: Yes.

Lackey: Did you feel yourself trying to lay out the nature of that dysfunctional psychology?

Oates: Oh yes. I wrote another novel about this idea, which is called *My Sister, My Love*. It is based on the JonBenét Ramsey case. I particularly look at the use of drugs given to children, like child athletes, and in this case a little girl figure skater. But there I changed the name and the family is different. But many things are different. My focus was on the exploitation of a child in *real* life and also in the novel.

Lackey: In *Blonde* you include a character that you refer to as "the Sharpshooter" and this character is very fascinating but also eerie. How does this character function? Is it an allegorical figure? And your narrator also makes the comment that this character does not know how to interpret. It's not that the character puts up false interpretations but that the character just doesn't know how to interpret.

Oates: One interpretation might be seeing the novel as a postmodernist, posthumous movie about Norma Jeane's life and Norma Jeane is watching her own movie and narrating it and she's going to die. So she invents this character the Sharpshooter who's going to come kill her at the same time that she's going to kill herself. It could be a postmodernist, posthumous movie that she's telling herself, and that she's created the Sharpshooter. Some people thought, and still think, that Marilyn Monroe had been killed, so this is a way of giving a dramatic form to that interpretation.

Lackey: The Kennedy family takes a big hit in your fiction as in *Black Water* as well as *Blonde*. Why is this?

Oates: I see them more as allegorical figures. I refer to JFK as The President. He did use Marilyn Monroe. The President and the Blonde Actress are sort of these figures like big puppets. She was so addicted to drugs at that point and he was such an exploiter of women. I'm sure he was a very nice person to his family and could be very wonderful to his friends, but he exploited people. He's exploiting Marilyn Monroe. The meeting between them is like a cartoon situation. At that point in her life, she left behind her own real life. When she was Norma Jeane, when she had real feelings toward her foster mother, that is one of the tenderer relationships that she has. And there is one of her foster mothers and she is so sorry to leave the woman. But she goes into this world where she's known as the Blonde Actress and people appropriate her, like the athlete Joe DiMaggio, who has seen her picture in the paper and wants to meet her. It's that sort of thing. But actually Joe DiMaggio is ultimately very nice to her. He's the one who paid for her funeral. That's not in the novel because you don't know that until after she dies. Her corpse was in the Los Angeles county morgue for a while because nobody had enough money to pay for a funeral director. But Joe DiMaggio came along and he paid for it and the funeral. He was so angry when all these Hollywood producers and all this scum of Hollywood came to her funeral. He didn't want them to come because he felt that they had killed her. All that I would have liked to have put in the novel, but I couldn't because it's after her death and that was sort of narrated by her.

Lackey: One last question. Of the biographical novels that have been written, can you tell me which ones you think are the best and why?

Oates: I like *Cloudsplitter*. Russell's my good friend.

Lackey: That's an extraordinary one.

Oates: Yes, it's very eloquent. The novels that mean the most to literary people are works of language and the biographical-historical elements are part of that. But it is more about the speech and language. I think that's why people write. If I'm writing a story it's because I'm basically trying to give voice to something that hasn't been said before. So that's why we like it. And Ralph Ellison's *Invisible Man* has wonderful language, this funny, unexpected sense of humor. Styron's *Nat Turner* I haven't read in so long but I would sort of wonder whether it would hold up. People say that the voice of Nat Turner is not very good.

Lackey: A lot of people say that it's just not a believable novel.

Oates: That's what people say, yes. What about Norman Mailer's *Executioner's Song*?

Lackey: That is an interesting choice. That novel won the Pulitzer Prize for fiction, but there was some debate among the members whether it was actually a novel.

Oates: Sometimes when prizes are given by committees, there are connections between the people who win or lose and the jurors. That maybe people don't know about. When I was doing my research into Robert Frost, I found that he won three Pulitzer prizes. The problem is that his very best friend was on the Pulitzer committee. And I wouldn't be surprised if the same thing were true with Norman Mailer and other people who win and people who *don't* win like Stephen Jay Gould. I was on the Pulitzer committee, and Gould was our unanimous choice. But he didn't win. Gould was disliked for political reasons: He was an outspoken Marxist, and his theory of "punctuated evolution" was not the prevailing theory of evolution in some quarters. There could have been no doubt that Gould's book—*Wonderful Life*—deserved the Pulitzer Prize in non-fiction that year, but the Columbia committee, that votes upon the jurors' suggestions, must have been persuaded by someone on the committee who was anti-Gould. No doubt, the bias against Gould's politics was masked as some sort of "aesthetic" disagreement. It is a rare juror who speaks openly and honestly in such circumstances. A much lesser book was given the Pulitzer Prize. So one can look around for theories of what Gould was doing in intellectual theories, but it was really personal animosities that led to the decision. Somebody else got the Pulitzer Prize but there was no reason for that other person to win except that he *wasn't* Gould. So if anyone's trying to draw a conclusion from the person who won in that year it's going to be wrong because there's no conclusion to be drawn. It was a personal dislike of Gould. And that may be the case with fiction, poetry or drama. There are subterranean connections between people and somebody gets a prize for that reason. I'm on many committees, and I certainly see that. It's not that you necessarily give a prize to your best friend, but if you have an enemy, you just don't give it to that person. All these things are sort of shifting but I think maybe generally speaking there's some general theory to be drawn from all this.

Lackey: With regard to the biographical novel, it seems that people lack a vocabulary for articulating what this type of fiction is doing. For instance, a number of people have odd notions about the biographical novel. They say that many contemporary writers are merely summarizing and paraphrasing biographies and then calling their work fiction. They think that biographical novels require less in the way of creativity than what they would call "true fiction."

Oates: It is not so different from what I was saying about the twentieth-century portrait painters. It's much more subjective, a feeling that you're getting an original interior truth that just wasn't displayed before.

13

The Biographical Novel's Practice of Not-Knowing

Lance Olsen

Lackey: As you know, Georg Lukács' *The Historical Novel*, published in the mid-thirties, is considered one of the most insightful and exhaustive studies of the historical novel. In that work, he argues that the biographical form of the novel is doomed to failure because the focus on "the *biography of the hero*" leads authors to overlook or misrepresent significant historical events and truths and thus "reveals the historical weakness of the biographical form of the novel." Given the nature of his critique, he would say that *Nietzsche's Kisses* and *Head in Flames* are not just failures—he would argue that they were doomed to failure from the outset because the very form of the biographical novel is limited and even flawed. How would you respond to Lukács's critique?

Olsen: I would begin by challenging some of Lukács' assumptions. He's working with a set that makes me uncomfortable—the quaint notion, for instance, that there is some kind of transcendental truth; the one that we can easily define what history is; the one that we can easily define what the novel is. Such taken-for-granteds reveal a modernist monologic imagination underway. Part of what *Nietzsche's Kisses* and *Head in Flames* are doing, part of what historical and biographical novels in general are doing, is problematizing precisely those assumptions—problematizing our relationship to "truth," "history," and, ultimately, narrative itself: how we tell ourselves, our past, our cultures, and so on. That is, I might, by way of my critique of Lukács' critique, invoke Mikhail Bakhtin's concept of "unfinalizability." Bakhtin suggests that the first thing we do when we meet another human is to categorize him or her so that we can better understand him or her—which is to say stabilize her or him, which is to say solidify him or her into something she or he isn't. You know: He's a short person, she's a conservative, he's from the Midwest. Bakhtin's claim is that humans are unfinalizable. The more you get to know one, the less you can develop "truths" about him or her, totalizing structures. The only time any of us becomes truly finalizable is when we're dead, when we have no more life before us through which to change, through which to keep the complication called being human active. And so it is, Bakhtin continues, with the novel. Our first instinct when we approach one is to limit it, totalize it, deaden it into a monologic discourse that gives the illusion of containment. But every time we enter the complexity called a novel, the thing before us becomes a different novel because we are always-already different people who are reading it at different times, in different places, in different contexts, through different frameworks. The unfinalizable is the only productive strategy to deploy when discussing biography, history, truth.

Lackey: Given your claims, would you say that it's problematic to even refer to your novels as "biographical novels"?

Olsen: A fruitful way to get into this is to discuss science fiction novels. Some of us read science fiction novels with the assumption they are out to make claims about what the future might look like. We read William Gibson's *Neuromancer* and say: "Oh, he predicted cyberspace accurately, but missed cell phones, and that's a point against him." But science fiction novels are about something else altogether. They are not about predicting the future at all. Just the opposite. They are a continuous lesson about how the future will never be knowable. They teach us again and again that ten minutes from now (let alone tomorrow, or the year 2500) will always be a mystery, always arrive as a shock. That is, what science fiction novels do is problematize our notions of prolepsis, futurity. Historical and biographical novels undertake a similar meta-project with respect to the past and identity. They are not about yesterday and/or selfhood. They are about the problematics of trying to capture the unfinalizability of yesterday and/or selfhood. They are how such spaces are continuously elusive, impossible to capture. If we are paying attention, they draw our attention to something other than what they seem to be drawing our attention to.

Lackey: Putting aside for the moment some of your quibbles with the designation "the biographical novel," can you explain why there has been an explosion of these kind of novels since the 1980s, and can you offer some sort of explanation? Can you explain why you decided to write such a novel with the focus on a particular character like Nietzsche?

Olsen: I'm not so sure the position I'm voicing with respect to "the biographical novel," or, better, perhaps, ~~the biographical novel~~, could be considered "quibbles." I want to suggest a set of problematics much more elemental than that. But I have to confess that, until I talked with you, I didn't realize that there *had* been an explosion of these novels since the 1980s. I've been interested for years in novels having to do with pastness, especially when the idea of pastness itself registers as a difficulty. Linda Hutcheon's term, "historiographic metafiction," is particularly helpful here. Historiographic metafiction refers to a kind of writing practice that's self-conscious about the complexities when narrativizing last week—a strange (for lack of a sharper term) postmodern beast that is both trying to tell history and think about telling history. Novels, for instance, like Coover's *The Public Burning*, which is in a sense about the events that lead up to Julius and Ethel Rosenberg's execution, but which is also about the predicament involved in narrativizing those events. There are parts of that novel that are linguistically explosive, hallucinogenic, in ways that destabilize all the other parts, call attention to their making, lead the reader to question the authenticity of any monologic perspective on history. Couple that impulse, in the case of *Nietzsche's Kisses*, with a much more prosaic one: I've always been interested in Nietzsche, interested in knotting the way Nietzsche has come down to us, drawing attention to the many different Nietzsches that ~~history~~ has written. I discovered that the more I investigated the noun Nietzsche, the less I understood it—and in certain really interesting ways. The more you look into the Nietzsche function, the less you can say about it from any sort of privileged position. To study that function is to study a mode of not-knowing. For some reason, such an enterprise delights me.

Lackey: One of the things I've noticed is that you alter historical fact in *Nietzsche's Kisses*. Is this fair to history? Or to the historical figure you represented in your work? I'm going to give you a quick example. You have Nietzsche's sister Elisabeth fire Peter Gast, who was a Jew and one of the first editors of Nietzsche's work. Historically, Elisabeth did fire Gast. But then she rehired him, which you do not mention in the novel, and eventually came to like him, something that you also do not mention. How can you justify your alterations of the historical record, and what kind of impact do you think that has on readers?

Olsen: Let me approach your question through two different optics. The first comprises a novelist's point of view. There is an aesthetic logic that drives novel writing. Continuously present in one's imagination is the relatively limited number of pages with which one has to work—250? 350? 450?—one can only pack so much stuff into those pages. When you're working with ~~history~~, when you're working with ~~biographical figures~~, the result is that you immediately begin to edit, erase, revise in the largest sense of the word. For my purposes, what was interesting to me wasn't the later relationship of Elisabeth and Peter Gast, but rather that moment when Elisabeth had begun to rewrite her brother, gain control over him by narrativizing him. This answer leads to the second optic I mentioned: historiographic metafiction. That is, I wanted a novel that wasn't only about a Nietzsche, or a series of Nietzsches, but also about the impossibility of wanting a novel about a Nietzsche, or a series of Nietzsches.

Lackey: Did Gast's Jewishness matter? Did that play a role in making your decision in creating that character or that moment?

Olsen: Honestly, I don't think it did. I want to say it was a technical decision I needed to make, one where Gast, given the novel's focus, had to play a smaller role in the whole, and one where Lisbeth had to operate as a means to get the reader to focus on how, from very early on, people began to write the Nietzsche they needed to write for very specific sorts of politico-cultural purposes—in Lisbeth's case, of course, proto-Nazi ones. Back to Linda Hutcheon for a minute, and the theorist's optic. Hutcheon makes a distinction between facts and events. Facts, she says, are discourse determined, while events aren't. The gesture historiographic metafiction performs is to make visible what for most of us is invisible. Most of us conflate facts and events. But to begin to narrativize an event is to begin to transform it into a constellation of chosen (and discarded, erased, manipulated) facts. We are always-already telling through ideology.

Lackey: In *Nietzsche's Kisses*, you focus on a character who is concerned about the condition of knowledge and who formulates a theory about knowledge. Can you briefly discuss what motivated you to focus specifically on Nietzsche, and in particular his obsession with the condition of knowledge?

Olsen: The novelist in me has a biographical reason. I was raised for my first couple years in the jungles of Venezuela. My dad was helping to set up an oil refinery there. The world into which I came to consciousness took a certain amount of unhinged reality for granted. A snake drowned in our washing machine and flopped out in the sheet in which it had become entangled. Six-foot-long iguanas hung on our screened windows. Thousands of butterflies would ascend out of the grass each spring. These were head-jarringly surreal images for a little kid from the northeast. So my family and I returned to the States and settled into the hermetically sealed, climate controlled malls called New Jersey, and the years went by. During show-and-tell in school on Friday afternoons, I would recount my childhood and be sent to the principal for lying. I would have to call my mom and have her vouch for me. When I was in my thirties, my sister and I would get together and try reminiscing about our childhood in South America, and it became immediately apparent that, whatever event we tried to bring to mind, the facts surrounding it were *completely* complicated, fuzzy, torqued. We could never settle on what happened to whom. Things I believed had happened to her ultimately turned out to have happened to me and vice versa. It became painfully clear that the past simply wouldn't settle down. That realization tracked me for my whole life. The theorist in me has from very early on been interested in epistemological questions—certainly from my undergraduate days, when I took my first theory courses. I quickly became interested, thanks to the poststructuralists, in how we come to know and understand texts and what our relationship is with those texts. It remains extraordinary to me that all of us sitting at this table could read the same text, and could try to talk about it, only to learn, again and again, that we were really talking about five different texts. That was one of the things, I believe, that drew me to Nietzsche early on: his sense of perspectivism in relationship to knowledge. One can never simply ask what I know. One must continuously ask: "What optic do I know it from? How am I framing my understanding of that knowing? How am I ideologizing my knowledge?"

Lackey: I want to shift now to a more specific question about the novel. As you point out, Nietzsche's sister married Bernhard Förster, who was a Christian anti-Semite. Elisabeth and Förster shared a dream of building a utopian community which would be free of Jews. In the late 1880s, they actually established such a community in Paraguay, and they called it "Nueva Germania." Nietzsche despised Förster, and he passionately opposed his utopian community. Nietzsche did this in part because he hated anti-Semitism, as you make clear in your novel. And yet, Nietzsche's sister, who took charge of the Nietzsche Archive after Nietzsche's mental collapse, revised and even forged some of her brother's texts, thus making them acceptable and even appealing to Hitler and the Nazis. Your novel brilliantly builds up to that scene when Hitler visits the Nietzsche Archive, and Elisabeth presents him with Nietzsche's walking stick. Why, in a novel about Nietzsche, did you shift the focus to Elisabeth, and specifically her meeting with Hitler? And why did you do this in a novel rather than a scholarly study? Put differently, what does the novel allow you to communicate about this history-making event that you could not communicate in a traditional biography or a scholarly monograph?

Olsen: Every genre exists because it can do things other genres can't. So the question behind your question is this: "What can novels do that things like scholarly monographs (or drama, say, or film) can't do?" One answer is simply language. Novels can do language—beautiful, uproarious language—for extended periods of time; can draw language to the surface, delight in its rhythms and textures, not for one page, or twenty, but for 500, 1,000. Another answer is that the novel can explore deep consciousness. Film can only try to do so for maybe 90 minutes, maybe 120, and it's going to have to do so from the outside, from an external point of view, because that's its generic nature. A novel can create the impression of diving fully into the consciousness of another human being, and place the reader in a position with respect to that consciousness for days, if not weeks. What a dazzling thing. Obviously, a scholarly monograph can't do that. Now, at the same time, the novel problematizes genre because it knows that the character that it is diving into isn't, in fact, a real character; it is a paper person, a construction of language. The noun on the page of my novel that says "Nietzsche" doesn't point to Nietzsche. Every time it's used it points to Nietzsche's absence. Novels by nature are these strangely disruptive zones. They both try to get you to believe that they are exploring a consciousness other than the author's *and* know that they're not doing so. And a final answer to your questions for right now. The novel can perform a number of thought experiments. So one of the things *Nietzsche's Kisses* is trying to imagine (at the same time understanding such imaginings are, in a sense, futile) is what Nietzsche might have been like, given the Nietzsche that Lance Olsen read and experienced when he was studying Nietzsche. I did extensive research for *Nietzsche's Kisses*, both in terms of reading various biographies and Nietzsche's work multiple times, and in terms of travelling extensively, following Nietzsche's life journey through Germany and Switzerland and Italy, taking extensive notes along the way, taking photographs and film footage, visiting the Nietzsche Archive, standing in the room in which he died, and so on. But I was also trying to move beyond those kinds of events into a series of conditionals about Nietzsche. Which is to say, at the end of the day, the novel always-already knows that Lukács is wrong. The best we can do is to set up these thought experiments about the relationship of the individual to history and then disrupt both those terms. The individual? How do we talk about identity? What are its limits, its substance? And history? Who's telling that history, and from what perspective, and with what sort of agenda?

Lackey: Building on this, you talk about how the novel accesses consciousness. I wonder if consciousness has undergone a transformation in the last fifty years—not necessarily consciousness itself, but our understanding of consciousness—and if that has any relevance to the rise of the biographical novel. Instead of writing a classical historical novel, which focuses on events, we now write novels that center on consciousness itself. Do you think that this helps account for the rise of the biographical novel? And if so, can you specify what happened to our understanding of consciousness?

Olsen: What you say feels right: the feeling, in this age of uncertainty, that our sense of consciousness has changed dramatically. I wouldn't want to speak for anyone but myself, here, now, but, with that as my caveat, my intuition is that we've moved away from early-twentieth-century (read: modernist) notions of Freudian depth-consciousness, for example. They no longer seem to fit—at least for me—lived experience. In part, of course, this is because of the troublings poststructuralism launched in the middle of the century, and in part because of the digitization of our culture: the data overload so many of us experience as experience these days, the splintering or multifaceted-ness of our consciousnesses. I'm speaking of that new way of being—you know, sitting at our computers, writing, say, but also researching on the web, perhaps checking out the news, our email program running in the background, Facebook floating behind that, a dictionary behind that, Wikipedia behind that, and, for a break, perhaps we flip over to YouTube to check out a video clip, and maybe we're listening to iTunes, and our friends are texting us on our cell phone lying on our desktop to the right of our computer, and someone in the next room is watching TV, and, well, you get the picture. Pictures. Compare that to the information intake for someone in, oh, 1347, or 1847. And you see what I'm driving at. By necessity, I should think, we process our worlds differently, have a different sense of what we mean when we say thinking and/or feeling. We have the continuous impression of mediation, remediation, unreadability, dispersion—something closer, perhaps, not to Freudian thought, but, perhaps, Baudrillardian: schizoid selves as pure screens, switching stations for all the data networks flowing within us and without. So the question for authors is this: How do we write the contemporary? That is: How do we write our experience of experience? Such questions don't in any way divorce us from the historical. Rather, they're a result of the historical. Authors I'm most interested in now are trying to tackle these problems. When reading a novel like David Foster Wallace's *Infinite Jest*, I can't help being aware how profoundly it couldn't have been written 100 years ago. Or there's this *beautiful* hyper-medial work by David Clark called *88 Constellations for Wittgenstein* that employs audio, nonlinear narraticules, video, images, and text in a consciously failed attempt to understand the philosopher and his thought. Throughout, it's aware of the reader, or the viewer, or the listener, or whatever you want to call this new person who's trying to navigate this new thing—aware of that person's presence, aware of trying to activate that presence by making the navigator continually choose how to maneuver through this hypermedial field. That is to say, one is keenly aware that one is constructing narrative as one proceeds, that reading has become a form of writing even as writing has become a form of reading. That moment is pointing to exactly what you're talking about, Michael. To a much lesser extent *Head in Flames* and *Nietzsche's Kisses* partake of the same kind of project. The latter is structured in groups of three. Each chapter has a first person, a second person, and a third person point of view. The first person constitutes the real time of Nietzsche on his deathbed, his last mad night on earth. The second point of view chapters constitute irrational, hallucinatory moments of Nietzsche's semi-consciousness. The third person point of view chapters constitute attempts by Nietzsche to narrativize his life. The structure, then, is insistently polyphonic—that is to say, it insistently privileges multiple perspectives, multiple voices. The result of that is to immediately bracket questions like truth, or history, or the world, or a thinker like Lukács' totalizing systems. The very structure of the book works against any sense of totalization, and with that against any stable view of consciousness and its corollary: identity. Those points of view don't add up to a consistent narrative any more than they add up to a consistent self.

Lackey: Shifting focus again, there has been a tendency among biographical novelists to emphasize the role of religion in shaping major historical events. Here I am thinking about Jay Parini's *The Last Station*, Bruce Duffy's *Disaster Was My God*, and David Mamet's *Old Religion*. This focus on religion stands in stark contrast to what we see in canonical interpretations of Western intellectual and political history, which tend to emphasize secularization. Can you explain why there is this emphasis on religion in contemporary biographical novels? And in particular, can you explain why there is this focus in *Nietzsche's Kisses*, as when you mention the Christian anti-Semitism of Elisabeth and her husband, Bernhard Förster?

Olsen: All writing—whether novel, poem, newspaper article, scholarly monograph, whatever—is, at the end of the day, an act of spiritual autobiography. You will, that is, always learn more about the person writing it than you will about the alleged subject matter. One of the reasons I decided—and it was, as I recall, a very clear decision on my part—to bring religion to the fore in *Nietzsche's Kisses*, and *Head in Flames*, is to help me think about how in the United States in the last, say, ten or fifteen years, there has been this resurgence of a kind of Fundamentalism, a dangerous overstated Christianity that in many ways is reminiscent of Förster's undertakings—religion in the service of repressive politics, a generation of politicians who had begun to deploy religion in ways that were hauntingly familiar. I wanted to use *Nietzsche's Kisses* and *Head in Flames* as reminders of how religion can be used to justify all manner of horrendous acts. In a sense, needless to say, this observation is the opposite of new. Yet it is one our culture is very good at forgetting. Religion can be used—and usually is—to close down debate, to categorize, and (back to Bakhtin) to finalize things that in fact are inherently unfinalizable.

Lackey: At this point I want to open up the discussion. If you have a question for Lance, please feel free to ask.

Question 1: I have been pondering the importance of authorship, specifically with respect to creative, historical narratives, and how you use the term "spiritual autobiography." I was wondering, given the theory of the death of the author from Roland Barthes, how we can perhaps liberate the reader from the tyranny of an author who wants to impose their particular perspective. Do you think that concept of liberated readership is a new kind of transcendentalism, where one actually can't escape the author's framing? Or do you think that Barthes was right, and actually saying something Nietzschean where, like the death of God through the creation of new systems of thought, we claim our identity when we're reading literary pieces by imposing our own interpretations?

Olsen: Here's what happened after World War Two. Generations of authors, instead of, say, coming to writing on their own while working second jobs like, say, Hemingway as a journalist, attended university and soon came across a new kind of course: one on literary theory. There they read and became self-conscious about questions concerning how texts might mean. And those generations, I would argue, have come to think of their writing practices differently because of it. Certainly I have. Exposure to theoretical engagements with textuality trouble romantic myths of authorship, put writers in a strange position with respect to their own work, ask us to unlearn or at least trouble certain intuitive responses to our being in the textual world. The operative word through our interview has been "problematization," and here we come across it again. Now, if you're a theorist, or you're a literary critic, you get that, and we move on. If you're an author, you live with it in a complex way every day. Every day we need to ask ourselves, in a very practical way, what our relationship is to our work, how much of what we're doing, or think we're doing, partakes of the very magisterial space of authorship Barthes seeks to overthrow, how right Barthes is with his claim that the text is a kind of nexus where a number of other texts come together and clash. The short answer is I honestly don't know, again and again. That is: Such a series of questions excites me, makes me want to think deeply about the issues they raise, examine my own practices and goals, forces a self-awareness to be perpetually active—which, in a sense, is my definition of the writer, of the artist: one who spends a lifetime practicing curiosity, practicing how to pay attention. So if you think back to how I've tried to engage with Michael's questions, I think you'll discover that that self-consciousness with respect to narrativity shapes them all, that that's my larger project, and it's one, I would argue, that someone like Hemingway didn't possess. That self-consciousness produces a different sort of narrativity, or ~~narrativity~~, altogether, varieties that I find extraordinarily interesting, ones by the likes of Anne Carson, David Markson, Lydia Davis, Kathy Acker, Mark Z. Danielewksi. Of course, what I've just said could be utterly wrong. Nassim Nicholas Taleb's discussion of narrative fallacy may help us here. He argues that, confronted with a whole bunch of chaotic data (some of us would call this life), the human mind's first instinct is to search for pattern, create pattern (which is to say to create narrative) where it doesn't exist. That is, Taleb's point is that we're pattern-recognition machines. We seem hardwired to create narrative (which is to say meaning) whether or not it actually exists. When writers begin indulging in talk of intentionality in their work, I begin to suspect narrative fallacy may be in play, that I may be as guilty of it as any of them, that my account of my own writing is an unconscious attempt to make cosmos out of chaos. I'm not convinced that I'm the same person that wrote *Nietzsche's Kisses*, and when I was writing *Nietzsche's Kisses*, I wasn't convinced I was the same person who was writing *Nietzsche's Kisses*. I'm not sure I want to answer your question, then, so much as agree with the complications that your question suggests, the problematics you just raised by naming Barthes's extraordinary essay. Let me say this another way. Sometime in twelfth grade, many of us had it all figured out. Since then, it's been a slow slide into not-knowing, into unlearning. In other words, I used to know a lot more than I do now, and that delights me. I'm sure (in an unsure way) that's why I'm drawn to writers like Nietzsche, Barthes, Derrida, Cixous, Foucault, why I'm increasingly comfortable with the discomfort they create. Their thought gestures are about unlearning, not learning. And, of course, this is why Lukács and I don't get along, can't sit at the same table. He knows too much. I love the definitiveness with which he states his cases. At the same time I acknowledge his totalizing impulse strikes me as utterly foreign, enviable, and nonsensical. What I can talk about with absolute assuredness is precisely what I *don't* know, whereas I think Lukács really thought he knew what he was talking about. I *know* I never know what I'm talking about. And I can articulate that not-knowing, as you can tell, for very long periods of time.

Question 2: I have a very specific question about *Nietzsche's Kisses*. I am wondering about the conflict of saying that Nietzsche got syphilis from being a medic in the war or from having sex with a prostitute. In this novel, he has sex with the prostitute Ingrid. Ingrid, I thought, was a really interesting character or placeholder for the three or four other times she seems to come up in the novel or her similarities with the girl at the Wagnerian opera in the "Liver" section. So I'm wondering why you chose that scenario. Was it purely aesthetic or is there more to it than that?

Olsen: Syphilis was for a long time the only answer to what was going on those last few years of Nietzsche's life. Now, apparently, it's not so clear. Certainly, even if it were, the details aren't. So, for me, Ingrid was an aesthetic choice, a narrative necessity, rather than a person based on historical facts. The thing about tertiary syphilis—if what Nietzsche had happened to be tertiary syphilis—is that it takes your brain out completely. Which is to say, if we're to agree with that diagnosis, this novel couldn't have happened. One of the assumptions the book makes is that Nietzsche possesses a mind with which to think, hallucinate, narrativize on his last night alive, but that couldn't have been the case if he had tertiary syphilis. During his final days, given the descriptions that come down to us, he was in something a lot closer to a catatonic state. So the novel's premises are contrary to received knowledge—a gesture I found engaging to make because it strikes to the heart of the larger problematics concerning historicity which the book explores.

14

Reflections on Biographical Fiction

Jay Parini

Lackey: Georg Lukács published *The Historical Novel* in the late thirties, and many scholars consider it one of the most insightful and exhaustive studies of the historical novel. But there's something really troubling about the book, especially in relation to your work. He argues that the biographical form of the novel is doomed to failure because the focus on "the *biography of the hero*" leads authors to overlook or misrepresent significant historical events and truths, and thus "reveals the historical weakness of the biographical form of the novel." Given the nature of Lukács' critique, he would say that your *Last Station, Benjamin's Crossing*, and *The Passages of H.M.* are not just failures—he would argue that they were doomed to failure from the outset because the very form of the biographical novel is limited and even flawed. How would you respond to Lukács' critique?

Parini: First, let me say that I did read that book. I read it in 1968 or 1969. So I read it a very long time ago, when I was at St. Andrews, in Scotland. So I had in mind for quite a long time the idea that the biographical novel might be a flawed form, potentially lethal for a novelist! But I'd always been drawn to and read a lot of historical fiction, admiring such books as *Lotte in Weimar*, Thomas Mann's biographical novel. I was drawn to the idea of books centered on real historical figures. Having been a great reader of standard biographies, I realized at a certain point that it was simply all narrative, and that narrative is necessarily a form of fiction. In the course of time, I came to realize that Lukács had it wrong; that, in fact, there's no appreciable difference between history and fiction in terms of narrative technique. It's all narration. Lukács' argument, for me, didn't hold much water. It was flawed, in my view, because if you look at the examples of biographical fiction that we have before us in the last twenty years, we see again and again that the form can actually bring us closer to certain kinds of truths, truths unavailable in other genres. Biographical fiction shapes our ways of thinking about not only specific figures in a landscape, but it also takes us into that intellectual and cultural landscape and political landscape as well. It opens up our imaginations to a particular era. I have long believed that anything processed by memory is fiction. I don't know what kind of writing is *not* fiction, if truth be told.

Lackey: A number of people have referred to your novels like *The Last Station* as an instance of historical fiction. Do you think it's useful to call your novels historical fiction, or is there a benefit to actually saying these are biographical novels?

Parini: I don't think it's actually historical fiction, if only because that's a very specific genre that smacks of third-rate, dime store novels which give you a sweeping panorama with invented characters deposited in a fictional landscape. I'm doing something very different. And biographical novels are, too, when they focus and take as their main character, or at least as significant characters, actual people who lived in time, and open outward from that narrative, and while keeping to the agreed-upon-facts, nevertheless shine a flashlight into the darker corners of history and try to imagine what was really going on. So I think we are opening up perspectives here.

Lackey: So when you say "what was really going on," are you talking about the nature of human motivation? Are you talking about things that happened in the society that we don't really know about, that have not been recorded? What do you mean by that?

Parini: Just to play a little bit of a devil's advocate here: I recently read an interview with Bob Dylan where he says, "You can't do anything to change the present or the future, but the past is something you can change." I thought that was a crafty way of saying that we don't have any access to the future, and we barely have any purchase on the present. What we have is everything that happened behind us. So we are like the Angel of History in Walter Benjamin: an image from a painting by Paul Klee. We turn our backs to the present and to the future, and we have the wreckage of history piling at our feet. In this wreckage, our job is to try and sort out *something* that fits into the category of "truth." That can be an emotional truth. It can be a factual truth. Obviously, in the biographical novel, we're not trying to excavate historical truth in the way professional historians are—although we sometimes do work with documents, interviews, and other materials that historians use. Nevertheless, we are trying to *imagine* truth. We are attempting to imagine ways of thinking about what might have happened, what could have happened. Rarely do we know what *really* happened. That's almost inaccessible. But at least we have the possibility of trying to imagine our way into the reality of something: Nietzsche's last night, or the reality of Tolstoy when he's dying in *The Last Station*, or the reality of Lincoln when he's dealing with the Civil War... We don't really know about the "truth" that lies behind such things. What can you do as a conventional historian with such events or situations? You can sift through limited documents, and you can quote those documents. But any time you begin to speculate on what those documents mean, you're moving into the area of imagining the past. So the biographical novelist simply gives himself or herself extra license and says, "I am going to open this up. I'm going to let the floodlight of the imagination shimmer on what facts are there and try to see if there are pathways between those rocks."

Lackey: Let's move to a specific example. In your novel *Benjamin's Crossing*, your Walter Benjamin believes that a Copernican revolution in thinking needs to occur. Here's how you describe the revolution: "Fiction would replace history, or become history." Can you clarify what this means? Would you say that we could use this idea in order to explain not only the rise, but also the value of the contemporary American biographical novel?

Parini: I agree with what Walter Benjamin says, that fiction ultimately should replace history. What I mean is that history should acknowledge its debt to fiction. History should understand that no matter how much it protests, it remains a form of fiction; that narrative involves the illumination of certain facts and the suppression of other facts. It has to do with the ordering of events. It has to do with trying to guess at motivation. And these are things that novelists do by trade. So ideally, the perfect historian of the future, if there is a new Copernican revolution, will acknowledge the fact that he's a fiction-maker, and that his work involves a grand ordering of events, the illumination and highlighting of certain things, and repression or suppression of other things. Shaping, in other words.

Lackey: Can you briefly talk about the title of *Benjamin's Crossing*? How are you using the word "crossing" here? Specifically, how does the idea of crossing relate to Benjamin's experiences and philosophy?

Parini: Well, crossing means many things. On the most literal level, it's about Benjamin's crossing from France into Spain in 1940. There is a literal journey over the mountains. But it is really a symbolic phrase. It is about his transfiguration—his transformation—from, in some ways, a selfish, self-contained man who really had dismissed his own family, sent them off to England, and was living a life of narcissistic isolation, almost solipsism, working on his consummate project, a lost manuscript, in the national archives in Paris. History, in a sense—contemporary history –pried him loose from this cocoon and set him fleeing. In sending him afoot, he came into contact with Lisa Fittko, whom I interviewed at length, with Henny Gurlund, and José, her son. These were real people who crossed the mountains with Benjamin. So there was a figurative crossing of Benjamin from the narcissistic self-enclosed state he had been in for twenty years, sitting in the *Bibliothèque nationale*, to a much more humane person who was having to deal with the practical realities of getting over the mountain and dealing with his physical problems—he had a bad heart, for example, and the more spiritual realities of having to open himself up to these people, not only for his own sake, but for their sake as well, in order to get safely across the mountains into Spain. Ultimately, I believe he sacrificed himself so that they could proceed without him holding them back. It was almost a Christ-like act of self-sacrifice for the sake of other people, for their welfare. So this was a tremendous crossing for Benjamin—crossing in the sense of transfiguration. I think people are often transfigured. We don't know when or how or who. But I think there are transfigurations going on all the time. This is one of those crossings. I mean, the word "crossing" bears with it, of course, things like Charon's crossing of the River Styx in Greek mythology. I was thinking of all the different versions of crossing: from one state to another, from one mental state to another, from one literal place to another… It's a multivalent image.

Lackey: Can you talk just briefly about him crossing with regard to his identity? Benjamin was raised Jewish, and he was considered Jewish. Yet he would never really embrace his Jewish heritage. Not because he didn't want to be Jewish, but because he had a philosophy of crossing in the sense of ethnic crossing, moving from one kind of identity to the other. Did that play a role at all?

Parini: It did, in fact. I was thinking of this in a postmodern sense. Benjamin embraced so many different philosophies. He couldn't be pinned down. He couldn't be a Zionist. He couldn't be an Orthodox Jew. He couldn't even be a mystical Jew, even though he was very interested in moving toward Kabbalah and mysticism. I think he was in many ways an Emersonian figure who is in touch with the spirit, and he moved in ten directions at once. So his person-ality becomes *extremely* difficult to pin down or categorize. I think he, as a writer and intellectual, was an inveterate resister of categories. I mean, what *was* he? He wrote stories. He wrote fiction. He wrote book reviews. He wrote philosophy. He wrote art criticism. There was almost nothing he didn't try his hand at. His postmodernity involved shape-shifting, slithering among identities, taking on and jettisoning ideas with ease, a gleeful eagerness to resist being pinned down.

Lackey: Shifting to another topic here, you insist that your work is fiction; that it's not history or biography. This claim seems to establish a strict division between fiction and history, fiction and biography, as if fiction could not be used to shed significant light on a historical period or a biographical figure. Do you think it is possible for scholars like myself to use your work to shed new and important light on historical events and biographical figures? In other words, is it possible for biographical novelists to access a type of truth that traditional historians and biographers overlook? And if so, can you define the nature of that truth?

Parini: Well, I think you pointed out the fact that in each of these novels, I put up a warning sign saying "Don't be reading this as history, because it's fiction." That's my way of warning rather naïve readers not to imagine that they hold in their hands a work of history. If you bring those conventional expectations into play, you're in danger of possibly misreading the book that's before your eyes. But I'm speculating, again and again. In *Passages of H.M.*, for example, there was no way to know for sure the degree to which Herman Melville and Nathaniel Hawthorne were emotionally attached to each other—to what degree that relationship might have been homo-eroticized. We can't know what happened behind closed doors. But I like to open those doors and try to imagine what could have happened. Again, the authors left traces, so one is not just grasping at straws. We have the journals of Hawthorne. We have Melville's letters to Hawthorne. So we have traces we can follow. But there is no clear path to truth. It stops well short of the door. The work of the fiction writer is to open closed doors and say, "Well, here's what might have happened on the other side of those doors." I think historians will have to become more comfortable with the fact that, whether they like it or not, they themselves are opening closed doors. The doors are there to be opened, and if they're not willing to step through them, they're limiting the possibilities of knowledge. What's the use of saying that there was this wonderful room, only the door was closed? You want to know what might be going on inside that room.

Lackey: But for the historians to make that move, wouldn't they have to first acknowledge that history is in some measure fiction? Once they make that concession, then they can see fiction as potentially getting to history. Is that right?

Parini: Yes. I think that the work of the historian would be amplified by the acquisition of skills that novelists have. One might ask for a greater use of the imagination and a freer use of the facts—I don't want to suggest that you should distort or misuse the facts—but I think you need to know what to make of the facts, and maybe allow yourself more room to play with them. It's a joyfulness of the imagination that I'm asking for, in myself and others.

Lackey: Shifting to a slightly different topic, one of the things I have noticed is that canonical scholars of intellectual and political history—and here I'm thinking about Erich Auerbach, Max Horkheimer, Theodor Adorno, Hannah Arendt, and Benedict Anderson—suggest that Western culture has either been secularized or is in the grip of a rapid secularization process. But reading your novel *The Last Station*, it seems that religion and spirituality are very much alive. They may be changing form, but they are certainly not disappearing. Would you say that something in the nature of the biographical novel gives us a very different, indeed, a contradictory perspective about intellectual and political history from what we get in traditional scholarly studies?

Parini: Yes. Traditional scholarly studies tend to close out the spiritual aspect of human beings because that is not something you wander into easily, without personal, even moral, consequences. People tend not to be open about their spiritual lives. So it's difficult. Whenever you deal with an actual human being—we know this from everyday experience—there are layers and there are layers, and conventional historians often stick with, or get stuck with, a superficial layer. Many of the great intellectual historians that you've talked about—Adorno, Erich Auerbach—stick to historical surfaces, as if afraid to penetrate into the layers. (I admire their work, of course; but I still would argue that they turn away from aspects of the subjects before them, bound by conventional approaches.) I'm more interested in, say, the approach of Borges, who will take history and then will turn it into fiction; will turn it inside out and backwards. Borges is the great teacher, someone who understood how when he's writing a piece of literary criticism, it actually becomes a narrative, becomes a story. He starts imagining his way into the material, breaking through layers. In "Pierre Menard, Author of the Quixote" or "Tlön, Uqbar, Orbis Tertius," for example, you see him parodying conventional scholarship, upending conventional criticism and historical writing, showing his readers a literal mindedness at work in the academic world that is actually *killing* the truth. In order to find the truth, one has to imagine it. I have always loved that Oscar Wilde line that the English are "always degrading truths into facts." This is often true of literary critics and it's true of historians, intellectual historians especially. They are always degrading truths into facts. As a result, they often fail to arrive at spiritual truth. We now live in an incredibly religious age. If there's anything true about the modern world, it is this: Religion is alive and well. People are trying to open doors to the spiritual life everywhere you look. The fact that modern secular history and historical science aren't willing to acknowledge this only shows that resistance is going to look more and more foolish as it completely contradicts the experience people have every day.

Lackey: Can you briefly discuss the narrative technique of your biographical novels? In all cases, there are multiple narrators, multiple perspectives. Why is this so crucial to your work as a biographical novelist? Finally, can you clarify how this technique sets the contemporary biographical novel apart from the traditional historical novel?

Parini: Well, traditional historical novelists, as in Sir Walter Scott, simply assume that history is verifiable and solid and ontologically stable, that a third person narrator can say, "In 1799, this army marched against that army," and believe they are getting somewhere near the truth. I suspect that the modern biographical novelist believes that truth is subjective and that every person's viewpoint is subjective and that truth is therefore idiosyncratic and resides in ways of framing the world and picturing it in language. People with their own linguistic gifts (or lack of them) have different degrees of access to interior realities. In my novels, I tend to layer subjective viewpoints. For example, in *The Last Station*, you are hearing from Tolstoy's wife, one of his daughters, his publisher, and his secretary. The narrative unfolds in five or six subjective viewpoints. You are hearing the same story told from different angles of experience. By layering these viewpoints, there is a technique here for accessing truth. Now, what on earth would *conventional* historians have to do with any of this? They can't get at subjective truth. So, in many ways, a tremendous breakthrough in historical work has occurred. By analogy, this technique reaches back to the insights of Cubism. Picasso defined Cubism as a dance around the object. Whether the object is Tolstoy or Walter Benjamin or Herman Melville, I use these many voices to dance around this object, trying to open up the truth, looking for recesses where I can dig in and try to grow truth.

Lackey: This whole "question of truth" raises some serious questions about the responsibilities of the author and also the rights of the people who are the subjects of your novels. On your acknowledgments page of *Passages of H.M.*, you say that your book is a novel, not a literary biography. Even though your work is acknowledged to be fiction, is it possible that it infringes upon the rights of the subject under consideration? For instance, you say, "Very little is known about Lizzie Melville, so I made her up." Do you have any responsibility to Melville and Lizzie? An obligation to represent their lives accurately? Can you specify the kind of liberties you feel justified in taking with the facts? And can you specify the kind of liberties that could not be justified?

Parini: That's a tricky but important question. If you look at the essay "Borges and Myself" by Jorge Luis Borges, he talks about how there's this fictional character Jorge Luis Borges who in many ways stands apart from the real self, who is Borges. These are different people. There will be a Jay Parini who exists in the public world and has a life apart from me. I think whenever you start launching representations of yourself into the world via letters or short stories or poems or novels or whatever, you sign on the dotted line a contract with the future. And in this contract, you say, "Okay, I have launched forth a character with a name similar to my own. I acknowledge therefore that this person—this projection—can be open to interpretations, and that the people in the future, posterity, will have the privilege of interrogating that projection and coming to terms with it." So we come to terms with a figure called James Joyce. We know some dark things about that figure. We know that he had a scatological obsession with his wife's underwear, for example. We know all kinds of horrible things about all kinds of people, from Napoleon through Hitler or Franklin Roosevelt or John Kennedy. Some of these things will be true, some will be exaggerated, some will be distorted… But again, we don't know anything *really* about Franklin Roosevelt, for instance. What we know are something about the traces he left behind and some of the projections that people had in their own heads about "Who was Franklin Roosevelt?" I think one could do a weird, wacky, surreal novel in which Franklin Roosevelt spends much of his time flying in air balloons over France, and I think that would be within the boundaries of a surreal novelist. If he or she thought that that would get us closer to some aspect of the personality of F. D. R., let him fly air balloons over France for thirty years. He can live in that air balloon over France and call himself Franklin Roosevelt. He can spout ideas about the New Deal while flying over the fields of Provence. I don't see that anybody should worry about that. I doubt that Franklin Roosevelt himself, the *actual man*, would have cared. Roosevelt signed the deal that I've signed, allowing people of the future to project out this name and attach certain language to it. Posterity has the rights and privileges accorded to all imaginative creatures, which means they can play around with public material. They can move it around, rearrange the elements in ways that might have a clarifying effect. If people do this in an immoral or irresponsible way, that will show up. I hope so. To be frank: I felt a little guilty, for example, prying into the homoerotic impulses of Herman Melville. But I felt less guilty about it only because he opened himself up to this kind of inquiry in his own fiction. I mean, there's homoeroticism in everything from *Typee* through *Moby Dick*, and of course *Billy Budd*. There's a homoeroticism in all this work that's pervasive. So Melville—probably without being conscious of this—invited posterity to play around with that aspect of his soul. I thought I was fairly discreet on this matter. I didn't actually have Melville engage in any homosexual acts in my novel. I simply had him entertaining mild homoerotic fantasies and walking close to the line but never crossing it. My guess is—and that's, again, the hunch of the historian/fiction writer—that what I imagined might actually be true. I assumed I could get beneath his fictional world by probing into an imagined sexuality. So I think there are places that it would be immoral to go, but I think those lines, if they are crossed, become pretty bloody obvious to people, to readers. People will say, "You can't do that. That's just crazy." I think readers understand that when you are reading a work of history or a work of fiction, you need to trust the integrity of the writer, his or her fidelity to experience of the kind under examination, subjected to representation.

Lackey: One of the benefits of interviewing you is that you have a commanding grasp of literary history, so you can talk about the evolution of certain aesthetic forms. And in this case, I want you to briefly talk about the way the historical novel has morphed into the biographical novel in recent years. Here's what I'm thinking. You were friends with Robert Penn Warren and Gore Vidal. *All the King's Men* is a traditional historical novel in that it is based on Huey Long but it changes his name to Willie Stark in order to give Warren considerable freedom to alter historical facts. Vidal's *Lincoln* is different in that it retains the names of the original figures. Can you locate your work within this genre of writing? And can you explain why this particular genre has become so popular in the last thirty years?

Parini: This is a fairly recent phenomenon, for the most part. I mean, there are isolated examples going back to the eighteenth century. It's not as though it was invented from whole cloth. In various European languages, early versions of this kind of writing occurred. Thomas Mann, for example, played around with biographical fiction in fascinating ways. Some of the African American writers of the Harlem Renaissance toyed with it. In *All the King's Men*, written in the mid-forties, Robert Penn Warren felt tightly bound to the traditions of conventional historical fiction. I don't think he could see his way toward the contemporary forms of the biographical novel, or else he would have called his protagonist Huey Long, not Willie Stark. I wish he had. I think he could have written a better novel if he'd actually dug into Long, because I know he was obsessed with him. I had long conversations with him about Long. I recall sitting at the dining room table with Warren and Cleanth Brooks, his old friend, and they spent a whole evening telling wild stories about when they were at LSU and editing *The Southern View* and things that Huey Long said, did, and so forth. In many ways, those stories were wilder and more interesting than anything in *All the King's Men*. So I think Warren in *All the King's Men* drew on the energies of the modern biographical novel without quite understanding what he was doing and where he was going. Warren's thinking and writing—his example—shaped my thinking at a very early stage. He was in many ways the most gifted and influential figure in my life. But when I began working on *The Last Station*, my first biographical novel, I was lucky to be living in Amalfi, in southern Italy, and my next door neighbor and close friend was Gore Vidal. He had just published *Lincoln* in 1984. This was in the middle of the 1980s. I spent long evenings over glasses of wine talking with Gore about the nature of the biographical novel. And he kept saying to me, "We've got to put historical figures up front and center in our novels and use all the techniques and tools of the conventional historian, and yet bring to bear on this material the imagination that a good novelist has." And so I talked through the writing of *The Last Station* with Gore at every stage of its composition. He read it in rough draft form, several times. I think he really pioneered the genre with *Burr* and with *Lincoln*. He found ways of putting front and center a real character. Of course he'd read conventional historians carefully. He really understood everything about Lincoln and his era. Gore was a real historian at heart. And he was a true novelist and creative artist. So he was able to illumine Abraham Lincoln in a way that his version of Lincoln will stand beside a dozen other Lincolns. The truth will reside somewhere amid all of them. Gore would be the first to say, "I cast up on a screen one version of Lincoln. Somebody else will cast up on that screen another version of Lincoln. And when you get the accumulation of all these different Lincolns, eventually people in the future will have a sense of this man: his motives, his triumphs, his failures, his difficulties." Novelists sensed an opening that postmodern theory created, and they have rushed into that space.

Lackey: Actually, that is my next question. What role do you think postmodern theory has played in the formation of the biographical novel? Here I am thinking about the way the postmodernists claim that truth is more a fictional construct than an ontological reality. How has this idea inflected our understanding of biography and history? And is there a logical connection between the ascendancy of postmodernism and the rise of the contemporary biographical novel?

Parini: I would guess that the rise of the biographical novel and the rise of postmodernism, with postmodern theories of truth, are directly linked. We couldn't possibly have the biographical novel in its current form if it weren't for the fact that truth has been—not so much deconstructed as *re*constructed. That's to say, we now understand that truth is situational and that perspective plays a huge role in how we view anything. It's the old idea that if you look at the sedimentation in a rift in Africa, one person sees a certain kind of rock. Another person sees snails. It depends on what you're looking for. If you're coming at something from, say, a Christian perspective, you are going to observe patterns of self-sacrifice and bearing the cross and transfiguration. If you are looking at it from a secular viewpoint (or a purely capitalist or Marxist viewpoint), you are going to see a very different kind of pattern. You will look for economic motives, for example. The fact is, every person brings an idiosyncratic lens to the camera and looks at reality through that lens and views different colors and different objects. So the same historical object will appear different to different people coming with different perspectives. So if you apply a Marxist approach, you are going to see certain things in history. If you apply a religious approach, other things. If you apply any one of a thousand different viewpoints, you are going to get a thousand different versions of reality. I think that the postmodern insight is that truth is not some hard, objective thing; it is an accumulation of subjective viewpoints. Truth is, in fact, constructed very carefully, although often unconsciously, because everybody is a gigantic prejudice-making machine. We all generate ideological formations that color everything we see. So it is almost impossible for two or three people to see the same thing and describe it in exactly the same way. The biographical novel affords an *amazing* possibility for the future, a way to translate history into a kind of truth that has been unavailable until this time.

Lackey: When you think about biographical novels—other people working in the genre—has anybody done something that strikes you as totally groundbreaking? Something that expands the borders of knowledge through fiction?

Parini: I think Peter Ackroyd in England has done some astounding work, both as a biographer and as a biographical novelist. When he wrote his book *Chatterton*—he did that maybe thirty years ago—he examined the life of the Romantic poet Chatterton in very interesting ways. Julian Barnes in *Flaubert's Parrot* was, I think, exploring biographical fiction in a unique and interesting fashion, too, opening up the life of Flaubert in ways that had never been done before. When Ackroyd in the early eighties wrote his massive biography of Charles Dickens, he included a number of fictional dialogues between himself and Charles Dickens. To me, these innovations illumined and shaped the biographical passages written in a more conventional vein which preceded and followed it. So I think that some of these English writers, especially Peter Ackroyd and Julian Barnes, have been pioneers. In his book *Libra*, Don DeLillo showed how the biographical novel can add immensely to our understanding of key historical events such as the assassination of JFK. The main thing I came away with after reading *Libra* by DeLillo was the thought that the Warren Commission counts among the great fictional works of all time. I think we're going to see this happen eventually with 9/11. I mean, what's desperately needed for 9/11 is the imagination of history. Someone has got to go into that sequence of events from unique angles, perhaps try to get into the mind of Mohamed Atta, the Egyptian who flew one of the planes into the World Trade Center. A good writer has to grapple with the historically complicated, endlessly fascinating, tragic realities associated with 9/11, a multi-dimensional event that will never be fully understood.

Lackey: What project is next? And how will it be a logical extension of what you have already done? And how will it chart new ground for you?

Parini: Well, the main book I'm working on now is called *FDR*, which is a very long novel in which one takes this projection, the initials of Franklin Delano Roosevelt, in bright letters and throws them up into the sky like in Hollywood with those search lights that flash in the sky at night when there is a premier of a film. From 1920 up until 1944, the world, especially the United States, was utterly in the spell of this incredible creature who became a kind of blank screen on which countless ordinary citizens projected their ideas. I think that F. D. R. *was* a genius, in his odd way. He was able to recreate American politics. We have not yet come to terms with the full range of his genius, not even begun to explore the wild, almost Dionysian aspects of his life. His sexual energies were productive and strange and complicated. His own wife's homosexuality—her lesbian life—needs a good deal of sensitive exploration, as it played into her husband's sexuality, affected his politics. The open-mindedness that F. D. R. showed on this topic and so many other topics remains of huge interest to me. I'm hoping that in moving from literary figures to a political figure like F. D. R. I can extend the range of the biographical novel as I conceive of the genre. I want to use all the techniques of the conventional historian and the novelist in ways that hover on the edge of a new kind of history. That's my hope—maybe a fantasy. I don't know whether I will succeed. I've always believed in aiming high, even if I miss.

15

The Masking Art of the Biographical Novel

Joanna Scott

Lackey: Let me start by telling you about the nature of this project. I'm trying to figure out why, starting in the 1980s, so many prominent writers began to author biographical novels. I am also trying to define the nature of this genre of fiction. Can you start by explaining what led you to write a novel about the Austrian artist Egon Schiele? And can you explain why you decided to write a novel rather than a biography or a scholarly study?

Scott: I was still in my twenties, and I was feeling very energetic as a writer. *Arrogance* is my third book. With my first novel, I discovered the fun of writing away from myself, in the voice of a narrator utterly different from me. With my second novel, *The Closest Possible Union*, narrated by a captain's apprentice on an illegal slave ship, I began my lifelong quest to mine history for lost stories. Coming out of that book, I was wondering what I might write next. It was during that time, a twilight period between books, that I went to an exhibit at the Museum of Modern Art in New York. The show focused on *fin de siècle* Vienna, the art, music, and architecture of the time, which was a very rich period. Most of the work on display was by the artist Gustav Klimt. But there was a back room with drawings by a lesser-known artist named Egon Schiele. While I was in the room, people were walking through expressing some startled reactions to Schiele's work. One couple stopped in front of *Self Portrait of the Artist Masturbating* and the man looked at the woman and said, "Would you buy a used car from that guy?" "Ho ho ho!" they laughed. But when I looked at this portrait and then looked back at the people, I was struck by their condescension. I was also struck by Schiele's ferocity of expression. It just made me wonder about him.

I didn't know anything about Schiele, so I went home and started to explore. I paid a visit to the art library at my university to see what I could find out. At that point, Schiele really was not well known in this country, and there weren't many books about him available in English. I did find a book by Alessandra Comini about his time in prison, along with a translation of his diary from this period. I read these with intense interest, trying to understand the artist who had provoked the viewers in the back room of the Museum of Modern Art to be contemptuous.

In his diary, Schiele mentioned a girl he thought was his accuser. This caught my attention. I'm always on the lookout for lost stories that deserve attention, stories that have been forgotten or haven't been told. Also, following my experience with my previous novel, I was feeling the drive to investigate pivotal moments in history and see if there was more to say and tell. I will never stop wondering about the voices that have been suppressed or ignored. I found a suppressed voice in the girl Schiele thought was his accuser. Her story hadn't been told, as far as I knew, so I decided to tell a story about Schiele's time in prison from *her* perspective. To my surprise, the story kept going. The girl became the opening narrator of each chapter and gave me access into Schiele's life. She is as central to the book as he is.

Lackey: What ultimately made you settle on Schiele? In other words, what was it about him that made you think he is so pivotal?

Scott: I felt that the exposure Schiele was offering in his drawings was very daring. And the more I read about him, the more I admired the risks he was taking with his art. I wasn't totally won over by the work, but I was fascinated and impressed. It's important to remember that he died at the age of twenty-eight. He did incredible work as a young artist, in a relatively short amount of time. I would have *loved* to see the work he would have done as a more mature artist. His ambition didn't have much chance to evolve. So while I admire him, I also see some limitations in his work. But from the start, I admired his daring, and I felt that he was important to our time. Artists need to be able to take risks, we need to be able to make ourselves vulnerable, and I found a model in Schiele.

Lackey: One of the striking things about your novel is the relationship between Klimt and Schiele. Schiele initially admires Klimt, and he is certainly in Klimt's debt. But as the novel progresses, he becomes increasingly more critical of him. He thinks of Klimt as a bourgeois optimist, while Schiele adopts a much bleaker view of the world. Could you discuss that relationship in the novel?

Scott: Yes, and in a way you are probing a dirty little secret in the novel. I couldn't help but consider my own position as a young artist while I was writing the book. I wrote the book when I was twenty-eight—Schiele's age when he died. I felt his relationship to Klimt's more decorative, playful art was not without resonance in my own life. Schiele was passionate, dedicated, and very serious. As a young writer, I found the work of certain more established writers provocative and even nurturing, but I felt some impatience with the jokiness of the new postmodernism, the satire for satire's sake. Some of the playfulness seemed frivolous to me. In fact, as time goes on, I have more of a taste for lightness and playfulness in art. Back then, though, I wanted to write something more expressive than decorative. I was very serious, in my own way.

Lackey: Shifting to a different topic, there was a famous debate in 1968 with Robert Penn Warren, Ralph Ellison, and William Styron about the ethics and the wisdom of naming a protagonist in a novel after the original figure. Ellison praised Warren for changing Huey Long's name to Willie Stark in *All the King's Men* and he criticized Styron for naming Nat Turner after the original person in *The Confessions of Nat Turner*. Ellison's critique was two-fold: naming the protagonist after the original would necessarily lead the author to misrepresent the complexity and details of the original figure and it would make the novelist vulnerable to attack from historians. How would you respond to Ellison? Also, can you explain why you didn't write a novel loosely based on Schiele but change his name in order to give yourself more creative license? Were you tempted to do that at all?

Scott: No, weirdly it never occurred to me not to use his name. And that's something we could probe a little bit, though I'm not sure I can offer a good explanation. I could talk, and will, about certain precedents I think I had in mind as I was writing. But in terms of Ellison's critique here, that's a slippery road. It seems to me that if the name of a person is off limits, then why wouldn't the name of a place be off limits? Why wouldn't every verifiable fact be off limits?

Lackey: In *Invisible Man* he does exactly that. Many readers, for example, think that the Brotherhood in the novel is the Communist Party, but Ellison is absolutely insistent that it is not. As a symbol, the Brotherhood could be used to illuminate the Communist Party, but it could also illuminate many other organizations.

Scott: Absolutely, and it's significant that his main character does not have a name. Ellison makes sure we understand that a name can become fraught with meaning. It can carry dangerous cultural baggage. I respect his nervousness about naming. But then I'm all for keeping open as many doors as possible. If we say we can't use the name of a historical figure, why should I be able to use the name of a woman no one remembers but is inscribed on a nineteenth-century tombstone? And if I can't use her name, I can't use the name of the cemetery, and if I can't use the name of the cemetery, then

I shouldn't be able to set down my characters at the Alamo, or in Times Square for that matter. All these names signify something unalterable. By appropriating them for fiction, I signal that I will alter them. I will do something other than what the historian does with them. I will reshape facts to create an imaginative experience rather than use them as supportive evidence. If we follow Ellison's restriction to its ultimate end, it's not just names that are sacrosanct. Words tend to come with their own baggage. So I can't use words! Then we are done. We end in silence. I suppose it is unfair to exaggerate the implications of the restriction to such an extent. But it's important to remember that every fiction writer is involved in an effort of distortion. As soon as we call something "a fiction," we are indicating that it cannot be relied upon for historical accuracy. Readers usually know to look elsewhere for historical accuracy, and if they don't, good luck to them. The deeper I got into writing *Arrogance*, the more my attention went to creating something new rather than repeating what was already known.

I find myself thinking about the artificial nature of fiction more than ever these days, and I keep coming back to the metaphor of the mask. I'm probably closer in spirit to a masked performer wandering through the fog of Venice during Carnivale than to a historian. Say someone is wearing a mask that recreates the face of Napoleon with leather and paint—you are not going to worry if the person wearing the mask is imitating Napoleon exactly, word for word, gesture for gesture. What is more interesting is the way that the mask is put into action and the dynamic relationship between the mask wearer and the mask itself. Sometimes fiction writers happen to wear a mask that resembles an identifiable historical figure, but it is the ingenuity of the performance rather than the precision of the resemblance that counts.

Lackey: Virginia Woolf had some very serious problems with the concept of the biographical novel, and I don't think she could have seen her way to it. She claims that it is illegitimate to mix fact and fiction. The novelist creates, whereas the biographer gives us fact, and if the writer were bound by fact, this would necessarily prohibit the artist from doing what he or she does, which is to create. So she wanted to make sure that she was going to protect the artist's freedom to create a living and breathing character. Do you agree with that?

Scott: I'll guess that Woolf's motive was to protect the freedom of the novelist rather than to define limits. And certainly in her own fiction she gives us many opportunities to consider how facts mix with the imaginative entities we have come to call "characters." I think of Mrs. Dalloway walking through London—through Woolf's fictional version of factual London. I also think of the panoply of voices in *The Waves*. The characters in that novel are given names and identities, but Woolf makes sure that we keep thinking about how identity is constructed with words. And if we pay attention to how names are given meaning, then we can start thinking about how unstable meaning is, how it is revised and even invented with every new sentence. It seems to me that Woolf was expressing concern with the way the past can be sneakily misrepresented in conventional historical fiction. Given her own experiment in *Orlando*, I would assume she wasn't worried about the brazen distortions of history in imaginative literature. And maybe she was also pointing to an inherent limitation of biography. We want to be able to trust that the facts in a biography will hold up to scrutiny. If the author of a biography, or of any historical work, has mixed fiction with the facts so the different genres are indistinguishable, then that can be problematic.

Of course, I can hear my historian friends reminding me that the act of interpretation is in itself creative and skews everything. It impacts our ability to ascertain causes, trajectories, patterns. But if we are thinking about the biographer's responsibility to the reader, and to the material, I have to agree with Woolf. Fiction does not mix well in a biographical soup. In the soup of the novel, however, fact is a basic ingredient. And I think, looking at Woolf's own fiction, she works beautifully with history. She may veil specific times and places and blur what we think we know about London in the 1920s, or an historical event like World War One, yet she manages to make these subjects newly vivid.

Lackey: And she veils them so she can give herself more creative freedom, so that she is not bound by these actual figures.

Scott: Yes, I don't want to be bound, but I am willing to use a much more transparent veil. I don't think we need to hide the relationship to the real or the factual. Fiction is always made up of stuff drawn from the past—even if the past is only yesterday. And I side with Defoe who says of *Robinson Crusoe* that his version is truer than history! Absolutely.

Lackey: Jay Parini makes a similar observation. In a conversation with Peter Ackroyd, Jay asked: "What's the difference between your biographies and your biographical novels?" Ackroyd said: "In my biographical novels I have to tell the truth."

Scott: Novelists have always been a little nervous about this and we say it perhaps more fervently than we need to, that our made up stories are truer than the truth.

Lackey: It gets a different kind of truth, doesn't it?

Scott: That's the goal. And in this Information Age, when the race is on to make ourselves immortal by gathering up all that can be known and making the facts work to our advantage, I feel a need to reassert that the inquiry of fiction has its own legitimacy. I just heard a talk last night in which a novelist came around to this very topic. His ambition, he said, is to get it right, to do a whole lot of research and make the fiction an accurate historical representation. My ambition is to get it wrong. Am I going to get in trouble for saying that? I want to make something new and intricately expressive, even as I try to honor the richness of the past. There's immense satisfaction in looking back into history and trying to find what is hidden. But the fundamental joy for me is in the act of invention.

Lackey: Russell Banks has an argument that might resonate with yours. He noted a consistency in biographies about John Brown. For most white writers, Brown is either insane or criminal. But for most black writers, he is a hero, almost a saint. Russell said that he began to realize that the biographers deal with the same facts, but they come up with radically different interpretations of the man. So he realized that there's something very naïve about assuming that facts give us an authoritative or accurate picture of history. As a novelist, he wanted to give us something very different, a kind of internal truth that cannot be converted into a metaphysical or absolute claim. To the contrary, he wanted to give us something much messier, something not nearly as codifiable. You can't fit human experience into easily categorizable systems, which is why he thinks there is something fundamentally false about the histories and biographies that presume we can do such a thing.

Scott: Since fiction is by definition fundamentally false, it offers a good venue for exposing unsupportable claims about the world. I like Russell's idea that a novelist provides an internal reality that is messier than history. I've been rereading *Les Misérables*—talk about messy! It certainly isn't the book I'd go to for an accurate account of French history, no more than I'd trust it on its claim about the nature of women. Yet it's thrilling to be suspended in its imagined world.

Lackey: Almost all biographical novels include a preface, an author's note, an afterword, or an epilogue, something as a disclaimer saying that this is just a work of fiction and it's not to be confused with biography or history. Why do you think so many biographical novelists feel this need to make this qualification? And why did you decide not to include such a statement in your work?

Scott: I thought it was obvious. It is called a novel so it is fiction. I would never want to say that it is "just" fiction. I don't like disclaimers. They are redundant and silly. It is a good thing they tend to be in very small font on the copyright page. Publishers put them in for legal purposes, I guess. But I would rather claim than disclaim. If I am calling a book fiction, if it is being presented as a novel, that should be enough.

Lackey: Shifting to the concept of the historical novel, Georg Lukács produced in the mid-thirties one of the most insightful and exhaustive studies of the historical novel. In that work, he argues that the biographical form of the novel is doomed to failure, because the focus on "the *biography of the hero*" leads authors to overlook or misrepresent significant historical events and truths. Given the nature of Lukács' critique, he would say that your novel is not just a failure. He would argue that it was doomed to failure from the outset, because the very form of the biographical novel is limited and even flawed. How would you respond to his critique?

Scott: I'm just glad Lukács is not around now to call me a failure. Worse than a failure! I would say, nothing is doomed to failure. If one hasn't written it, it could very well succeed.

Lackey: He would say it could succeed, but not as a historical novel.

Scott: Right, and only narrative methods associated with social realism are valid? Mann is good, Kafka is bad. I am all for widening the field, making it as inclusive as possible rather than restricting it. I know others find Lukács a useful guide. Nadine Gordimer has written persuasively about his importance. But if I understand the hypothetical situation here, a novel about a historical figure is doomed to failure because of its focus on the individual.

Lackey: His argument is that, because of the biographical novelist's investment in and focus on a particular character, he or she is necessarily going to give us a distorted picture of history and the world. By centering the novel in a person's consciousness, the biographical novelist exaggerates a person's importance, so everything appears through a distorted lens.

Scott: Wasn't it the modernist immersion in individual subjectivity that Lukács was reacting against? I, as a late twentieth-century writer, was nurtured by that immersion and it is absolutely what I love. I came to be a writer because I was reading Woolf and Faulkner and Conrad, all good distorters who remind us of the value of individual existence.

Lackey: But what can they give us in terms of understanding history that is different from and perhaps superior to the classical historical novel?

Scott: We've spoken about how any approach to history needs to consider the act of interpretation. Fiction writers spend a lot of time thinking about and showing us how we interpret the world. If we are going to think about how truth is constructed, than we need to get deep into the impressions of consciousness. I am certainly learning about experience when I am deep inside Benji's mind in *Sound and Fury*, or deep inside Mrs. Dalloway's mind in *Mrs. Dalloway*.

Lackey: Or a biographical novel like Cunningham's *The Hours*?

Scott: Or *The Hours*, absolutely. Michael Cunningham gets us thinking about how we read the world, how we understand reality through the slant of personality. Writers can show us what is at stake in life without insisting that our existence becomes meaningful only when it is spread out on a vast scale. In terms of exploring what is involved in being human, a story about a single mind actively at work, responding to the world, can be as illuminating as a sprawling story of a famous battle.

Lackey: The mind is illuminated, but is history?

Scott: Even with an emphasis on the individual, maybe because of this emphasis, a fictional work set in the past can make us think about the reality of history. I go back to that mask of Napoleon again. We want to see what the person wearing the mask will do with it. But a good performance won't let us forget about Napoleon. The past may be distorted, but it is not erased in the kind of fiction we have been talking about. Even the most outlandish fiction—Barthelme's rendering of Cortes and Montezuma, for example—will get us wondering about the past. I think that when it comes to art, there is more to learn from the act of distortion than from mimicry.

Lackey: Can you clarify the kind of truth you seek to represent in your novel *Arrogance*? More specifically, what is it that the biographical novel can communicate?

Scott: Well, here I would say that the phrase "biographical novel," as a category, makes me a bit nervous. I am nervous about all categories. They necessarily create restrictions. The challenge is to create the category but avoid relying on equations to define it. As soon as we have the equations, then the problem is solved. Unless, of course, the equations are wrong.

Lackey: I want to briefly address the ethics of a novel such as *Arrogance*. Even though your work is acknowledged to be a novel, is it possible that it infringes upon the rights of the subject under consideration? Can you talk about the ethical responsibility you have to Schiele and the other characters in the novel, that is, the obligation to represent their lives accurately? Also, can you define the kind of liberties you feel justified in taking with the facts? And can you specify the kind of liberties that you could not justify?

Scott: There is a lot packed into that question. In order to talk about ethics, I need to talk about precedence. Shortly before beginning *Arrogance*, I saw a beautiful production of Shakespeare's *King John* in London. In fact, I saw it twice. I wasn't thinking at the time of taking a major historical figure and fictionalizing him like Shakespeare did. But as a precedent, King John made very plain that there is a huge tradition of building fictions around historical characters. I was also familiar with Robert Coover's book *Public Burning*, which takes extraordinary liberties with Richard Nixon. Given these precedents, I don't think I hesitated at any point in taking some liberties and creating what seemed necessary in order to build this living, breathing thing we call a novel. I suppose the only kind of unjustifiable liberties would be the ones that don't contribute anything meaningful to the story.

Lackey: Can you discuss some scenes you created?

Scott: There are plenty of scenes in the novel that do not coincide with the biography. But I also took documented experiences and invented dialogue and thought to fill them in. There is a line in Grace Paley's "Conversations with my Father" in which the narrator says about a fictional character in a story she is writing, "she was my knowledge and my invention." Schiele was both my knowledge and my invention. I wanted to get my readers thinking about the limitations of my knowledge and the boundaries of the factual material, and at the same time to accept the invention on its own terms. One of the ways I tried to accomplish this was by opening each chapter with the comments of my narrator, who takes liberties with the life of Schiele. The best image I can use to describe my efforts in that novel is to point your attention to the scene in which the narrator as a girl is looking through the window at Schiele and Vallie sleeping. She can't possibly know what they are dreaming. But she can imagine. She creates her own versions of the two characters by watching them and then imagining what is happening in their minds as they are sleeping. Like her, I am standing outside of history, looking in through the window. I offer that scene as an example of my own relationship to the factual material that went into this novel.

Lackey: But we see her as an extremely flawed narrator. We don't trust her a whole lot.

Scott: Absolutely! She shouldn't be trusted.

Lackey: But I trust you more.

Scott: But you shouldn't! That is why it is a novel, don't trust me! Certainly don't count on me for accuracy. If my fellow novelist wants to get it right, as I said, I am going to get it wrong. Never trust a novelist.

Lackey: At one point in the novel the narrator says that "it is the artist's responsibility to educate" people's "eyes." Your novel is about an artist, and you spend considerable time clarifying how Schiele's art can educate our eyes. But what is it that the biographical novelist educates?

Scott: I've been learning what I can about the history of the novel since my own early years as a writer and have been aware of the somewhat fraught position that education has for novelists. Didacticism is something that has both energized the novel and has created terrible constraints for it, and many writers reacting against the didactic purposes of novels have created really interesting things in the name of self-expression. Yet it is a great thing when language educates, when art educates. Sitting here talking to you, I am being educated by your questions. We are educating ourselves through conversation about writing. I was and remain interested in trying to improve my understanding of experience. I learn from stories about mistakes. I like to read them and, if possible, write them. I like to write about how easily our impulsive responses can mislead us.

My young Schiele takes it upon himself to tell people what to think. He isn't always right, but he is often certain. There is some authorial ambivalence behind that comment about the artist's responsibility to educate. We need to be allowed the right to be impulsive if we are going to feel deeply, and we need to feel deeply if we are going to create worthy art. First impressions are valuable. On the other hand, we can easily misjudge things that are unfamiliar. And when we make art, the work is easily botched if we rely only on impulse. The Schiele in *Arrogance* is not always the best teacher. And yet he recognizes that if we want to give a full experience of art, we need to act boldly, without worrying about pleasing the audience.

Does this make sense? I'm trying to unknot the ambivalence behind the claim that the artist teaches people how to look at the world. I believe it, and I don't believe it. I wanted to spur readers to recognize the usefulness and dangers of impulsiveness. Schiele, as I have drawn him, is an impulsive artist. His passion is productive and gives him fierce insights. But the same passion can make him unwaveringly certain about the legitimacy of his views. So when he lectures about the importance of the artist, I am hoping there is a note of caution ringing softly in the background.

Lackey: Something in the nature of the biographical novel is inherently multidisciplinary. As a biographical novelist of Schiele's life you must have a commanding grasp of Viennese Secessionist art, Austrian history, Schiele's biography, and European politics, etc. Can you discuss both the challenge and value of the biographical novel in giving readers a multidisciplinary picture of character and history?

Scott: Well, there we go. This is the answer to Lukács: The biographical novel is multidisciplinary, varied, mosaic—as vast as those big sprawling novels by Mann and Balzac—which I do love, I have to add. So maybe my efforts aren't doomed to failure.

No, I do not claim expertise, I never did. I am trying to express fascination with my subject. The period known as the *fin de siècle* in Vienna was very fruitful. It deserves to be pondered, and it is exciting to explore. As a novelist, I can share my enthusiasm. I can give my own version of a tour through the period. I can say to my readers, "Come with me. Take this trip, so come along with me and let's see what we see." But I am no expert. I have always insisted that as a novelist I am not an expert. If I have any expertise, it is with the basic material of fictional language. By this point in my life, I should be able to say something useful about the arrangement of words in a work of imaginative prose. But I will leave history to the historians and thank them for the groundwork that they have done.

You ask about the challenge of the biographical novel. The challenge follows very clearly from this discussion of expertise. If one doesn't have expertise, then there are areas of ignorance that are profound. That is part of the package; to me that is true of any novel I have written and will ever write, whether it is about Vienna at the turn of the twentieth century or the street in Connecticut where I grew up. There are a lot of things I will never know. Even within the mind of a single invented character, there are a lot of things I don't know. The individual is so complex, fictional or biographical. And then the time period, any time period, is *so* complex. Trying to honor the complex beauty of an individual, a place, a time, without knowing everything—that is the challenge. But if we only took on subjects about which we have absolute knowledge, we wouldn't have fiction, or any art. So much of the pleasure I get from art is in understanding what the artist has done with her subject. It is not the accuracy of the representation that concerns me. It is the way the artist works with the subject. To watch the artist in action, working on or responding to something—I learn from that, I learn about what we can do and what we can think and what we haven't thought before. Every new sentence teaches me something new about the potential of the mind.

Lackey: You are working on a biographical novel right now. Can you talk about the differences between dealing with somebody like Egon Schiele and the person you are working on now?

Scott: My main subject in this new book is a man named Armand de Potter, who ran a travel business in the late nineteenth century and led tours through Europe and around the world. While he was doing this, he also was assembling a notable collection of ancient Egyptian art. He died mysteriously at sea in 1905. The book tells the story of that mystery and is an attempt to solve it drawing from archival materials that have turned up in my family. I started working on this book after I discovered a set of diaries that his widow left behind when she died. All the challenges we've been talking about, and the values associated with biography and fiction, or history and fiction, seem really relevant to me now. There is an added challenge in that this figure is my ancestor and has been somewhere in my imagination since I was a child. I heard stories about him for years and had wondered what happened. I was told that he disappeared at sea. What does that mean, to disappear at sea? This figure, this ancestor, came alive to me when I started to read my great-grandmother's diaries. But still it is very challenging to work with him, to take him out of history, out of the factual swamp, and to reinvent him as a fictional character. It is exciting but difficult.

Lackey: And how is it difficult in a different way from the Schiele novel?

Scott: I think because I am older. I was young and reckless when I wrote *Arrogance*. I am far more mature.

Lackey: Were you arrogant?

Scott: I was! The original title of that book was *Travels and Confessions of a Pair of Shoes*. Don't ask me to explain that! Then it changed to *Travels and Confessions of a Wunderkind* and then it changed to *Arrogance* at the end. I found myself thinking about the arrogance of Schiele himself, the arrogance of the audience, and my own arrogance as a twenty-eight-year-old American woman taking on this material and trying to make it my own. I think I am probably more cautious now in treating the factual material than I was, even though I still insist that what is important is the invention. The other thing is that even though there wasn't a whole lot of material available about Schiele—that had been translated into English at least—there was enough. And the subject I am working on now—there is a ton of material, volumes and volumes of diaries, letters, legal documents, but it is not enough. So the ground is a little bit more precarious for this new project, which is part of the fun.

Lackey: To conclude, could you identify some of the best biographical novels being written today? And could you explain why they are, in your estimation, some of the best?

Scott: Well, since early on, I have been interested in the way representations of history can mix with the expressions of fiction. Earlier this week I found myself opening up Angela Carter's book of stories *Saints and Strangers* and rereading her "Fall River Ax Murders," which is about Lizzie Borden. I saw that I marked it up with comments. I must have reread it several times when I was younger. She works with history in other ways throughout that collection. I found her explorations exciting when I was a young writer. She was a freeing kind of influence for me. So I cite her as a really fine example of the kinds of mixing we have been talking about. Thinking back over the past thirty years, I can track other influences. When I was just out of college and trying to learn how to be a writer, I had the opportunity to read Salman Rushdie's *Shame* in manuscript. I was enthralled by his brazen interruptions in the story, when the narrator stops a fictional scene to explain the sources he used to create his fictional characters. Another writer who has done some of the most interesting work in these terms is Sebald. He includes visual material to create a really provocative relationship between facts and fiction. It is very exciting work, I think. Michael Cunningham has managed to mix history and fiction in innovative ways. Parini and Banks are able to absorb us beautifully in their re-creations and revisions of history. I am intrigued by John Coetzee's fictional version of John Coetzee. Also, I have come to love the collage of quotations in David Markson's late novels. Somehow he makes a moving fictional narrative out of other writers' words. I am drawn to any art that offers evidence of ingenuity without seeming self-congratulatory. I like to see fiction tested and expanded so that the genre itself becomes freshly relevant. Really, I am looking for anything that introduces me to an idiosyncratic way of thinking and at the same gives insight into the expressive potential of language.

16

Gay Interiors and the Biographical Novel

Edmund White

Lackey: Let me start by telling you about this project. My objective is to clarify why the biographical novel has become so popular in recent years. It is also to define the distinctive form of the American biographical novel. Before the 1980s, there were, as you know, only a handful of major American biographical novels. But starting in the eighties, this genre became very popular with prominent novelists. This seems odd since so many prominent writers thought that the form couldn't work. For instance, Virginia Woolf says that the biographical novel is an impossibility, because you can't blend fact and fiction. What I want to know is what prevented her from understanding that we can blend fact and fiction in the form of a biographical novel. Also, I would like to know what enabled you to blend fact and fiction so skillfully in your biographical novel *Hotel de Dream*.

White: I think other people just think that there is a good story to tell. In my case, I felt like I wanted to fill a lacuna, or a possible lacuna, in the story. So in the case of *Hotel de Dream*, one very unreliable witness says that Stephen Crane began to write a gay novel called *Flowers of Asphalt*. Then he was talked out of it by another writer, a friend of his, Hamlin Garland, who said it would just ruin his career. I mean, Stephen Crane had already done *Maggie: A Girl of the Streets* about a female prostitute. Then he met in real life, according to this one witness, a male prostitute. He was fascinated by him. Crane was a young journalist who died at twenty-eight, so he was pretty young when he worked on this. He liked prostitutes. In fact, he married one. The Hotel de Dream was the name of a house of prostitution in Jacksonville, Florida that his wife, Cora, owned. She was the madam. She was a bit older than him. So anyway, he felt comfortable with prostitutes. He had even been condemned by the police of New York for being too friendly with prostitutes and always defending them against the police. So I don't know. I think he was a guy fairly secure in his own sexuality who didn't get freaked out by gay people and, as a journalist, was very curious about them.

Lackey: But Woolf couldn't imagine this form of fiction. She couldn't imagine somebody actually filling in the lacuna the way you did. But you could imagine this. What was the shift in literary history that made you say that we could blend fact and fiction? And why couldn't Woolf see her way to the biographical novel?

White: Well, I don't know why she was so opaque about that, because, I mean, she got into the mind of her *dog* after all.

Lackey: But the dog is a created character versus a real person. You decided to fictionalize a real person, and most people would change the name. For instance, they would take Huey Long, and they would call him Willie Stark, as Robert Penn Warren did in *All the King's Men*. But you decided to name your character Stephen Crane. What happened? This is the question I am really trying to answer.

White: I guess that part of it is that her fiction was a real exploration of extreme subjectivity. I mean, that is really what all of her novels are about. There is not that much plot, and there is not that much milieu, but there is *almost* a stream of consciousness pursuit of the individual's thoughts. Like in *Mrs. Dalloway*, she gets into the mind of a madman, Septimus Warren Smith, and tries to recreate all of his thoughts. I suppose that would seem very daunting about a historical figure. You wouldn't feel confident that you could do it. That is the only real difference I can imagine. I think that, in a way, the exploration of historical subjects came on the heels of the era of the autobiographical novel. I think people got sick of saying "I," and they wanted to enter into a historical period and also recreate some of their favorite authors and so on. Sheila Kohler is a friend of mine, and she has a book, *Becoming Jane Eyre*. It is about the bedside vigil of Charlotte Brontë and how she is sitting by her sick father in London and how she begins to conceive this story and why. So I suppose it is always speculative. Roz Brackenbury, a Key West friend, has written a novel about George Sand. Another historical novel that occurred to me to write is to take *The Great Gatsby*. We are told that there is a moment in his life when he spent ten years aboard this yacht with this rich man, and that he changed his name from James Gatz to Jay Gatsby; changed his character; changed his attitudes about the world. That experience made him much more worldly. Yet Fitzgerald just skips over that period. It is treated in half a page.

Lackey: So you would fill that in.

White: Yes. I think that that would be a good subject for a book or at least a story.

Lackey: But that would be a very different kind of novel. That wouldn't be a biographical novel, because that is already a created character, whereas people are now writing about real people.

White: But the impulse is the same, to fill in a missing part of the story.

Lackey: With regard to the biographical novel, you are trying to access the internal reality of these people who have actually lived. But there are more restrictions with this kind of novel, right?

White: Yes. I did a lot of research, for instance, on *Fanny*. It was a book I wrote about Mrs. Trollope, Trollope's mother, who was called "Frances Trollope," and also Frances Wright, who was the head of a utopian colony in America on the Mississippi in the 1820s, which turned out to be a disaster. So anyway, I thought it would be fun to explore two very different personality types: one who is very principled, because she is rich and she can afford to be, and has high ideals and is slightly unbending about them—that is Frances Wright—and then Frances Trollope, who is very much more accommodating to the circumstances of her life, partly because she was in rags. She was in extreme poverty, and she had to survive somehow or other. So those two personality types were what I was trying to explore in *Fanny*.

Lackey: This gets to an important distinction. To date, you have written three separate biographies about Genet, Proust, and Rimbaud. But you have also written a biographical novel about Stephen Crane. Can you tell me: What is the difference between the two genres? And what is it that we can get in a biographical novel that we cannot get in a biography?

White: I was very frustrated when Paul Russell this last year brought out a biographical novel about Nabokov's brother. Nabokov had a gay brother, Sergey Nabokov, who was killed in the concentration camps as a gay. That is a story that I would have loved to have heard for real. I didn't want a novel, and I found the idea of that novel very frustrating, because no biography already existed of that man. He is somebody that everybody who likes Nabokov is curious about. I mean, Nabokov was very uptight about gay people, because both his brother and his uncle were gay, and he thought it was hereditary. Anyway, so there is an example of a biographical novel that I think was pointless. It should have been a biography. But I think when the biography is already well established, like in the case of Stephen Crane, and there is an important lacuna, then I see a need for a biographical novel. For instance, Crane didn't write autobiographically. The person who wrote the first biography of him, Thomas Beer, was a liar who was unmasked later and who created lots of letters from Stephen Crane that Crane had never really written. He did lots of falsification of his material. So very little is really known firsthand about Stephen Crane. Various people, like Ford Madox Ford and Henry James and other people who knew him, wrote tiny sketches, but nobody ever really wrote a proper biography who *knew* him. So he is a fairly shadowy figure.

Lackey: But what is it we can get through your novel that we can't get through a biography? What kind of truth, if we want to call it that, can we access?

White: If the story that he was trying to write a gay novel is true, that would have been very remarkable for the period really. Nobody else did it. That would have changed the whole course of American fiction. It would have extended people's sympathies in an unimaginable way. Because I am a gay writer and interested in gay history, I was interested in that. It also gave me a chance to recreate gay life of that period, including the gay slang and what the first gay bars were like, which I did research on. But I tried to stick with the facts, not to introduce anything that was contra-factual. On the other hand, there were just many gaps in people's knowledge, including mine. This whole novel, which I have him deciding to write again on his deathbed and then Henry James destroying the manuscript—that was all imagined. The book itself is imagined. So in other words, it was partly an act of ventriloquism, because that is a book that we have no record of. If it existed, it was destroyed, and I needed to recreate it, and also the thought process behind writing it, which we don't really think about, entirely.

Lackey: One striking thing about contemporary biographical novels is that *so* many deal with homoerotic desire. Bruce Duffy's *The World As I Found It* and *Disaster Was My God*, Jay Parini's *The Last Station* and *The Passages of H.M.*, and Michael Cunningham's *The Hours* are just a prominent few. In Russell Banks' *Cloudsplitter*, the narrator, Owen Brown, is John Brown's son, and Russell made him a repressed homosexual. Russell said he talked to you about this. In fact, Russell told me that he was delighted to hear that you considered his representation of Owen's struggle as a repressed homosexual to be believable and insightful. Why do you think so many contemporary biographical novels focus on homoerotic desire?

White: I think it is a great gap in knowledge. The necessary conditions for people coming out and calling themselves gay—that they live far from their families, that they be self-supporting, and that they live in a big city and be anonymous—weren't met for women, for instance, until the beginning of the twentieth century. There is really no trace of lesbian activity in the lower middle class before that. Suddenly, all these women were earning their living as typists and so on. So in other words, it is really a practical, sociological, economic dimension. The word "homosexual" was invented in the 1870s by a Hungarian doctor. There was a crime called "sodomy," and people were killed for it over the centuries. But it was a pretty wide spectrum—it included sex with animals and other things, too. It seems like Louis XIV's brother was gay, but he had to make his so called "gay" courtiers take a pledge that they would *stay* gay, because they were always drifting back into heterosexuality. All you have to do is read Foucault's *The History of Sexuality* to see how changeable the definition of homosexuality was. It really was constantly transforming itself. I think that modern homosexuality that we know of really started in World War Two. There is a very interesting book by Allan Bérubé about that, and James Lord wrote a book called *My Queer War*. I just read a new biography of John Horne Burns, who was in World War Two, and wrote an early novel with gay characters, *The Gallery*.

Lackey: But in terms of the biographical novel, there has to be a reason why so many of these novels have focused on homosexual characters.

White: To imagine the unimaginable! It hasn't been recorded yet. There is no record of it. Novelists like a challenge in trying to imagine something that hasn't been documented. So I think that is it—that's why so many have turned to that. After all, novelists like to invent things, and with ordinary middle-class urban homosexuality in the nineteenth century—everything has to be imagined. We don't know whether people thought they were feminine or members of a third sex or Uranians or degenerates or Ancient Greeks (Marius Bewley, the Rutgers professor who was educated at Cambridge, used to call gays "Athenians"). It must all be explored and speculated about.

Lackey: Let's shift to another question. In the context of the contemporary biographical novel, *Hotel de Dream* is unique in that there are two separate levels of creation. On one level, you have to imagine how Stephen Crane responded to his encounter with the boy-prostitute. But on another level, you have to imagine the kind of novel Crane would have written about this boy-prostitute. Something strikes me as very daring in creating scenes about a historical figure in order to communicate something substantive about that person and his or her age, but there is something even more daring about writing fiction in the voice of such a famous writer, like Crane. Can you talk about the challenges of doing this kind of writing? I am specifically interested in your reservations and ambivalence, if there were any, in doing this.

White: My task was to ventriloquize him. I was interested in his very lean style, which is very shocking, if you compare it to the other things being written at the time—even if you compare it to Henry James, let's say. It is so lean. It is much closer to Hemingway than it is to James. I did try to aim for that in a general way. But I never did any statistical analysis of what words he used or what turns of phrase he had. I just boldly went on and did it. The plot of the novel was a true imaginative act for me, because there was no history of it. I invented the banker, Theodore, who is in love with the boy.

Lackey: So you ventriloquized an earlier work, specifically *Maggie*, which was written in the early 1890s. Your novel takes place during the last few weeks of Crane's life in the year 1900. Each time a novelist produces a work, the new material propels him or her forward. Did you see your Crane as utilizing the same style as we see in *Maggie*? Or did you imagine some development in his style and thinking as you sought to represent the lives of Elliott and Theodore?

White: I saw it as an imaginative act for Crane in the sense that he wasn't gay, and he hadn't had any gay experiences, and yet he had interviewed this boy extensively, let's say, and as a reporter, he was very interested in him. I always feel that with fiction, it is always half a fairy tale and half a newspaper article. I mean, there is a dimension of truth and research in almost every novel. So I imagined him doing that. Very incidental, journalistic pieces were what I imitated his voice from more. Like, for instance, he covered a fire for a newspaper. His whole description of the horses dragging the fire engine to the side of the fire is very impressionistic. He doesn't really break it down in a logical way. He just tries to recreate the feeling of this conflagration. Well, that was kind of a hint to me. There is a fire in *The Painted Boy*, and I tried to treat it that way, too.

Lackey: You mention that Crane was heterosexual, and you also point out that he was initially disgusted with the boy-prostitute that he meets. But throughout the novel, Crane undergoes a transformation. Do you believe that the actual Crane would have undergone a similar transformation? If so, what in Crane's writing and biography leads you to believe that this is the case?

White: I think he had very wide sympathies. He was very melancholy. For instance, there is a whole period of about a month and a half in his life when he was in Havana, and his wife was absolutely desperate for him to make a sign that he was alive. But he didn't. He just vanished into the bowels of Havana. Yet he was very friendly to the people that he met in his everyday life in Havana, including the landlady of the boarding house where he stayed and so on. He was a very friendly guy. Everybody attested to that. He was a big party boy. He liked to constantly have people around him in his stately home in England. They had food fights, and they were kind of juvenile. But he had a tremendous charm that seduced almost everybody who met him. He was one of the most popular Americans, you can say, in England at that time. His father was a minister. He was brought up in a very strict way, though he was the youngest child. He was brought up more by older siblings than by his parents, who died when he was quite young. I think that he rebelled against that narrow family upbringing. He had wide sympathies.

Lackey: Which we see in *Maggie*. He clearly has this capacity and gift to identify with someone from the lower or the poor classes. So it's only a matter of logical extension that, had he had contact with somebody like Elliott, he probably would have identified with him, as well.

White: I think so. It is hard to say. People's feeling that homosexuality was a disease and that it was dangerous and that it was degenerate and infectious, too... All these things influenced their thinking. But I think if anybody could have been a big enough spirit, it would have been Crane.

Lackey: Jay Parini says that some of the greatest works of literature shift human consciousness. Had Crane written and published something like *The Painted Boy*, do you think that it would have inspired more hatred of gays? Or, do you think that it would have shifted consciousness about gays? To be more specific, had something like *The Painted Boy* been published, let us say, in the year 1900, would E. M. Forster have been able to publish *Maurice* in the early twentieth century rather than in 1971?

White: I think that it is conceivable that it could have had a big influence. After all, he was an extremely prominent writer. He was paid top dollar for his writing as a journalist. He was constantly writing in order to pay the bills, because he and Cora had a very extravagant way of life. I think that, had he written this book, it might have broadened people's sympathies.

Lackey: Especially because of the way he writes. Because he could make us feel for Maggie, maybe he would have been able to make us feel for Elliott and Theodore.

White: Yes.

Lackey: But this gets to a really interesting point. Through the character of Theodore Koch, you imagine an inner world with all its confusions and conflicts of an average, middle-class banker who has homosexual yearnings but has been psychologically and culturally coerced into a heterosexual marriage. Would it be right to say that *The Painted Boy* is not really about the life of Elliott? That it's primarily about Theodore Koch? His conflict? His state of mind? Did your Crane start with one idea—the life of a boy—but then shift to another idea—the life of a closeted homosexual who is even in the closet to himself?

White: I think when I was writing it, I was very influenced by an article that I read by James Fenton in the *New York Review of Books* years ago in which he talked about Maillol, the French sculptor, who was commissioned by Harry Kessler, a German homosexual, to do a statue of a boy. Maillol was famously a womanizer who always did the most beautiful, luscious women. But he was broke in the 30s, so he accepted this commission to do this sculpture of a boy in a telegraph delivery boy's uniform. The statue is now missing, but we have a photo of it. Somehow, that stuck in my mind. I imagined Theodore commissioning a sculptor to do this sculpture of Elliott nude in marble that he could have sitting in his living room, because it would look like the kind of neoclassical work of art that everybody had. I guess that gave me the germ for the idea. But then once I did that, I started to do research. A lot of my plot ideas came from the research. I was working at the Cullman Center at the 42nd Street library, and I had access to seven million books and to lots of librarians who would help me. So I asked a particular librarian, "If you were commissioning a sculpture in 1890 by a mediocre artist, how much would it cost?" He did a lot of rummaging around in *The Stone Cutter's Manual* and in various auction catalogues, and he came up with a price. Then I began to think, "Who would be the sculptor?" And I thought, "Well, who did the lions in front of the library?" It was a guy named Piccirilli. Then I thought, "Well, it would be very convenient for me if he were gay." Then I read a 1,000 page biography of him, and he *was* gay! He didn't get married until he was fifty. He lived with the Italian ambassador to America who was constantly being arrested for molesting boys and so on. So it is only circumstantial evidence, but still. I began to get very interested in Piccirilli who had a big atelier in the nineteenth century, because in the nineteenth century, no American knew how to sculpt a heroic statue in marble. All they could do was create a little maquette, which they would send off to Italy—to Carrara, usually—and there the workmen would render the maquette into a big thing. The Lincoln Memorial, for instance, wasn't really done by Daniel Chester French, but by stone carvers in Italy. Piccirilli moved here with five of his brothers. They were from Carrara. They had been trained by their father. They set up a big studio in the Bronx, in Morrisania, and they took on these giant commissions like that.

Lackey: That Theodore would commission such a statue testifies to the depth of his feeling for Elliott. What does the biographical novel tell us about the inner life of a character like Theodore? What kind of emotional response did you want to elicit in your reader about him?

White: I suppose because it's a *novel* the reader is more likely to accept it or to entertain it without subjecting it constantly to doubts of plausibility. If I had included Elliott's story in the so-called biographical parts about Crane, the reader would have been more skeptical, more suspicious.

Lackey: Your Henry James has a very negative response to Crane's story about homosexuality. Why target James? On what basis do you suggest that he would have done something so incredibly cruel as to burn Crane's manuscript? Through this act, do we learn something specific about James, or do we get more insight into the culture of which James was a part?

White: I think both. James was a self-hating gay man. There's one moment where Hugh Walpole, an English writer, young and handsome, came toward him with his arms extended, and James just cowered and said, "I can't. I can't!" As far as we know, he never really had sex with anybody, but he developed a tremendous crush on a Scandinavian sculptor, Hendrik Christian Andersen. There is a big exchange of letters. The sculptor lived in Rome.

Lackey: This is in the Tóibín novel, *The Master*, right?

White: Yeah. The Tóibín novel, I think, really shows quite well what it is like to be in the mind of a closet queen. He veers away constantly from any realization of where his desires might be taking him.

Lackey: And also intimacy. He never experiences true intimacy because he is blocking off such a key component of his own humanity.

White: That's right. Like when he is in Ireland at some lady's stately home, she arranges for her gay butler or whatever... But it doesn't come off because James resists it. I took my clue from that.

Lackey: From the Tóibín novel?

White: Yes. His book came out three years before mine.

Lackey: But your novel seems a bit harsh on James, whereas Tóibín...

White: ...is very generous. Well, you couldn't write a major figure that would be so harsh, but you could write a minor figure my way. I did want to suggest that the worst enemy of gays then and now are other gays.

Lackey: So what would your Joseph Conrad have done with *The Painted Boy*, had your Crane directed Cora to give it to him to complete?

White: I think he would have hated it. Conrad had a military bearing and consciousness and was not very sympathetic, I don't think, toward this dimension of human behavior. I think a woman would have been the best bet, really. *Maybe* a woman could have finished the book. But I don't think that any of those men would have been able to deal with it.

Lackey: There was a famous forum with Robert Penn Warren, Ralph Ellison, and William Styron. The historian C. Vann Woodward moderated it. It is a debate about the ethics and wisdom of naming a protagonist in a novel after the original figure. Ellison praised Warren for changing Huey Long's name to Willie Stark in *All the King's Men*, and he criticized Styron for naming Nat Turner after the original person in *The Confessions of Nat Turner*. Ellison's critique was twofold. He said that naming the protagonist after the original person would necessarily lead the author to misrepresent the complexity and details of the original person, and it would make the novelist vulnerable to attack from historians. How would you respond to Ellison's critique?

White: I was very conscious of that. So, for instance, I managed to get a blurb out of Paul Sorrentino, a historian who is writing the definitive biography of Stephen Crane. I thought I would be much more attacked than I was, but I guess that people have forgotten Crane, largely. Or they don't think about him much. There aren't too many academics who are worrying about him anymore.

Lackey: Part of it, however, could be that we are now more accepting of the biographical novel. This has become such a legitimized art form that people are willing to give us more freedom to take these kinds of liberties. Do you think that is part of it?

White: Yes, but see, in one sense, I don't feel like I did take liberties. I feel like nothing I said about Crane was contra-factual. I might have added things— that he wrote this book or that he had sympathies toward gay people—but it was all an extension of what was known. I never said anything in the book that was not true, to my knowledge.

Lackey: At this point, I want to pose a challenge to your approach to Crane. In his fiction, Crane emphasized the role the environment plays in shaping character's lives and destinies. Given the logic of this model, do you think Crane would have understood homosexuality as a consequence of a warped and twisted environment? Or, do you think he would have recognized that there are people who have natural inclinations for same-sex partners, that this is something not environmentally determined?

White: I think that the most progressive thinking of that period would have taken the environmental stance. There are many people who did have biological ideas, including Nabokov, who was born in 1899. He thought of homosexuality that way. There was a famous Italian, Cesare Lombroso, who had a theory about people—about the criminal, for instance—that you could measure his skull. Criminal anthropometry. I know about it because Genet was forced by law to carry around his papers that showed the measurements of his skull, all by these Lombroso principles, because he had been convicted. He was a multiple offender. He was arrested once for not having those papers on him. But Lombroso himself renounced those ideas by 1900 or so. He said that they weren't scientific, that the facts had proved him wrong. I think most people did feel the environment was the decisive factor at that point in history.

Lackey: I think that it would have been difficult for Crane, who was so influenced by the view that environment determines human behavior, to see Elliott or Theodore as having natural or legitimate desire, because he would have just interpreted that desire through an environmental lens. He would have interpreted it as a form of perversion or distortion.

White: A form of decadence... But the positivists tried to show genetics determined everything. Lombroso even tried to prove that artistic genius was a form of inherited madness. But there is still no reason why you can't be sympathetic or charitable toward people who have been "ruined" by their environment.

Lackey: This is one of the central reasons why the biographical novel is so valuable. You imagine the inner life of Stephen Crane, and how his aesthetic sensibility would have been impacted by a particular experience. Can you briefly discuss the power writing would have in shaping and expanding a person's sensibility and sensitivity? Here I am thinking specifically of your Crane's imagined response to gay characters insofar as it could have translated into a literary work.

White: There is something about the act of elaborating a novel that expands our mind-set. For instance, I have heard that Tolstoy wanted originally to show that Anna Karenina was a she-devil, *une dévoreuse d'hommes*, but that he set the book aside for a long time and when he returned to it she was a far more sympathetic character, far from its initial conception. He became more human because of artistic, not ethical reasons.

Lackey: One of the things that I have noticed is that there has been a shift in our attitude about the biographical novel. Let me explain why I think this. I started this interview by saying Virginia Woolf couldn't have imagined her way towards the biographical novel. Ralph Ellison condemned the biographical novel; he praised Warren for changing Huey Long's name to Willie Stark, and he condemned Styron for not changing the character's name. Georg Lukács is very negative about the biographical novel; he said it is a perversion and distortion of the historical novel, because it necessarily misrepresents history. But then there is 1999, which is a big year, because Michael Cunningham's *The Hours* and Russell Banks's *Cloudsplitter* are both up for the Pulitzer, and Michael won it. Put simply, the literary establishment decided in that year that the biographical novel is now a legitimate art form, and it gave an American biographical novel the highest honor in literature. Why did it take so long? And why 1999?

White: I don't know. I think that in the English language, as opposed to French or German, there has, for a long time, been an interest in biography and autobiography. I think that those were considered very high literary forms—especially the literary biography—throughout the century. That is not true in France. It is always dismissed as an American perversion of the biography. So the biography was a high-prestige form and many prominent novelists, like Sylvia Townsend Warner, who wrote a life of T. H. White, turned out distinguished biographies. But they called them biographies— they didn't call them novels. Then there was a thing called "*la biographie romancée.*" In other words, it was a biography that had been novelized. That was considered a fairly low form. So I guess for this form to be elevated, it was necessary to see that real writers were doing it. And why did real writers let themselves do it? I think it was because a lot of them became older people, and like a lot of older people throughout the world, they got interested in history. And also, they had read so much—so many memoirs, biographies, and histories—that they could see that it would be interesting to recreate a period. I mean, after all, so many great novels, like *War and Peace*, are historical novels. There was also the desire during a period of low sales of a novel to attach a new work to a canonical figure.

Lackey: But there is a difference between a historical novel and a biographical novel. Why center them in the consciousness of a character?

White: *War and Peace* has a general who was a real general, Kutuzov, who won the battle of Borodino. That writer has to imagine what it would be like to be a Russian general, endlessly retreating in front of Napoleon. It is not unheard of.

Lackey: But you wouldn't consider *War and Peace* a biographical novel?

White: No. But it has principal characters that were based on real people— like Kutuzov.

Lackey: Right. And I do wonder what has motivated so many of these contemporary writers to center their narratives within a particular consciousness.

White: Well, I think oftentimes people see a parallel between an earlier period and their own. They see a chance of dramatizing a contemporary problem through talking about its roots in the past.

Lackey: Russell Banks does exactly that in *Cloudsplitter*. He examines the race issue in the nineteenth century, but he decides to make Owen Brown gay, and there is no documentary evidence to suggest that he was gay. But as Russell recently said to me, "Look, the novel is not just about the past. It is also about our present." He realized that, when you think about the make-up of society, there had to be gay people back then. The problem is that we don't know how they lived, what they suffered through, and what they experienced. What he realized is that the race issue and the gay issue could be aligned here in an important way, which is one of the reasons he decided to go back to create a gay character in *Cloudsplitter*. It was partly because of the contemporary situation, the big transformation that we see going on now about gay rights and the gay lifestyle, the radical affirmation of that lifestyle we see today.

White: Yes, I think that is a real issue. I read lots of articles on microfilm at the library about a raid on this bar called The Slide, which was the first gay bar. The journalist, though he is pretending to be horrified, is going into lots of juicy details, explaining how these transvestite prostitutes were all sitting. And I used to go to that bar. It was called "The Bleecker Street Tavern" when I first arrived in New York. I had no idea it had been the first gay bar and that that derelict balcony, which was condemned in my day, had been *the* balcony where prostitutes would sit and entertain their clients. I learned something recently, while I was writing the book, and I went to visit the place, which is now called "Kenny's Hideaway." The owner was standing in front. He said, "There are little rooms down below that were the *chambres d'assignations* where the prostitutes would take their clients—and they are still there." You know, I found all that fascinating. I really love history, and I love research. As for Ralph Ellison, I think what he might have criticized people for is actually what other novelists today admire: that they are able to invent these very dramatic experiences that aren't recorded anywhere which are perfectly coherent with what we know as historical fact.

Lackey: I think part of Ellison's critique was that the specific historical reference de-universalized the universal. Specifying an individual or party would take away from the power to have universal significance. So in *Invisible Man*, he never mentions the Communist Party, but we know the Brotherhood could be a representation of the Communist Party. The reason why he wanted to do that was because he wanted to say, "this isn't just about the Communist Party. This could apply to so many other organizations."

White: All my life I have heard the most conservative and bigoted views defended as "universal." Whenever a gay man hears the word "universal" he reaches for his sword. The family, physical courage, fidelity, the "glory" of war—these are among the conservative values that old-fashioned writers defend. Virgil Thomson once said to me about my early avant-garde writing, "Well, this is all very fine, but you are like those twelve-tone composers who do their best work by the time they are thirty and then never write again. If you are not interested in the real world, you will dry up as a writer." I thought that was brilliant advice. I saw Toni Morrison introduce Styron toward the end of his life in a very generous and wholehearted way, because those race wars and cultural wars had all blown over. It is true that he encountered a tremendous amount of resentment at the time of his Turner book. I know about that because Genet, in writing *The Blacks*, was at first acclaimed by the American blacks, and then the so-called Negro Ensemble Company put it on. It was the longest running play up to that time off Broadway. But then later, Ed Bullins and lots of other black writers denounced it, saying that no white had the right to write about the black experience. That period of the late sixties, early seventies was terribly polemicized around race, especially by young black writers who wanted to claim that territory for themselves.

Lackey: When you think of the best and the worst biographical novels, which ones strike you most? Here, I am trying to figure out: What are the ones that work, and what are the ones that don't work? And can you explain why they work or don't work?

White: I wrote a terrible review of a book by a Scottish woman called Alison Fell. It was about medieval Japan, and the women were marching around as feminists! It borrowed lots of information from *The Tale of Genji* and *The Pillow Book* of Sei Shōnagon, but it didn't respect the spirit of that age. It had what I call "modern figures in period drag," and I think that is the kind of historical novel I hate. Paul LaFarge's novel about Haussmann, the man who rebuilt Paris, ignored this man's achievement and invented all sorts of trivia that had nothing to do with him. But maybe I was tone-deaf to the book's appeal, which was praised by Dave Eggers.

Lackey: So in your view, it is this spirit of the age idea that is really central. It has to capture that in some way.

White: Yes. It has to be the archeology of the past in terms of mores and attitudes as well as clothes and everything else. I think a bad historical novel is one that dresses up modern people in old-fashioned clothes. I remember my stepmother used to read things like *Désirée*, which was about this Swedish queen, Désirée Clary, who was engaged to Napoleon and who was married to that Napoleonic general who founded the royal house of Sweden. She was just some modern girl with all the attitudes of the 1950s.

Lackey: What are the positive ones? What are the best biographical novels? And can you explain why?

White: Well, I think Russell's book is wonderful, and I liked *The Hours*, too. I thought it was very, very good, because I thought he did try to really recreate Virginia Woolf's persona; also, the subsequent readings of her book and the way it had ramifications on people of the present day. But I think that the most important thing for me is that the person should have done his research and not have things that are jarring, in terms of the historical fact—both the attitudes and the details of everyday life. The best biographical novels flesh out and clarify what historians know but in terms that are true and characteristic of the period and not of ours.

Contributors

Julia Alvarez was born in New York City, and spent the first ten years of her life in her family's native country, the Dominican Republic. In 1960, her family was forced to flee to the United States because of her father's involvement in a plot to overthrow dictator Trujillo. Alvarez has been practicing the craft of writing for over forty years. She has brought a variety of work to readers of all ages, including novels, like *How the García Girls Lost Their Accents* and *In the Time of Butterflies*; picturebooks; the Tía Lola stories for middle readers; novels for young adults; collections of poetry, including *The Woman I Kept to Myself*; and non-fiction, most recently *A Wedding in Haiti*. With her husband, Bill Eichner, she founded Alta Gracia, a sustainable farm and literacy center in the Dominican Republic. Currently, she is a writer in residence at Middlebury College in Vermont.

Russell Banks is the internationally acclaimed author of seventeen works of fiction, including the novels *Continental Drift*, *Rule of the Bone*, *The Book of Jamaica* and *Lost Memory of Skin*, as well as five short story collections. Two of his novels, *The Sweet Hereafter* and *Affliction*, have been adapted into award-winning films. Banks has been a PEN/Faulkner Finalist (*Affliction*, *Cloudsplitter*, *Lost Memory of Skin*) and a Pulitzer Prize Finalist (*Continental Drift*, *Cloudsplitter*). His work has received numerous other awards and has been widely translated and anthologized. Banks is a member of the American Academy of Arts and Letters and was New York State Author (2004–8). He lives in Miami, Florida and in upstate New York with his wife, the poet Chase Twichell.

Madison Smartt Bell is the author of twelve novels. His biographical novel, *All Souls' Rising*, was a finalist for the 1995 National Book Award and the 1996 PEN/Faulkner Award and winner of the 1996 Anisfield-Wolf award for the best book of the year dealing with matters of race. *All Souls' Rising* is the first novel in his trilogy about the Haitian Revolution, which includes *Master of the Crossroads* and *The Stone That the Builder Refused*. Bell also published *Toussaint Louverture: A Biography*. Born and raised in Tennessee, he has lived in New York and in London and now lives in Baltimore, Maryland. Since 1984 he has taught at Goucher College, along with his wife, the poet Elizabeth Spires. He has been a member of the Fellowship of Southern Writers since 2003.

M. Allen Cunningham is the author of the novels *The Green Age of Asher Witherow* and *Lost Son*, the illustrated limited edition short story collection *Date of Disappearance*, and a volume of nonfiction, *The Honorable Obscurity Handbook*. Cunningham's debut, *The Green Age of Asher Witherow*, set in nineteenth-century Northern California, was a #1 Indie Next Pick and a finalist for the 2005 Indie Next Book of the Year Award alongside Marilynne Robinson's *Gilead* and Philip Roth's *The Plot Against America*. *Lost Son*, Cunningham's novel about the life and work of Rainer Maria Rilke, was named a Top Ten Book of 2007 by *The Oregonian*. Cunningham lives in Portland, Oregon where he has recently completed two new novels.

Michael Cunningham is the author of the novels *A Home at the End of the World*, *Flesh and Blood*, *The Hours*, *Specimen Days*, and *By Nightfall*, as well as a non-fiction book, *Lands End: A Walk Through Provincetown*. *The Hours*, which was made into a film in 2002, received the 1999 PEN/Faulkner Award and the Pulitzer Prize. Cunningham's essays, reviews, and short stories have appeared in such publications as the *New Yorker*, the *Atlantic*, and the *New York Times*. His short fiction has been included in the annual *O. Henry* and *Best American Stories* collections. He lives in New York City, and teaches at Yale University.

Anita Diamant (www.anitadiamant.com) is the Boston-based author of twelve books, including *The Red Tent*, an international bestseller published in twenty-five countries and twenty languages. Her other novels include *Good Harbor*, *The Last Days of Dogtown* and *Day After Night*. She has published a collection of essays and six non-fiction guides to contemporary Jewish life, including *The New Jewish Wedding* and *Choosing a Jewish Life*. Her feature stories and essays have appeared in such publications as *The Boston Globe*, *Boston Magazine*, *Real Simple* and *Hadassah Magazine*. Diamant is also a lyricist, blogger and script writer. She is the founding president of Mayyim Hayyim Living Waters Community Mikveh and Education Center in Newton, Massachusetts, an inclusive and expansive twenty-first century reinvention of the ancient Jewish ritual of immersion. www.mayyimyayyim.org

Bruce Duffy's first novel *The World As I Found It* (1987) has been reprinted as a New York Review Books Classic. He is also author of the 1997 semi-autobiographical novel, *Last Comes the Egg*. In 2011, Duffy's third novel, *Disaster Was My God*—based on the turbulent life of French poet-prodigy Arthur Rimbaud—was published. A former Guggenheim Fellow, Duffy is the recipient of the 1988 Whiting Writer's Award, a three-year Lila

Wallace-Reader's Digest Award, and a 1991 National Magazine Award nomination by *Harper's* for his essay "Feeling Something." As a journalist, Duffy has written for *Harper's*, *Life*, *The New York Times Book Review* and *Magazine*, *Discovery*, *The Village Voice*, *GQ* and *The Daily Beast*, covering everything from third-world war zones, to riding the rails with hoboes, to the Hubble Space Telescope. Duffy is now at work on a new novel, *A Towering Brilliance*, built around the birth and aftermath of the atomic bomb.

Ron Hansen is the author of eight novels, including *Desperadoes*, *The Assassination of Jesse James by the Coward Robert Ford*, *Mariette in Ecstasy*, *Hitler's Niece*, *Exiles*, and most recently *A Wild Surge of Guilty Passion*, as well as a children's book and *A Stay Against Confusion: Essays on Faith & Fiction*. Twice nominated for a PEN/Faulkner Award, he was a finalist for the National Book Award for his novel *Atticus*, and is a recipient of an Award in Literature from the American Academy and Institute of Arts and Letters. Scribner published his *She Loves Me Not: New and Selected Stories*. Married to the novelist Bo Caldwell, Hansen is Director of Creative Writing at Santa Clara University where he is the Gerard Manley Hopkins, S. J. Professor in the Arts and Humanities.

Sherry Jones's debut novel, *The Jewel of Medina*, sparked international controversy in 2008 with its ground-breaking portrayal of the relationship between the Muslim prophet Muhammad and his young wife, A'isha. Its original publisher, Random House, canceled its publication out of fear of terrorist attacks, setting off a worldwide debate about free speech, censorship, and the portrayal of religious figures in biographical fiction. The book became a best-seller with translation rights sold in nineteen languages. The sequel, *The Sword of Medina*, telling of the spread of Islam after Muhammad's death and A'isha's role in the first Islamic civil war, won a silver medal in the Independent Publisher Books Awards and is also an international best-selling novel. Her biographical novel *Four Sisters, All Queens* and e-novella *White Heart* were published by Simon & Schuster. Jones continues to write biographical fiction from her home in Spokane, Washington.

Rebecca Kanner is the author of the biographical novel *Sinners and the Sea*, which examines the life of Noah's unnamed wife. She has won an Associated Writing Programs Award and a Loft Mentorship Award. Her stories have been published in numerous journals including *The Kenyon Review* and *The Cincinnati Review*. Her personal essay, "Safety," is listed as a Notable Essay in

Best American Essays 2011. She is a freelance writer and teaches writing at the Loft in Minneapolis.

Michael Lackey is a scholar of twentieth-century intellectual, political, and literary history. A recipient of the Alexander von Humboldt Fellowship, a University of Minnesota Institute for Advanced Study Residential Fellowship, and an NEH Summer Stipend, he has published articles in dozens of academic journals. His first book, *African American Atheists and Political Liberation: A Study of the Socio-Cultural Dynamics of Faith*, was named a "Choice Outstanding Academic Title" for 2008, and Bloomsbury published his most recent book, *The Modernist God State: A Literary Study of the Nazis' Christian Reich*. He is also the editor of *The Haverford Discussions: A Black Integrationist Manifesto for Racial Justice*, which contains a previously unpublished manuscript from African American writers such as Ralph Ellison, John Hope Franklin, St. Clair Drake, Kenneth Clark, Adelaide M. Cromwell, and Phyllis Wallace.

Kate Moses is the author of *Wintering: A Novel of Sylvia Plath*, which has been published in fifteen languages. She is the recipient of the Janet Heidinger Kafka Prize and a *Prix des Lectrices de Elle*, and her book *Cakewalk, a Memoir*, was a finalist for the Northern California Book Award for Creative Nonfiction and chosen by NPR as one of their favorite memoirs of the year. A founding editor of Salon, Moses coedited two critically acclaimed anthologies of essays inspired by the site: the national bestselling, American Book Award-winning *Mothers Who Think: Tales of Real-Life Parenthood* and *Because I Said So: 33 Mothers Write About Children, Sex, Men, Aging, Faith, Race & Themselves*. Moses' other honors include fellowships from the Lannan Foundation, the Djerassi Foundation, the MacDowell Colony, and Headlands Center for the Arts, and selection for Barnes & Noble's "Discover Great New Writers" program. A native San Franciscan, she now lives in upstate New York.

Joyce Carol Oates, 2011 recipient of the President's Medal of Honor in the Humanities, is the author most recently of the novels *The Accursed, Daddy Love,* and *Carthage*. She has been awarded the National Book Award, the PEN/Malamud Award, and the Common Wealth Award for Literary Achievement. Since 1978, she has been on the faculty at Princeton University. Her biographical novel *Blonde* was the 2010 Deauville American Film Festival Literary Award winner.

Lance Olsen is author of more than twenty books of and about experimental writing practices, including the historiographic metafictions *Calendar of Regrets*, *Head in Flames*, *Anxious Pleasures*, *Nietzsche's Kisses*, and *Girl Imagined by Chance*, and the anti-textbook *Architectures of Possibility: After Innovative Writing*. His short stories, essays, and reviews have appeared in hundreds of journals, magazines, and anthologies, including *Conjunctions*, *Fiction International*, *Village Voice*, *Time Out New York*, *McSweeney's*, and *Best American Non-Required Reading*. A Guggenheim, N.E.A., and Berlin Prize fellowship recipient, he serves as chair of the Board of Directors at Fiction Collective Two and as fiction editor at *Western Humanities Review*. He teaches experimental theory and practice at the University of Utah. With his wife, assemblage-artist and filmmaker Andi Olsen, he divides his time between Salt Lake City and the mountains of central Idaho.

Jay Parini is D.E. Axin Professor of English and Creative Writing at Middlebury College, a former Guggenheim fellow, a former Fowler Hamilton Fellow at Christ Church, Oxford, and a former fellow of the Institute for Advanced Studies at the University of London. In 1990, Parini published *The Last Station*, a biographical novel about Leo Tolstoy's last year which has been translated into more than twenty-five languages and made into a Hollywood film. Parini has published biographies about Robert Frost, John Steinbeck, and William Faulkner, and he has published biographical novels about Walter Benjamin (*Benjamin's Crossing*) and Herman Melville (*The Passages of H.M.*). He has also published *Some Necessary Angels*, a collection of essays that contains some of the most important discussions about the shifting and collapsing borders between biography and the biographical novel.

Joanna Scott is the author of eight novels, including *Follow Me*, *Liberation*, *Tourmaline*, *Make Believe*, *The Manikin*, and *Arrogance*, and two collections of short fiction, *Various Antidotes* and *Everybody Loves Somebody*. Her books have been finalists for the Pulitzer Prize, the PEN/Faulkner, and the LA Times Book Award. Awards include a MacArthur Fellowship, a Lannan Literary Award, a Guggenheim Fellowship, the Ambassador Book Award from the English-Speaking Union, and the Rosenthal Award from the American Academy of Arts and Letters.

Edmund White has written some twenty-five books. He is perhaps best known for his biography of French writer Jean Genet, for which he won the National Book Critics Circle Award. He is also the author of a trilogy of autobiographical novels—*A Boy's Own Story, The Beautiful Room is Empty,* and *The Farewell Symphony.* He has written brief lives of Marcel Proust and Arthur Rimbaud and a book about unconventional Paris called *The Flâneur.* His most recent published works of fiction are *Chaos, Hotel de Dream* and *Jack Holmes and His Friend.* His latest non-fiction is *City Boy,* a memoir about New York in the 1970s. In 2014 Bloomsbury will publish *Inside a Pearl: My Years in Paris.* He is a member of the American Academy of Arts and Letters and an officer in the French Order of Arts and Letters. He teaches writing at Princeton and lives in New York City.

Bibliography

Alvarez, Julia (1994 [2010]), *In the Time of the Butterflies*. Chapel Hill: Algonquin Books.

Banks, Russell (1998), *Cloudsplitter*. New York: HarperPerennial

Bell, Madison Smartt (1995 [2004]), *All Souls' Rising*. New York: Vintage Books.

Bontemps, Arna (1936 [1992]), *Black Thunder: Gabriel's Revolt: Virginia, 1800*. Boston: Beacon Press.

Butler, Judith, Ernesto Laclau, and Slavoj Žižek (2000), *Contingency, Hegemony, Universality: Contemporary Dialogues on the Left*. London: Verso.

Capote, Truman (1965), *In Cold Blood: A True Account of a Multiple Murder and Its Consequences*. New York: Random House.

Carnes, Mark C. (2001) *Novel History: Historians and Novelists Confront America's Past (and Each Other)*. New York: Simon & Schuster.

Cezair-Thompson, Margaret (2007 [2008]), *The Pirate's Daughter: A Novel*. New York: Random House.

Chakrabarty, Dipesh (2000), *Provincializing Europe: Postcolonial Thought and Historical Difference*. Princeton: Princeton University Press.

Charyn, Jerome (2010), *The Secret Life of Emily Dickinson*. New York: W. W. Norton & Company.

Coover, Robert (1976 [1977]), *The Public Burning*. New York: The Viking Press.

Cunningham, Mark Allen (2007), *Lost Son: A Novel*. Denver: Unbridled Books.

Cunningham, Michael (1998), *The Hours: A Novel*. New York: Picador.

Danto, Arthur C. (1981), *The Transfiguration of the Commonplace: A Philosophy of Art*. Cambridge MA: Harvard University Press.

Davis, Lennard J. (1996), *Factual Fictions: The Origins of the English Novel*. Philadelphia: University of Pennsylvania Press.

DeLillo, Don (1991), *Libra*. 1988. New York: Penguin Books.

Diamant, Anita (1997), *The Red Tent: A Novel*. New York: Picador.

Doctorow, E. L. "False Documents." *American Review* 26 (1977): 215–32.

Duffy, Bruce (1987 [2010]), *The World As I Found It*. New York: New York Review Books.

—(2011), *Disaster Was My God: A Novel of the Outlaw Life of Arthur Rimbaud*. New York: Doubleday.

Ellison, Ralph (1947 [1995]), *Invisible Man*. New York: Vintage International.

Ellison, Ralph et al., "The Uses of History in Fiction." *Southern Literary Journal* (Spring 1969): 57–90.

Endore, Guy (1956), *King of Paris*. New York: Simon and Schuster.

—(1961), *Voltaire! Voltaire!* New York: Simon and Schuster.

—(1965), *Satan's Saint: A Novel about the Marquis de Sade*. New York: Crown Publishers, Inc.

Fischer, Heinz-D. and Erika J. Fischer (2007), *Chronicle of the Pulitzer Prizes for Fiction: Discussions, Decisions and Documents.* Munich: K. G. Saur Verlag.

Foley, Barbara (1986), *Telling the Truth: The Theory and Practice of Documentary Fiction.* Ithaca: Cornell University Press, 1986.

Foucault, Michel (1969 [1972]), "The Archaeology of Knowledge & The Discourse on Language." New York: Pantheon Books.

—(1970 [1994]), *The Order of Things: An Archaeology of the Human Sciences.* New York: Vintage Books.

Frus, Phyllis (1994), *The Politics and Poetics of Journalistic Narrative: The Timely and the Timeless.* Cambridge: Cambridge University Press.

Hall, Brian (2003), *I Should Be Extremely Happy in Your Company: A Novel of Lewis and Clark.* New York: Viking.

Hansen, Ron (1983 [2007]), *The Assassination of Jesse James by the Coward Robert Ford.* New York: HarperPerennial.

—(1999 [2000]), *Hitler's Niece: A Novel.* New York: HarperPerennial.

—(2009), *Exiles: A Novel.* New York: Picador.

Hogan, Patrick Colm, "Literary Universals," *Poetics Today.* Vol. 18, No. 2 (Summer 1997): 223–49.

Hollowell, John (1977), *Fact & Fiction: The New Journalism and the Nonfiction Novel.* Chapel Hill: The University of North Carolina Press.

Hurston, Zora Neale (1939 [1991]), *Moses, Man of the Mountain.* New York: HarperPerennial.

Hussey, Mark (2012), "Woolf: After Lives," in *Virginia Woolf in Context.* Bryony Randall and Jane Goldman (eds). Cambridge: Cambridge University Press.

Hutcheon, Linda (1988), *A Poetics of Postmodernism: History, Theory, Fiction.* New York: Routledge.

Iggers, George G. (1997), *Historiography in the Twentieth Century: From Scientific Objectivity to the Postmodern Challenge.* Hanover: Wesleyan University Press.

Jackson, Lawrence P. (2011), *The Indignant Generation: A Narrative History of African American Writers and Critics, 1934–1960.* Princeton: Princeton University Press.

Jones, Sherry (2008), *The Jewel of Medina: A Novel.* New York: Beaufort Books.

—(2009), *The Sword of Medina: A Novel.* New York: Beaufort Books.

Kanner, Rebecca (2013), *Sinners and the Sea: The Untold Story of Noah's Wife.* New York: Howard Books.

Kundera, Milan (1986 [1988]), *The Art of the Novel.* New York: HarperPerennial.

Lukács, Georg (1962 [1983]), *The Historical Novel.* Lincoln: University of Nebraska Press.

Lyotard, Jean-François (1979 [1984]), *The Postmodern Condition: A Report on Knowledge.* Minneapolis: University of Minnesota Press.

Mailer, Norman (1979 [1998]), *The Executioner's Song*. New York: Vintage Books.

Malmgren, Carl Darryl (1985), *Fictional Space in the Modernist and Postmodernist American Novel*. Lewisburg: Bucknell University Press.

Mamet, David (1997), *The Old Religion*. New York: The Free Press.

McIlvanney, Liam and Ray Ryan (eds) (2011), *The Good of the Novel*. New York: Continuum International.

Monk, Ray, "The Fictitious Life: Virginia Woolf on Biography and Reality," *Philosophy and Literature*. 31(2007): 1–40.

Moses, Kate (2003), *Wintering: A Novel of Sylvia Plath*. New York: Anchor Books.

Nietzsche, Friedrich (1967), *The Birth of Tragedy and The Case of Wagner*. Translated by Walter Kaufmann. New York: Vintage Books.

Oates, Joyce Carol (1992 [1993]), *Black Water*. New York: Plume.

—(2000 [2009]), *Blonde: A Novel*. New York: Ecco.

—(2008 [2009]), *Wild Nights: Stories about the Lasts Days of Poe, Dickinson, Twain, James, and Hemingway*. New York: HarperPerennial.

Olds, Bruce (1995), *Raising Holy Hell: A Novel*. New York: Henry Holt and Company.

Olsen, Lance (2006), *Nietzsche's Kisses*. Tallahassee: Fiction Collective Two.

—(2007), *Anxious Pleasures: A Novel after Kafka*. Emeryville: Shoemaker & Hoard.

Parini, Jay (1997), *Benjamin's Crossing: A Novel*. New York: Henry Holt.

—(1997), *Some Necessary Angels: Essays on Writing and Politics*. New York: Columbia University Press.

—(1990 [2009]), *The Last Station: A Novel of Tolstoy's Final Year*. New York: Anchor Books.

—(2010 [2011]), *The Passages of H.M.: A Novel of Herman Meliville*. New York: Anchor Books.

Rampersad, Arnold (2008), *Ralph Ellison: A Biography*. New York: Vintage Books.

Rorty, Richard (1979), *Philosophy and the Mirror of Nature*. Princeton: Princeton University Press.

—(1989), *Contingency, Irony, and Solidarity*. Cambridge: Cambridge University Press.

Ryan, Judith (2012), *The Novel After Theory*. New York: Columbia University Press.

Said, Edward W. (1993 [1994]), *Culture and Imperialism*. New York: Vintage Books.

Scott, Joanna (1990 [2004]), *Arrogance: A Novel*. New York: Picador.

Southgate, Beverley (2009), *History Meets Fiction*. Harlow: Longman/Pearson Education Limited.

Styron, William (1967 [1993]), *The Confessions of Nat Turner*. New York: Vintage International.

Vidal, Gore (1973 [1993]), *Burr: A Novel*. New York: Ballantine Books.
—(1984 [2000]), *Lincoln: A Novel*. New York: Vintage International.
White, Edmund (2007 [2008]), *Hotel de Dream: A New York Novel*. New York: HarperPerennial.
White, Hayden (1973), *Metahistory: The Historical Imagination in Nineteenth-Century Europe*. Baltimore: Johns Hopkins University Press.
—(1978 [1992]), *Tropics of Discourse: Essays in Cultural Criticism*. Baltimore: Johns Hopkins University Press.
—(1987 [1989]), *The Content of the Form: Narrative Discourse and Historical Representation*. Baltimore: Johns Hopkins University Press.
Wilde, Allen (1981), *Horizons of Assent: Modernism, Postmodernism, and the Ironic Imagination*. Baltimore, Johns Hopkins University Press.
Woolf, Virginia (1942), *The Death of the Moth and Other Essays*. London: The Hogarth Press.
Wright, Richard (1940 [1998]), *Native Son*. 1940. New York: Perennial Classics.
Wright, Terry R. (2007), *The Genesis of Fiction: Modern Novelists as Biblical Interpreters*. Hampshire: Ashgate Publishing Limited.
Yalom, Irvin D. (1992 [2005]), *When Nietzsche Wept: A Novel of Obsession*. New York: Perennial Classics.
—(2005 [2006]), *The Schopenhauer Cure*. New York: HarperPerennial.
—(2012), *The Spinoza Problem*. New York: Basic Books.
Zavarzadeh, Mas'ud (1976), *The Mythopoeic Reality: The Postwar American Nonfiction Novel*. Urbana: University of Illinois Press.

Index